INFORMING PRACTICE DECISIONS

INFORMING PRACTICE DECISIONS

SHARON B. BERLIN

JEANNE C. MARSH

The School of Social Service Administration
The University of Chicago

Macmillan Publishing Company
New York

Maxwell Macmillan Canada
Toronto

Maxwell Macmillan International
New York   Oxford   Singapore   Sydney

Terry Franklin Berlin
In Memoriam

This book was set in Clearface by Publication Services, Inc.
and printed and bound by Book Press.
The cover was printed by New England Book Component.

Editor: Linda Scharp
Production Supervisor: Publication Services, Inc.
Production Manager: Aliza Greenblatt
Text Designer: Publication Services, Inc.
Cover Designer: Cathleen Norz
Cover Illustration: Steven Alcorn

Printed in the United States of America

Macmillan Publishing Company
866 Third Avenue, New York, New York 10022

Macmillan Publishing Company is
part of the Maxwell Communication
Group of Companies.

Maxwell Macmillan Canada, Inc.
1200 Eglinton Avenue East
Suite 200
Don Mills, Ontario M3C 3N1

Library of Congress Cataloging-in-Publication Data
Berlin, Sharon B.
    Informing practice decisions / Sharon B. Berlin and Jeanne C.
Marsh
        p.   cm.
    Includes bibliographical references and index.
    ISBN 0-675-20628-6
    1. Social service–Decision making.   2. Needs assessment.
I. Marsh, Jeanne C., 1948-   II. Title.
HV41.B426   1993
361'.0068' 4–dc20   92-40418
                                                      CIP

Printing: 1 2 3 4 5 6 7   Year: 3 4 5 6 7 8 9

Preface

The central question behind this book is "How do clinicians generate useful ways of understanding their clients and decide what to do to be helpful?" From the standpoint of direct service practitioners who must sort through overwhelming amounts of information to generate judgments, plans, and actions, this is a critical question. The purpose of the book is to explore the nature of clinical decision–making and provide guidelines to assist clinicians in making informed, thoughtful, and useful judgments.

Over the past 20 years, the idea that the practitioner should approach clinical work with the mindset of a researcher has been advanced as the main way to ensure better clinical judgments and generate a more dependable knowledge base. The contributions of empirical data to practice decisions are undeniably important, but on their own they provide an insufficient knowledge base for practice. Optimally, clinical practice is informed by multiple sources of information (e.g., data, theory, experience) and a variety of thinking processes (e.g., critical thinking, creativity, empathy, reflection-in-action, and observation).

By pulling together ideas from literature on social cognition, decision making, intervention theory, clinical processes, and qualitative and quantitative research and then fitting them to our experience as social work practitioners, we describe ways to generate and organize information from several sources in order to address a series of fundamental clinical tasks. These tasks include making judgments about the (1) nature of the client's problem, (2) what to do about it, and (3) how the intervention work is going (e.g., is the client improving? what processes are promoting change? what needs to happen next?).

The book starts with a review of basic concepts related to clinical thinking. Subsequent chapters focus on the nature and purpose of specific decision-making tasks; they include discussions of how practitioners and clients commonly think their way through these tasks, the nature and effects of probable thinking biases and pitfalls, a range of strategies for overcoming them, and numerous examples of how these organizing strategies fit into real-life clinical encounters. Additional attention is devoted to describing how empirical data can be integrated into decision-making processes.

Although this book was written with social workers in mind, the content is applicable to clinical work in all of the direct service professions (e.g., psychology, nursing, psychiatry, rehabilitation). It is written from the perspective of the practitioner, from the first-hand experience of trying to make good clinical decisions and trying to figure out how that is done.

We would like to thank the following reviewers for their invaluable feedback: Albert S. Alissi, University of Connecticut; Lewis W. Carr, Howard University; Laura Epstein, University of Chicago; and Len Gibbs, University of Wisconsin–Eau Claire.

We wish to acknowledge and thank colleagues, friends, and family members who frequently expressed interest, encouragement, and even enthusiasm for this project. We are grateful for the intellectual legacy passed on to us by colleagues and forebearers at the University of Chicago School of Social Service Administration who pioneered the problem-solving tradition in social work. In particular, we acknolwedge the work of Charlotte Towell, Helen Harris Perlman, William J. Reid, and Laura Epstein. We are especially indebted to Professors Laura Epstein of the University of Chicago and Leonard Gibbs of the University of Wisconsin-Eau Claire for their careful and perceptive reviews of the manuscript and for suggestions that improved the final product. We thank Lynne Campbell for her support of the enterprise; Barbara Ray for editorial assistance, especialy her suggestions for avoiding sexist language while maintaining clarity and ease of expression; and to Juantia Denson who, with extraordinary equanimity, made her way through numerous drafts to produce the final manscript. We also thank our students at the School of Social Service Administration, especially those in courses SSA 302 (Research and Evaluation), SSA 445 (Clinical Research), and SSA 413 (Congnitive Intervention) whose questions, critiques, and class participation provided inspiration for the book as well as several case examples. We credit Lee and Lauren Marsh Shevell for the graphics in Figure 1 and thank Lee, Lauren, Steve, Winnie, and Betsie for sticking with us throughout a project that took much longer than we ever thought possible.

S. B. B.
J. C. M.

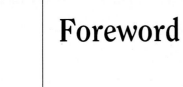

Foreword

A unique collaboration produced this original book. Two social work experts, combining the talents of research and practice, have broken out of the mold of contemporary practice studies. Considering the subject of how to practice successfully in the helping disciplines, Berlin and Marsh present their views about processes that enable us to understand clients sensitively and appropriately, and decide what to do that will be helpful.

INFORMING PRACTICE DECISIONS could be considered a new version of John Dewey's classic HOW WE THINK,[1] adapted to the subject matter of clinical intervention in social work, modernized in style of thought, and applicable to any of the related or similar helping professions. Dewey discusses in his first chapter the subject: "What is Thinking?" He then goes through an analysis of thought processes and the training of thought. Berlin and Marsh examine what thinking is in clinical practice, how it is done, how might it be done better, and what the thinking process consists of. Answers to the Deweyan question, "what is clinical thinking?" will equip today's practitioners with intellectual instruments for stocking, observing, and managing their own mental processes, and organizing the modes through which they influence and clarify the thinking and feeling of clients.

Dewey had a presentient grasp of the problem-solving process that is now a building block of thought in the physical and social sciences. In a sense, he laid down the framework for constructing Berlin and Marsh's book on informing practice decisions. This is Dewey[2]:

"Given a difficulty, the next step is suggestion of some way out—the formation of some tentative plan or project, the entertaining of some theory that will account for the peculiarities in question, the consideration of some solution for the problem."

[1]Dewey, John, *How We Think*. Lexington, Mass., D. C. Heath and Co., 1933.
[2]Ibid., p. 15

This is Berlin and Marsh:

"How do clinicians generate useful ways of understanding their clients and decide what to do to be helpful?"

Taking this to be the puzzle or the difficulty, the present authors proceed to explore the nature of clinical understanding and decision making and provide guidelines for making useful clinical judgments. This book takes its place as the latest work in the continuously evolving attempt to identify the components of clinical intervention, and to put ideas about intervention in a form that makes sense in the consciousness of the present generation, considering the contemporary state of knowledge.

Before the arrival of the current emphasis on practice models and attempts to standardize their use, practice texts were not explications of technologies but statements of "good intentions," driven by personality theories. Frameworks for problem identification and problem reduction, for diagnostic formulations or assessments of pathology, were embedded in theories that guided practitioners into ways to analyze persons. Observations of social situations were added to the mix to round out the picture and to conform to the special person-situation mission of social work. In the premodern period, the present problem, although not avoided, was de-emphasized on grounds it was primarily a result of the personality state. The social situation, regarded as background, was viewed partly as a product of personality and problem, and considered usually not capable of being remedied by clinical intervention.

During the 1970s and 1980s, serious scholarly and practice work developed what we now refer to as "approaches" and "models." These were characterized by increasing specificity and empirical validation. They were on the way to becoming intervention technologies, that is, manualized rules and formalized customs. Ideas from social ecology and systems theory were incorporated into the approaches and models, making it possible for us to think in more complex terms about the relations between social situations and individual personal conditions. These broad ideas about problems enabled us to sometimes take social situations out of the background position and put them in a place closer to being causes, precipitants, underlying conditions, or maintainers of problems. Furthermore, the arrival of behavioral and cognitive approaches, and renewed attention to problem-solving processes, created conditions for a new comprehensive view of practice. Conditions were in place to advance the social scientific formulation of a modern clinical practice.

This is where Berlin and Marsh now come in. They succeed in joining and interrelating new themes and substance into a view that begins to transcend present practice. The authors consider practice to be an endeavor that merges intuitive arts with rigorous thought. They analyze cognitive processes involved in professional thinking; and they support the work with practice experience. They explore how to work with one's own knowledge and how to consider features of one's own character and experience in relation to case activity. This view takes the troublesome concept of "counter-transference" and handles it in a more empirical manner, with a modern rhetoric.

Although many parts of the book are familiar, the reader will not have seen this particular analysis of patterns of clinical thinking before. This is what makes the work an exciting reading experience. The book's viewpoint evolved from the past two decades of effort by contemporary clinical scholars (including the two authors) to construct empirically based practice that is in harmony with philosophical humanism. The work is part of a fieldwide endeavor to join practice wisdom to empirical findings. The authors make a presentation of a literature on thinking and judgment in clinical decision making that is not well known to the clinical field. This body of work can help clincians understand how they acquire, store, arrange, and extract different kinds of knowledge in the course of regular client encounters and how they make the best use of what they know.

While existing in a practice world that the readers easily recognize, this book plunges into previously unexplored territory to discover and use scientific methods in the context of immediate and real feeling and caring interactions. An interesting example of dealing with heretofore unexplored regions is Chapter 2 in which assessment is explored anew. In this chapter the authors get beneath the familiar rhetoric to touch real thoughts and sensibilities, making acutely specific what usually is written in heavy generalities. In Chapter 10, which deals with the use of task analysis to assess change, another novel application is examined, again in terms of a high degree of detail that makes the processes ring true. They reveal application of theory in a practical and learnable fashion. In this chapter and throughout the book, this attention to detail illustrates and clarifies ideas to a degree that is rare in clinical writing.

Practical ways of combining research and practice has been the goal of most progressive academics in clinical social work, but a synthesis in a manner usable in the field has been elusive. It is this kind of synthesis that Berlin and Marsh have in mind; and this is a book that the present generation of practice teachers have hoped for. The authors took on a daunting enterprise. The job of identifying, sifting, and combining research studies and connecting that information with the myriad variations of treatment circumstances has had clinical scholars on the ropes. Nobody has known how to do this in a way that is both sufficiently straightforward and accurate enough. These authors took this challenge head on. The result is a definite advance in getting hold of concrete means for managing research in practice in a way that makes sense to practitioners who are first clinicians and later researchers. This book is a jump-start toward an advanced round of modernizing clinical practice. Future work will have to contend with these new ideas.

Laura Epstein

Contents

INFORMING PRACTICE DECISIONS

1 GENERAL THEORETICAL OVERVIEW

1 Overview: Thinking and Judgment in Clinical Decision Making

This chapter describes the thinking processes relevant to clinical decision making. It focuses on how clinical thinking is influenced by specific knowledge and information as well as mental processes available for using that information.

  I. Introduction
 II. Knowledge Structures
     A. Schemas
        1. Schema development and change
        2. Perseverance effect
        3. Polarization effect
        4. Expert schema
        5. Schemas about clinical practice
     B. Theory
        1. Theories about clinical practice
        2. Theoretical pluralism versus theory integration
III. Informational Cues
     A. Cues from direct experience
     B. Systematically collected information
 IV. Thinking Processes
     A. Reasoning
     B. Heuristics and biases in the reasoning process
     C. Availability heuristic
        1. Vividness
        2. Personal relevance
        3. Frequency, recency, familiarity
        4. Dispositional bias
        5. Observer-role characteristics
        6. Helper-role characteristics

INTRODUCTION

The clinician engages in three interrelated and fundamental activities: (1) understanding the client's problem; (2) doing some things to help her resolve it; and (3) evaluating the change so that the intervention can be adjusted and the outcome of the work can be known. In carrying out these steps, the practitioner makes an inestimable number of judgments. These judgments are influenced by universal characteristics of human information processing, the practitioner's individual knowledge-generating tendencies, her or his fund of knowledge, and the general context of practice. Under ideal circumstances, the clinical practitioner (social worker, psychologist, nurse, psychiatrist) takes a stance of open inquiry in order to discover new facets of meaning. Such discoveries are based on multiple sources of information and a variety of thinking processes. Rather than following the common *first* inclination to fit incoming information into usual patterns of thought, the clinician consciously reflects on how he or she is thinking and considers additional ways of understanding the phenomenon in question.

Although the human mind is capable of amazing feats and on a daily basis seems to serve us quite well, close scrutiny reveals its predictable vulnerability to specific biasing influences. Understanding how our minds receive information, give it meaning, and transform that meaning into judgment, helps us to become sensitive to possible sources of bias, to check and correct for them, and ultimately to make more adequate decisions. A significant amount of recent research on human information processing, perception, problem solving, and judgment exists. The purpose of this chapter is to examine what we know about this process as it relates to decision making in clinical practice. We are concerned here with what goes on in the mind of the practitioner and how that shapes the way he or she collects, organizes, and uses information in practice.

A fundamental dilemma for the human mind is that it is confronted with enormous quantities of information. Psychologists estimate that only one-seventieth of what is available in the visual field can actually be perceived. As a result, our minds must select among available cues and construct individual versions of the "real picture." Evidence about decision making indicates that most decisions, including clinical decisions, are based on limited cues and a small number of thinking strate-gies. Even though a social worker may gather a great deal of detail about a client's problems and strengths, he or she is necessarily selective in what is considered. The social worker's clinical thinking is dominated by prior knowledge and information-processing shortcuts.

Figure 1.1 provides four perceptual tasks that require selecting and using cues to understand a complex situation. The ambiguities in each of the four pictures can be understood as analogous to the complexities in a client's situation. After examining the pictures for a few moments, it becomes clear that attending to particular cues in the pictures leads to one recognizable pattern, while looking at alternative cues results in a very different conclusion. In a similar fashion, the clinician selects and focuses on certain pieces of information to make judgments about the nature of the client's difficulties. From one perspective, the client's dilemma may look like a function of personal weakness; from another, it shows all the signs of environmental deprivation; and from yet another, the configuration of details may seem to be a classic example of a family-systems problem. Depending on the specific cues selected and the associations they evoke, the situation takes on very different patterns and meanings in the clinician's mind.

The task for the practitioner, as for any perceiver, is to select the cues, make sense of them, go beyond them to resolve ambiguities and, ultimately, to draw inferences and make predictions. To do so, as depicted in Figure 1.2, the mind relies on knowledge structures, informational cues, and thinking processes. This chapter is organized according to these three factors and is focused on describing the nature of their interaction and reciprocal influence.

KNOWLEDGE STRUCTURES

Schemas

According to perspectives from social cognition (Cantor & Kihlstrom, 1987; Fiske & Taylor, 1984; Markus, 1977), each of us attends to, interprets, and remembers in-formation according to our individual systems of categorizing internal and external events. These thematically organized sets of categories are referred to as cognitive schemas. "A schema is a cognitive structure that contains knowledge about the attributes of a concept and the relationships among those attributes. . . . [S]chemata guide perception, memory, and inference . . . toward schema-relevant information, and often toward schema-consistent information." (Fiske & Taylor, 1984, p. 149). At the most fundamental level, one can think of schemas as general impressions or mind-sets. Schemas are stored in memory as generalizations or condensations from specific experiences. Over the course of experience and time, we synthesize specific episodes into abstract memory structures (Abelson, 1976; Taylor & Winkler, 1980). Long after we have forgotten the particulars of certain episodes, we can remember the general conclusion. For example, we cannot remember exactly why we distrust a certain individual, but we know that we do. If we were to try to reconstruct the

(a)

(b)

(c)

(d)

FIGURE 1.1
Ambiguous visual images (Sources: (a) R. C. James, photographer, from J. Thurston
& R. G. Carraher, *Optical Illusions and the Visual Arts* ©1966. Litton Educational Publ.,
Inc. ; (b), (c), (d) Roger N. Shepard, *Mind Sights*, New York: W. H. Freeman and Co.,
1990, pp. 76, 57, & 72 respectively).

6

FIGURE 1.2
Knowledge structures, informational cues, and thinking processes

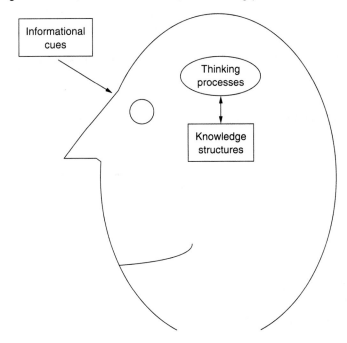

basis for our negative impression, we would no doubt recall an interaction, a report from another, or an observation that, while not significant or even memorable in isolation, provided us with evidence that this individual was not to be trusted.

In a powerful example of the way schemas operate in a clinical setting, Singer and Salovey (1991) describe a therapy session in which the therapist, using a standard Gestalt therapy technique called "the empty chair," asked the client to imagine her mother sitting in the chair across the room. The speech of the usually very articulate client became halting and uncertain, she finally blurted out to her male therapist, "Don't you realize you are asking me to perform just like my father did when I was a child? He was always trying to get me to sing, write poetry, and entertain the relatives when they came over to the house." Singer and Salovey write, "The therapist in this case only superficially resembled her father. Yet at that moment in therapy he summoned up in the client's mind a complex bundle of memories about the way her father treated her in front of others" (pp. 69–70). Freud's discovery of the redirection of these organized memory structures, which he called transference, was perhaps one of his most important contributions. In his recognition of the capacity for particular memory structures to influence therapeutic interaction, and human interaction more generally, Freud labeled a widely experienced clinical phenomenon that exemplifies the utility of the schema construct.

With respect to content, schemas may include descriptive concepts, including (1) descriptive self-concepts (persistent, shy, controlling, conflicted) (2) examples of types of people (depressed, hysterical, unreliable), (3) interpersonal scripts about the kind of behavior that is called for with particular people (mother, client, supervisor, ex-husband), and (4) procedural routines that specify how to carry out certain tasks (ordering lunch, assessing a client, checking out a book, making a referral). Although we cannot introspect the precise nature of our own schemas, by monitoring the content and patterns of our thinking it is possible to draw inferences about which categories are most salient and which pathways our associations seem to follow.

While schemas are the product of experiences in the world, they also shape ongoing experience by influencing the targets of attention, the meanings that are assigned to them, and the actions that are taken. The schema concept reflects the fundamental assumption that perceivers actively construct reality (Fiske & Taylor, 1984, p. 141).

SCHEMA DEVELOPMENT AND CHANGE   Schemas are developed as people form generalizations from similar experiences. The more they apply a schema to new situations, the more general, complex, organized, and capable of assimilating exceptions their memory structure becomes. For example, one instance of staffing a case will be stored in memory as a concrete episode: "I was nervous. . . . I gave the background history, and then the current situation. . . . No one paid attention." Add additional experiences and memory becomes progressively less concrete and specific and more abstract and general: "Staff meetings are useless; the only helpful part is the thinking I do to pull the information together." Additional experiences also provide new input to the schema so that it becomes more complex and organized. It includes more interconnected elements for constructing complicated meanings. "The staff psychiatrist is useful in cases that have to do with borderline disorders, but she usually doesn't have much to say about family problems. . . . On the other hand, if you can capture the interest of the social work consultant, he will. . . . " Having developed an abstract, complicated, and differentiated understanding of staffing, it is relatively easy to find a way to explain an unexpected occurrence: "His helpfulness to me was nothing more than a side effect of his trying to manipulate the program director." In this case, the "mature schema" has also become more conservative.

When informational cues do not readily fit an existing schema, these differences may either fail to register, be worked into an existing schema (as in the example above), or force the schema to change in order to accommodate the differences—the equivalent of changing one's mind. Schemas are more likely to change in the face of several intermittent, disconfirming events rather than a single, even intensely discrepant incident, which can more easily be taken as an exception to an otherwise intact rule. Moreover, if the discrepancies occasioned by these several instances are large, unambiguous, memorable (i.e., vivid and personally salient), and stable, they are more likely to alter the schema or, in other words, to alter the way one understands.

Continuing the previous example, imagine that the presence of new staff members alters the dynamics of the meetings and there is one staffing after another in which participants are attentive, involved, and helpful. The cumulative weight of the discrepant experiences can create a change in the staffing schema: "Staffing can be helpful . . . people seem to care about what is going on." On the other hand, if the discrepancy between existing memory and new information is moderate, ambiguous, and can be attributed to a temporary phenomenon, the schema will assimilate the event without being altered: "The new social worker tried to be helpful, but she was naive to think she could cut through all the resistance." Although assimilation may add complexity or variation to what is already believed, one's basic perspective remains very nearly the same.

PERSEVERANCE EFFECT   Each of us knows from experience that really changing our own mind, or someone else's, does not come easily. Although we may wish for more flexibility in ourselves and our clients, the stability or perseverance of schemas protects us from feeling overwhelmed and disoriented. On one hand, the perseverance effect biases us toward interpreting incoming information to support what we already think. On the other hand, it provides us with an important sense of continuity, predictability, and control.

POLARIZATION EFFECT   In the absence of new evidence, thinking about a topic that one knows a fair amount about is likely to reaffirm one's previous judgments concerning the topic (Fiske & Taylor, 1984). The more individuals think about something they believe, the more they construct justifications for their beliefs, and the more polarized their judgments become: "The more I thought about it, the more I knew I was right." This polarization effect seems to result particularly from re-flection in the absence of new information. On the other hand, encounters with new data lead to more complex schemas and more moderate judgments: "At first I thought . . . , but then I talked to the others and decided that it's not necessarily a catastrophe." As Fiske and Taylor (1984) note, "The more variety one has encoun-tered, the more complex the issues, the less clear-cut it all seems, and the less extreme one's judgments."

EXPERT SCHEMA   As we have suggested, the schemas of experts are more elaborate and organized than those of novices. Fiske and Taylor (1984) explain:

> One consequence of experts' well-developed schemata is that, despite the greater amount and complexity of their knowledge, its compact and well-organized qual-ity frees processing capacity. Consequently, experts notice, recall, and use schema-discrepant material more than novices do. In contrast, novices' simple, ill-defined schemata limit them to the more obvious schema-consistent material. In accord with their greater sensitivity to inconsistency, experts moderate their judgments to allow for the ambiguity of the information given.

Because experts are able to assimilate exceptions into their complex memory struc-tures, they are quite comfortable with anomalies. Discrepant information tends not to require a radical transformation of what they believe. On the other hand, the novice who is working to build a core of knowledge may be confused and threatened by ambiguous or contradictory data precisely because the data do not fit—because they seem to require revision of what he or she assumed to be a "given."

Consider the social work professor who has been teaching behavioral social work methods for years. She is well able to fit research findings about the utility of emotional expression into her complex framework of behavioral treatment. But the first year student who is just beginning to develop a behavioral conceptualization of intervention is completely thrown by this new data. "Where does this new information fit," he thinks. "What if all the behavioral ideas I've been trying to learn are wrong?" Or consider the social work intern who is certain her client presents a classic picture of manic-depressive illness. Her more experienced supervisor in the community mental health center questions the accuracy of this assessment based on (a) the numerous examples of manic-depression symptomatology that she has seen, and (b) the specific environmental characteristics of this case.

Although experts may have more cognitive capacity to attend to exceptions and sufficient complexity to assimilate them, the process of overlearning tasks (e.g., conducting an interview) may render them oblivious to unexpected occurrences. According to Langer (1975, 1989), this kind of automatic processing or mindlessness makes one vulnerable to a range of errors.

SCHEMAS ABOUT CLINICAL PRACTICE   As our preceding examples have implied, all the general descriptions about cognitive schemas can be applied to schemas about clinical practice. Clinicians' knowledge structures affect what they understand about their clients' problems and how they apply that knowledge. Their individual memory networks of categories and associations about human behavior pull their attention toward certain configurations of dilemmas and strengths and not to others; their networks provide ways of understanding what these patterns mean and of inferring intervention implications from them. Depending on the nature of the schemas, this understanding will fall somewhere along the continua between complex and simple, abstract and concrete, comprehensive and narrow, flexible and rigid.

Under the best circumstances, clinicians work toward a general awareness of the characteristics of their practice-related schemas. They are open-minded, they develop an overall sense of how they tend to think, and they consider taking other thinking pathways when the situation seems to warrant it. The clinician is able to take another path because he or she practices doing that—consciously considering other models for understanding—and because his or her professional self-schema includes attributes of openness, curiosity, and versatility. The clinician's ability to entertain a variety of explanations and responses provides flexibility in relating to a wide range of clients and in finding ways to assist them.

The actual experiences that clinicians abstract into general knowledge structures about practice come from many sources. When students arrive for their first course in professional social work, they already have schemas or "naive theories" (Evans & Hollon, 1988, p. 350) and some quite specific notions about human behavior and interpersonal interventions. They have acquired these schemas from life experiences or personal sources; for example, from the folk-psychology of the culture, from family interactions, and from their own experiences as a client or a helper. Students must rely on these structures to make sense of the ideas and exercises that make up their education. Although prior experiences affect how students select and understand their educational input, these new ideas also shape the ongoing development of practice-related schemas. As we have noted, the new information may be assimilated into existing schemas to make them more complex, or repeated and varied discrepant experiences may accumulate to the extent that preexisting knowledge structures need to be radically revised.

Professional education is explicitly designed to help students use new knowledge about how to help people. One important function of professional education is to expose students to theories of social science and social work practice that provide a formal explanatory structure to aid understanding. The next section shows how this theoretical foundation contributes to clinical decisions.

Theory

We begin our professional careers with knowledge structures about helping that are primarily the synthesis of experiences from our personal lives. The kinds of information we encounter and the ways we process it will shape the character of our professional development as we move from novice to expert. This new information comes from direct experiences (for example, feedback during fieldwork) and from indirect experiences, the things that others (authors, teachers, supervisors) tell us or show us. Although data from personal experience continue to influence the ongoing development of these knowledge structures, professional education alerts us to the importance of going beyond knowledge based on personal experience to integrating cues from the disciplined study of practice phenomena.

The practice-related theories that we study in school (and beyond) are the equivalent of the schemas of experts. They are experts' organized ideas about how people develop, how problems occur, how problems and people change, and about the superordinate moral principles that should guide our work. By disseminating their theories, experts make them accessible to the scrutiny of an interested public. Other experts may dispute the theories and add to them on the basis of alternative ideas, logical principles, and empirical tests, and practitioners can subject them to their own tests: "Do these ideas help me generate useful intervention options?" "Are these ideas consistent with my knowledge about effective intervention strategies?" These theories are thus added to the knowledge base of the profession.

Technically, the term "theory" connotes a comprehensive, precise, and parsimonious set of testable propositions that serve to explain or predict phenomena by specifying relations among variables (Kerlinger, 1973; Wallace, 1971). In common usage, the word "theory" is used more generically to include a wider range of explicit explanatory or predictive propositions as well: models, perspectives, approaches, and frameworks. The term is used here in this latter, broad sense. Although there is overlap between the concepts of theory and schema, we use "schema" to refer to personal knowledge structures (which may include knowledge abstracted from organized theories) and "theory" to refer to public knowledge structures that are subject to the scrutiny of scholars and practitioners.

THEORIES ABOUT CLINICAL PRACTICE   At best, theories give the clinician an expanded sense of how to understand and to act. They allow him to go beyond the client's account and beyond his own individual views in order to see alternative ways of approaching the client's problem. These are ways that also make sense to and empower the client. For example, a client's view may be that she is fated for misery and there is nothing to be done to escape this fate. The practitioner's view may be that hard work can cure anything. Theories about personal and social change enable the worker and client to go beyond these two limited perspectives.

Theories are useful for organizing information into meaningful patterns so that certain aspects become more or less salient and relations among facts can be examined. Theories alert us to some cues and not to others when we are trying to describe and understand a phenomenon. Theories provide preconceptions that serve as guides through large amounts of complex information and help us shape that information into new knowledge. For example, in Figure 1.1, once they are suggested, it is easy to see a dalmatian in 1.1(a), a woman's face or a saxophone player in 1.1(b), one irregular face or two regular faces (one in profile) in 1.1(c), and a row of balustrades or women's figures in 1.1(d).

As abstractions, theories are most useful in suggesting general explanations or hypotheses about what may be going on. They are less helpful in predicting or explaining specific, concrete instances. Even though theories are potentially useful in taking us beyond the narrowness of our own direct experience, they also can be limiting. Rigidly adhering to one theory or perspective as if it were true and useful for all client situations can blind the clinician to more valid and useful points of view (Beach, Abrahmson, & Levine, 1981). For example, describing the development of his ideas about clinical interventions, Arnold Lazarus (1971) discloses:

> The reason why not all the additional procedures were clearly apparent in my previous writings was due to the false selectivity of my own perceptions. Often my interest and attention were so firmly riveted to behavior therapy that I translated nearly everything I did into post-hoc S-R terms. At other times I erroneously failed to recognize the additional procedures I employed as anything more than incidental activity (p. xi).

The new perspective Lazarus developed to replace the old one also makes certain cues and interpretations more salient and excludes others. By necessity, his perceptions are still selective, but they also seem to be more inclusive.

THEORETICAL PLURALISM VERSUS THEORY INTEGRATION   Beach et al. (1981) recognize the dual pitfalls of operating without a theoretical framework or rigidly adhering to only one. As a solution, they propose a "models approach" for clinical work. A model is defined as a "sufficient explanation of some behavior problem" that identifies the specific elements of the problem that can be influenced through therapeutic interventions. Even though a number of models account for a particular set of difficulties, any given model "fits" only some subgroup of clients.

Thus, "the clinician's task is to determine which model best organizes the clinical data and identifies the most appropriate point of intervention for a particular patient" (p. 133). Assuming a multimodel perspective, the clinician avoids rigid adherence to any one model. At the same time, by self-consciously seeking to identify the most appropriate theoretical perspective, he or she insures that some organized framework will be applied to the clinical data to suggest directions for therapeutic intervention.

In a similar vein, Walsh and Peterson (1985) argue for theoretical pluralism but also take an explicit stance against integrating theories:

[The] acceptance of multiple world views encourages cross-fertilizations of ideas and enhances a cooperative, cross-school competition. More important, [theoretical] pluralism appears to be the most intellectually responsible course. Premature attempts at synthesis have consistently led to unsatisfying technical eclecticism and conceptual confusion. In contrast, pluralism emphasizes clearly defining the limits of a particular theory, while also acknowledging its unique contributions. (p. 152)

Much of the recent work on the synthesis of theories has advanced our knowledge about the common mechanisms of psychosocial change and the multiple ways to evoke those mechanisms (e.g., Goldfried, 1980; Horowitz, 1991; Wachtel & Wachtel, 1986). At the same time, there is also merit in the argument for theoretical pluralism. It emphasizes the importance of clarity about the merits and limits of specific approaches and explicitly encourages the clinician to develop a repertoire of perspectives and skills in order to identify those that best fit the circumstances at hand.

In summary, we rely heavily on experts' theories about clinical practice to take us beyond our personal views. Over the course of a professional education, our schemas about interpersonal helping progressively expand to contain our own versions of some number of prevailing theories (e.g., behavioral, psychodynamic, cognitive, problem-solving, systems). Nonetheless, at any point in our careers, our schemas about helping will be made up of a mix of information abstracted from experts' theories and personal experiences.

There is no shortage of experts in clinical practice and no shortage of theories from which to choose. One cannot and need not attend to them all. In choosing among theories, clinicians are best served by looking for ones that elucidate the experiences of clients and that suggest effective interventions. As we move along in our careers and become more knowledgeable and more comfortable with what we know, we still benefit by maintaining an attitude of openness and by looking for theories that say something new about how problems develop and change.

INFORMATIONAL CUES

Without constant feedback from direct experience, our theories remain abstractions—interesting ideas, unconnected to the moment-to-moment dynamics of human interaction. Although theories alert us to what to look for and how to organize what we see, cues from direct experience provide us with an ongoing readout about the fit between the theories and what we see, hear, and feel. Experience introduces novelty. It forces us to reconsider, try again, revise, add on, and come at things in a different way.

At the same time, we rely on systematically collected information as a basis for the decisions we make—information related to client characteristics, clients' previous interactions with the agency, information that is relevant to client goals, and information available in the research literature about the appropriateness and impact of specific treatment approaches. In this section, we will focus on explicit information relevant to practice decisions: both the information available from direct, ongoing experience and systematically collected information.

Cues from Direct Experience

Although the kind of information we seek is influenced by our knowledge structures and theoretical preferences, direct experience can overwhelm expectations, correct preconceptions, and lead to revised conceptualizations and actions. Indeed, it is primarily encounters with new experiential data that allow us to stretch and grow, that is, to accumulate "practice wisdom." The information we acquire in work with clients gives us ongoing feedback about the utility of our theories and our creative insights (and provides the raw material on which both are based): "Am I on course?" "Is this working?" "Was my idea correct?" "If I try this, then what?" Day to day and moment to moment, we depend on cues about the consequences of our clinical decisions and actions to guide us. We rely on our own casual and systematic clinical observations to enhance our understanding and increase our helpfulness.

Although all practitioners rely heavily on data, some are better observers and make better use of observations than others. What makes the difference? Good observers, we suggest, (1) know what to look for, (2) loosen up preconceptions in order to see the unexpected, (3) derive useful inferences from what is observed, (4) keep track of important configurations consistently and carefully so that small changes occurring over time can be discerned, and (5) have a system for organizing and remembering the emerging facts of a case.

A great many practitioners observe the first three criteria. However, only a few enhance their observational capacity by routinely relying on systematic methods for recording and organizing information referred to in criteria (4) and (5) above. Sometimes these practitioners rely on measurement instruments or qualitative criteria to assist them in reliably discerning changes in important patterns. Whether they are using these informational aids or relying on their own privately formulated notions, it is important for clinicians to have a relatively explicit sense of what things to watch for and what these things mean, as well as the ability to adjust their thinking and actions on the basis of what they see.

Systematically Collected Information

Despite the controversy related to the role of scientifically-based research in social work during the last two decades, almost everyone would agree that observations which result from the systematic collection and analysis of data are an important source of information for clinicians. The disagreements are more likely to arise concerning the relative importance of specific information or whether the practice of science and the reliance on empirical data should be the major guiding forces in the profession. During the late 1960s and throughout the 1970s, social workers were criticized for relying too heavily on theory (Briar & Miller, 1971) and ignoring research-based knowledge (Kirk & Fischer, 1976; Kirk, Osmalov, & Fischer, 1976; Rosenblatt, 1968). The trend in social work education during the 1970s was to teach social workers to integrate empirical methods into their practice procedures to ensure that evaluation components were built into each case. The outcry in the 1980s was that the utility of empirical methods had been exaggerated and that this overemphasis deprived practitioners of knowledge generated by other sources (Peile, 1988; Peiper, 1981, 1985; Rodwell, 1987; Weick, 1987; Witkin, 1991).

Empiricism is nothing more than using a set of rules for gathering and analyzing data so that the results are relatively unambiguous. It encompasses qualitative description as well as quantitative summarization. It can be used inductively to discover general principles at work in a sample of cases and deductively to test what is already assumed. The unique contribution of empiricism is demonstrable knowledge (Kirk & Miller, 1986). In contrast to personal opinion, organized theory, or intuition (which are also important sources of information), empiricism generates reproducible, reliable, observable demonstration. This observable quality gives empirical knowledge a measure of objectivity in the sense of agreement among observers. Nonetheless, the "facts" of experience are still open to question, changeable, and relative. They allow us warrantable conjectures, not absolute truth (Mahoney, 1976). Kirk and Miller (1986) further explain:

> A commitment to objectivity does not imply a desire to "objectify" the subject matter by "overmeasurement" or to facilitate authoritarian social relationships by treating human beings as though they were certain features they may happen to have. It does not presuppose any radically positivist view of the world; it emphatically eschews the search for final, absolute "truth".... (p. 11)

> Relaxing certain of the narrow definitions of the hypothetical-deductive mode... facilitates discovery of the new and unexpected. It would be an error, however, to drop the scientific concern for objectivity. The scientific credo is one good way to permit the resolution of a conflict of opinion. It is not the only way; the scholastic solution, still prevalent in many disciplines... relies on argument and rhetoric rather than on argument and demonstrations. (p. 18)

Despite the importance of empirical knowledge, it is insufficient for guiding practice. Clear theoretical conceptualization, commitments and values, and empirically derived data are interdependent contributors to a dynamic configuration of knowledge that is relevant to practice (Reid, 1990).

In sum, the kind of information we look and listen for in practice—information that is influenced by our knowledge structures and theoretical preferences—can and should be supplemented by information available from experience with clients as well as from relevant research. It is possible that the theoretically-oriented clinician may become so caught up in his or her own system of hunches as to neglect important evidence about the client's personal and environmental situation. It may also be possible for the empirically-oriented clinician to rely on such a limited fund of knowledge that he or she fails to grasp fully the narrowness of the findings. It is the clinician with access to the full range of theoretical and empirical tools who is most capable of considering the pertinent factors and weaving together plausible, encompassing, and useful explanations and action plans.

THINKING PROCESSES

A wise person once observed: "Thinking is hard work. That is why so few people engage in it." Clinical work requires a significant amount of thinking, of using available knowledge and evidence to reach an understanding, to plan a course of action, and to evaluate and revise that course of action. Thus, what we know about the clinician as a thinking, calculating being, in addition to what we know about the structure and character of knowledge and information, is important to understanding the clinician's task.

Psychologists and philosophers have done a significant amount of thinking about thinking. Four specific kinds of thinking processes are of particular relevance to understanding the cognitive processes of clinical practitioners: *reasoning,* including the use of heuristics, *problem solving, creativity,* and *metacognition.* Although we will consider each process individually, it is clear that, working singly and in combination, they unite to form the complex process that occurs when a practitioner reviews his or her work and determines what comes next. For example, this complex thinking process occurs when one writes out a progress note for a case session and ends up listing all the hypotheses about the client's current state and the data that support each one. It happens when a social worker recognizes that she has diagnosed five of the last six clients as suffering from depression. She ponders whether this can be attributed to the pervasiveness of depression in the population, or to the fact that most of her clients live in conditions where resources are minimal but demands are great, or whether her own academic interest in this problem has biased her. It happens when the clinician thinks about why things got derailed in the last session and how to get back on track. It happens when the worker, while preparing dinner, suddenly recognizes a new and more useful conceptualization of the client's problem. In short, reasoning, problem solving, creativity, and metacognition subsume much of the conscious review, synthesis, reflection, and correction that are fundamental to sensitive understanding and skillful performance.

Reasoning

To reason is to figure something out, to draw a conclusion according to certain rules. Traditionally, research on reasoning has focused on either *deductive reasoning,* using a set of rules in order to apply a theory to a particular case or set of observations, or *inductive reasoning,* using particular instances and specific facts to draw general conclusions and derive an overall theory. Both deductive and inductive reasoning are essential mental activities pervasive in everything we do.

The diagram derived from Wallace (1971) in Figure 1.3 shows that reasoning in research requires an ongoing interplay between deduction and induction. From theories we derive hypotheses that can be tested by examining their consistency with observations. Observations that are not consistent with the hypotheses may lead to alternative generalizations. These generalizations may be the basis for modifying the theory, which could generate a modified set of hypotheses, and so forth. For example, experience with and the prevailing understanding of addictive behavior could lead to a treatment approach that calls for immediate and complete abstinence from the target addictive substance (e.g., heroin). If evaluation revealed that such an approach resulted in the transfer of addiction or to the increased use of other addictive substances such as nicotine or caffeine, one might infer—from observing the

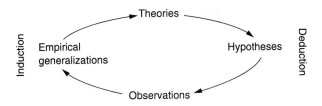

FIGURE 1.3
Cycle of inductive and deductive reasoning. (Source: adapted from Walter Wallace. *The Logic of Science in Sociology* [Chicago: Aldine Atherton]; seen originally in A. Rubin & E. Babbie, *Research Methods for Social Work* [Belmon, CA: Wadsworth Publishing Co., 1989])

way clients shift dependence from one addictive substance to another—that a more effective approach might be sequential targeting of specific addictive substances for abstinence. Thus, rational thought is increasingly understood as a goal-directed process that involves deductive and inductive reasoning as well as general knowledge and contextual knowledge (Anderson, 1990; Rips, 1983; Johnson-Laird, 1983; Holland, Holyoak, Nisbett, & Thagard, 1986).

   In many situations, there is simply too much uncertainty to permit conclusions to be drawn by applying rigid systems, even when pragmatic knowledge and knowledge of the context is taken into account. As a result, information processing shortcuts, sometimes referred to as heuristics, are employed to draw conclusions and make judgments.

Heuristics and Biases in the Reasoning Process

These shortcuts or "rules of thumb," sometimes referred to as *heuristics,* are automatic, not consciously contrived, and efficient; they lead to predictable conclusions and sometimes biased judgments. Depending on the situation, these biases may be constructive, as in the illusory optimism of nondepressed people (Alloy & Abramson, 1988) or harmful, as in gender or racial stereotyping.

   It often is assumed that rational people use "normative" strategies (that is, they apply empirical and logical principles to the available information) to make inferences about characteristics of people or events, about causes of events, or about future events. However, through an impressive program of research, Tversky and Kahneman (1974) demonstrated that in generating inferences under uncertain conditions, people tend not to follow normative strategies. Rather, lay people and scientists alike use information-processing shortcuts, or heuristics, that "reduce complex judgmental tasks to a set of simpler operations" (Evans & Hollon, 1988). These strategies should not be viewed as irrational or nonrational or in any way faulty mental mechanisms. On the contrary, they allow us to manage vast amounts of information and, for the most part, to render accurate judgments. However, because these nonnormative abilities occasionally produce inaccurate and detrimental conclusions, it is worthwhile for us to realize how we use them in making clinical decisions so that we can monitor their utility.

Tversky and Kahneman (1974) identified two kinds of heuristics that play a major role in decision making: "availability" and "representativeness."

Availability Heuristic

A major influence on decisions is information that comes readily to mind. When people make judgments about the frequency, likelihood, or even causality of something on the basis of the ease with which they remember or notice an instance of it, they are using the availability heuristic. In general, the most accessible or available information is that which is vivid, personally relevant, recently encountered, frequently encountered, or familiar. Its logical warrant notwithstanding, if the idea pops into the mind easily, it tends to be persuasive.

VIVIDNESS   Like all humans, clinicians find information that is vivid and specific easier to attend to and recall than more abstract information. A recent study showed, for example, that a detailed and vividly depicted account in the *New Yorker* of stereotypical welfare abuse had greater impact on attitudes than a more statistically valid but abstract presentation of overall welfare use (Nesbitt & Ross, 1980). Similarly, it is difficult to find a social worker who would not prefer to learn about a clinical phenomenon by reading or observing a richly detailed case account than by absorbing the most valid and reliable statistical description. For example, the case the practitioner read last week that revealed horrendous details of the sadistic abuse of a reticent wife by her charming husband remains more clearly in her mind than available statistics on domestic violence. This memory may serve to prompt the clinician to make very careful assessments of couple relationships, or it may reinforce a suspicious attitude toward all the more sociable men in her clinical work.

PERSONAL RELEVANCE   Information that matches up with something that is meaningful to us personally also tends to be readily attended to and recalled. Despite every care not to mix one's personal issues with those of the client, the clinician seldom pays such close attention to the client's account of a struggle as when it overlaps in some way with his or her own experiences. Similarly, inferences about causes, attributes, and treatment responses may also be shaped by the "ready to mind" nature of one's own experiences. For example, having just returned to work after taking several days off to attend her father's funeral and be with her family, the social worker responds very rapidly and assuredly to her client's comment about not knowing what to say to her ill mother with whom she usually argues. The worker advises her client of the importance of taking the opportunity to tell her mother some of the positive things that have been left unsaid. Drawing on Bower's (1981) work on mood and memory, Salovey and Turk (1988) extend the notion of the availability of personally relevant material to suggest that information that matches the clinician's mood is more likely to be noticed, learned, and remembered and thus be available for making clinical judgments than is information that is not mood-congruent. Thus, modifying Salovey and Turk's example, the student intern who just found out he will receive a full scholarship for his next year of school gives full and careful attention to his client's latest successes but does not attend very much to her worries and apprehensions. The practitioner may be able to remember easily many of the events the client talked about several weeks ago (on the same day he found out he got an A+ on a difficult computer assignment), but he may not recall much about the conversation with his client last week (the day someone ran into his car). The student practitioner in this case demonstrates the common effects of mood on the processing of information, that is, the tendency to (a) master material more easily when it is congruent with one's mood, (b) recall information more readily that is consistent with one's mood, and (c) more easily remember material when one's mood at the time of retrieval matches one's mood when the information was first stored (Salovey & Turk, 1988, p. 108).

FREQUENCY, RECENCY, FAMILIARITY   In part, the cognitive accessibility of a piece of information, say a diagnostic category, depends on how often we use the category, or how often we encounter people for whom the category seems to fit. For example, the clinician who works on an inpatient unit of a psychiatric hospital and encounters many clients suffering from paranoid schizophrenia is more likely to classify ambiguous clusters of symptoms as representing that disorder rather than employing other equally plausible diagnostic categories. Due to recency, frequency, and familiarity (e.g., having a detailed sense of the treatment protocol for people with paranoid schizophrenia), the diagnostic category "paranoid schizophrenia" is cognitively readily accessible (Snyder & Thomsen, 1988).

Although the relative frequency of events in the present is probably a valid indicator of the frequency of future events (Tversky & Kahneman, 1974), an individual's judgments are more often swayed by absolute frequencies. We do not typically have the information to make relative judgments readily at hand (e.g., total number of children to compare with number abused). Yet a clinician is likely to judge the situation based on the simple increase in absolute frequencies. For example, we know that the number of children who are abused is increasing (*absolute frequency*). However, we do not know how many children are abused in relation to the total number of children. If the total number of children is growing faster than the number abused, then the *relative frequency* of child abuse would be decreasing.

DISPOSITIONAL BIAS   One result of applying the availability heuristic that is of particular relevance to clinicians is dispositional bias, or the tendency for the observer to define the source of problem as within the "actor" (his or her disposition) rather than as within the client's situation. This phenomenon is so common in human information processing that it has been labeled the "fundamental attribution error." Dispositional bias is a well-documented phenomenon in social work (Mayer & Timms, 1970; Rubenstein & Bloch, 1978).

OBSERVER-ROLE CHARACTERISTICS   Batson, O'Quin, and Pych (1982) suggest that two aspects of the worker's role, that of observer and helper, make some decision possibilities more readily available than others. As an observer, the worker understands a client's situation from the outside looking in. The client is at the "center of the worker's attention." Compared with individuals actually involved in a situation, observers tend to impute more responsibility for what is going on to the individual than to situational factors. Social psychologists have documented the consistent tendency for individuals involved in a situation to attribute any difficulties to characteristics of the situation, whereas outsiders or observers tend to attribute the difficulties to characteristics of the individuals, that is, to look for ways in which the individuals themselves may have caused the problem (Jones & Nesbitt, 1972). For example, Snyder, Shenker, and Schmidt (1976) asked undergraduates to listen to an audiotape of a peer-counseling session and then to assume the role of the client or the counselor. Those assuming the client role tended to view the problem as more situational; those taking the counselor role viewed it as more dispositional. Moreover, a series of studies conducted by Taylor and Fiske and colleagues (Taylor & Fiske, 1975; Taylor, Fiske, Close, Anderson, & Ruderman, 1979, reported in Nesbitt & Ross, 1980) reveal that almost anything that draws attention to an individual—proximity, illumination, physical characteristics—results in the attribution of responsibility and influence to that person.

Batson et al. (1982) further suggest that if the client is seen individually and only in the office, the tendency to focus on the individual will be heightened. Although social workers more than other helping professionals are more likely to meet with clients in their homes, classrooms, or institutional settings, workers who meet with clients primarily in an office setting can become "office bound." Further, to the extent that a client is also seen in the absence of significant others, the worker will have little access to information about the social and physical context of the client. Clearly, the worker will have more information about the client than about his or her social context both for assessment and for implementing change.

There is also evidence to suggest that even when clients present situational information, workers tend to discount it (Maluccio, 1979; Mayer & Timms, 1970). Most clinicians would acknowledge the necessity of constructing an understanding of the client's problem that incorporates his or her perspective. This fundamental axiom of helping is based on the view that the client knows the most about his or her actions, perceptions, and situation. Nevertheless, evidence shows that helpers are often inclined to question the legitimacy or validity of the client's perspective. It may be that clinicians tend to give greater credence to information they have received about the client from referring agents or other third parties or because they are correcting for a conscious or unconscious sense that clients as "actors" tend to "blame" the situation rather than attributing responsibility to themselves.

HELPER-ROLE CHARACTERISTICS   As helpers, clinicians are trained and expected to facilitate some change or improvement in the client's situation according to organized theories of human behavior (e.g., psychodynamic, behavioral, or cognitive) that may also stress personal correlates of problems. Langor and Abelson (1974) found that when they showed a videotaped interview to psychodynamically and behaviorally oriented practitioners and told them that the interviewee was a job applicant, both groups perceived the applicant to be relatively well adjusted and attributed any problems they noticed to the situation. When the interviewee was described as a patient, however, the psychodynamically oriented therapists described him as maladjusted and indicated that his problems were dispositional in nature. In addition, Batson and Marz (1979) report that trained helpers who have been schooled in various perspectives on human problems were more likely to make dispositional attributions than untrained individuals (undergraduates). This finding was consistent for clinical psychologists, ministers, and social workers.

In addition, to the extent that helpers view their role as protecting society as well as helping individuals, there is greater risk in making a situational diagnosis than a dispositional one. If, in assessing a mother who has severely beaten her child, the social worker finds the mother to be unfit, with minimal impulse control, the child will be removed from her custody. If, on the other hand, she finds the mother's behavior to be a natural result of her social isolation, minimal economic resources, or limited knowledge of child development, she is more likely to recommend keeping the child in the home with a set of supportive educational interventions focused on improving the mother's circumstances. The first decision is the least risky for the worker. Any negative consequences of this decision will be felt by the child and the mother, not by the worker. On the other hand, negative consequences from the second decision—such as the child being severely abused or even killed—will have a radical impact on the practitioner, his or her supervisor, and the agency, as well as the child and mother. The risk for the practitioner, supervisor, and agency (personal guilt, negative news coverage, potential lawsuits, and job loss) is not as serious as the risk for the child and mother; nonetheless, it may be strenuously avoided.

Finally, practitioners know that the resources and skills available to them are predominantly oriented toward changing clients. As numerous researchers have noticed (Caplan & Nelson, 1973; Goffman, 1961), most resources and helping technologies are focused on assisting the individual adapt to his or her situation, rather than changing the social environment. Batson, Jones, and Cochran (1979) completed a series of experiments showing that decisions about how to help are heavily dependent on the helping resources available.

To sum up, when we make a judgment according to the ease with which we recall or notice what seems to be a relevant piece of information (the "ready to mind principle"), we are employing the availability heuristic. There is nothing inherent in the process that renders these judgments wrong; in fact, they are often accurate and useful. Nonetheless, it is important to remind ourselves that the availability of information is based on vividness, frequency, recency, personal salience, and familiarity and not necessarily the demands and opportunities of the moment.

Representativeness Heuristic

People employ the representativeness heuristic when they reduce complex judgment tasks into simple similarity judgments—for example, when they determine that a person, problem, event, or behavior is similar to phenomena with which they are familiar. The nature of clinical work requires us to perform many such classification tasks:

- Josephine Jones exhibits symptoms that are similar to those of alcoholics whom the worker has known and studied. Should she be diagnosed and treated as having an alcohol dependency problem?

- Joseph Patton is male, decisive, self-confident, bright, heterosexual, and white. He is similar to other agency executives. Is he the man for the job?
- Andrew Marder is grieving the death of his wife. His grief seems similar to that of other members of the bereavement support group who have profited from the group. What is the probability that he will benefit from joining the group?
- Annette Westberg is unassertive in her relationship with her husband. She and her husband are considering divorcing. According to several sources, lack of assertiveness in relationships contributes to resentment, dissatisfaction, and other major relationship problems. To what extent does Ms. Westberg's lack of assertiveness contribute to her marital difficulties?
- Bobbie Marshall draws several figures with no arms and big mouths during his play session. Does this mean that he is feeling dependent and helpless?

If the clinician relied on the representativeness heuristic in each of these situations, his or her answer to each probability question would be "yes." "Yes, Ms. Jones is alcoholic." "Yes, Mr. Patton is a good candidate for the agency executive position." "Yes, Mr. Marder is likely to benefit from the group." "Yes, Ms. Westberg's lack of assertiveness contributes to her marital troubles." And "yes" for Bobbie, too.

It may be that in all these situations, estimating probabilities based on representativeness serves the practitioner well. After all, matching characteristics of an individual, process, or problem to the criteria that distinguish a category is a logical way of proceeding—if the criteria are valid. Nonetheless, using this heuristic can lead to serious errors when the similarity is illusory and when it replaces other relevant considerations, specifically base rate, sample size, and the predictive capacity of information.

ILLUSORY CORRELATION   Certain associations between attributes and categories, say diagnostic categories, have been at least partly validated empirically. For example, the (DSM-III-R) represents some consensus about the clusters of signs and symptoms that constitute disorders. Other associations between attributes and the phenomena they are presumed to represent have been categorically invalidated, and yet they seem to persist. For example, Chapman and Chapman (1969) conducted a series of studies in an attempt to understand why clinicians continued to associate certain responses to projective tests with categories of psychopathology even though such associations had been shown not to exist. For example, on the Draw-a-Person test, they consistently reported that dependent patients emphasize the mouth and make childlike drawings while paranoid patients emphasize eyes. The Draw-a-Person test, however, has no predictive validity according to numerous objective assessments. Still, there are large numbers of clinicians who claim the Draw-a-Person test is a useful and predictive diagnostic tool.

Chapman and Chapman explain the "illusory correlation" phenomenon by suggesting that beliefs about the covariation between events is based on semantic associations (which amount to simple theories). To reach this conclusion, Chapman and Chapman randomly assigned to the undergraduates in their study pictures made by patients at a state mental hospital with symptoms of, for example, paranoia and dependency. They then asked the undergraduates to report which picture characteristics tended to be related to which symptoms. They found that the students identified the same relations, or covariations, between specific test results and symptoms using bogus data that were consistently identified by clinicians using real data. Both the clinicians and the undergraduates seemed to be relying on underlying verbal associations to make their judgments (e.g., mouths with dependency and eyes with paranoia). They strengthened this conjecture through an additional series of studies. In one, they simply asked subjects to rate the tendency of a symptom to "call to mind" a given body part. As expected, these ratings were highly consistent with the reported illusory correlations. Overall, this research indicates that detection of covariation can be more strongly influenced by expectations, beliefs, and simple associations than it is by actual covariation.

INDIFFERENCE TO BASE RATES   In a classic study, Kahneman and Tversky (1982) attempted to assess the impact of base-rate information on judgment. Base rate refers to the normal rate or pattern of occurrence in the population. For example, the best estimates we have suggest that 5 out of every 100 Americans suffer from a serious mental disorder. The base rate is thus 5 out of 100. Kahneman and Tversky were interested in how information about base rates affects judgments. They gave subjects brief personality sketches of several individuals allegedly sampled at random from a group of 100 lawyers and engineers. One group of subjects was told the sketches contained 30 lawyers and 70 engineers. The other group was told the opposite. Thus, the likelihood that any one description belonged to a lawyer was greater for the second group than for the first. Nonetheless, both groups judged exactly the same proportion of sketches to belong to lawyers. Both groups seemed to be relying on the match between the description and their stereotypes for lawyers and engineers and not considering the base-rate information at all. This conclusion seemed supported by the fact that subjects did use base-rate information in the absence of any other information, that is, when personality sketches were not provided. However, if any descriptive information was provided—even if it was completely irrelevant to the judgment to be made—base-rate information was ignored. For example, regardless of whether the stated probability of lawyers was .7 or .3, subjects judged the likelihood of Dick being a lawyer to be .5 when they received the following description.

> Dick is a 30-year-old man. He is married with no children. A man of high ability and high motivation, he promised to be quite successful in his field. He is well liked by his colleagues. Thus, base-rate information seems to be taken into account only when no other information is available. Any descriptive information, whether it is relevant to the judgment task or not, will be used in place of base-rate data.

INDIFFERENCE TO SAMPLE SIZE   A routine exercise in statistical sampling courses is to ask students to take 10 samples of two each from a "population" represented by a page of numbers from a random numbers table and to compute the mean or average for each of these 10 samples. They are then asked to take 10 samples of 10 numbers each from the same table and compute the means for these 10 samples. They are then asked to compare the two sets of means. The results based on samples of very different sizes are often a surprise. One might well expect the means from

the two samples to be basically the same—after all, they are drawn from the same population (i.e., the same page in the random numbers table). Instead, the means based on the samples of size 2 vary more from one another and from their overall mean (as measured by the standard deviation statistic = 1.6) than are the means based on the samples of size 10 (with standard deviation = .5). See the calculations in Table 1.1.

The idea that the variability of samples decreases as their size increases does not seem to be a natural intuition. Instead, the human mind seems to cling to two quite contrary and erroneous intuitions related to samples: (1) that samples (regardless of size) will be similar to one another and to the population from which they were drawn, and (2) that sampling is a self-correcting process. Tversky and Kahneman (1982) have shown that these biases are held with equal commitment by social scientists as well as by individuals relatively naive to statistical concepts. Insensitivity to the relation between sample size and variance often results in the design of studies in which samples are too small (and variances too large) for conventional statistical tests to detect existing effects. Cohen (1962, 1969) describes the numerous studies in the psychological literature with samples too small to detect important differences as self-defeating, wasteful, and pernicious. In a similar review of social work effectiveness studies, Crane and others have determined that most of the studies used to show that "casework does not work" were based on samples too small for any meaningful assessments to be made (Crane, 1976; Orme & Combs-Orme, 1986; Orme & Tolman, 1986).

The second faulty intuition related to sample size is sometimes referred to as the *gambler's fallacy*. This is the idea that sampling is self-correcting and that a

TABLE 1.1
Effect of sample size on mean and standard deviation

10 samples of 2 each:

3	0	2	1	1	4	9	6	9	5	
4	5	7	7	7	8	4	0	3	8	$\bar{X} = 5.3$
3.5	2.5	4.5	4.0	4.0	6.0	6.5	3.0	6.0	6.5	$s = 1.6$

10 samples of 10 each:

6	8	6	9	8	0	9	5	4	4	
7	9	5	7	9	2	3	6	5	9	
2	2	4	5	4	4	8	4	1	1	
8	0	4	5	6	7	9	3	8	2	
5	3	5	8	4	7	7	0	9	3	
2	6	7	2	3	9	2	7	6	7	
4	3	0	0	6	5	9	8	5	0	
5	2	7	0	0	5	4	8	3	4	
1	5	3	3	5	9	0	5	2	8	
8	5	1	3	9	9	2	4	4	4	$\bar{X} = 4.7$
4.8	4.3	4.2	4.2	5.4	5.7	5.3	5.0	4.7	4.2	$s = .5$

sequence generated by a random process will reflect the essential character of the process—even very small segments of the process. Thus, in a series of 10 coin flips, we expect to see heads 50% of the time and tails 50% of the time. If we get nine heads in a row and have the overwhelming sense that the next result will be tails or at least that the probability for tails is greater than 50%, then the *gambler's fallacy* is at work. Logically, we understand that for any given flip the chance of heads is 50% and tails is 50% and the outcome of one flip is completely independent of the previous flip. So what gives us this sense that we are "due for a tail?" We know that these processes are self-correcting, and we expect this self-correction to express itself over very short series. In fact, such series are self-correcting only in very long, that is, infinitely long, series. A sample of 10 flips is simply too small for the essential nature of the process to emerge.

INDIFFERENCE TO PREDICTIVE VALIDITY   Social workers are constantly required to make predictions: for example, about a client's performance in a particular program or about his or her performance in the absence of a program. Typically, these judgments are formed by relying heavily on the representativeness heuristic. For example, a client's similarity to another individual who failed in a particular program may result in a negative evaluation for the client. Often, judgments are made with little or no consideration for the relevance or predictive validity of the information used to make the judgment.

There are many examples from everyday experience of decisions made on the basis of fallible and sometimes irrelevant information. For example, interviews are the basis for most employment decisions despite the fact that there is little relation between interviewing skill and job performance. Psychological tests are relied on by clinicians despite the fact that they have demonstrated only modest validity for some groups. Academic achievement tests such as the GRE are used to make decisions about admission to graduate school even though they have been shown to have little predictive validity for some groups.

Kahneman and Tversky (1982) demonstrate our willingness to use unreliable information with little predictive capacity. They describe a study in which two groups of subjects read several paragraphs describing the performance of a student teacher during a practice lesson. One group of subjects was asked to evaluate the quality of the lesson. A second group was asked to predict the success of the teacher five years after the practice lesson. Despite the fact that the information at hand was more relevant to and predictive of the quality of the performance now rather than five years after the practice lesson, the scores of the two groups were equivalent. Quality of the information showed very little effect on the judgments made.

It is easy to criticize Kahneman and Tversky by pointing out that their subjects, like most of us making decisions in the real world (as compared with the psychology laboratory), were doing their best with the information available. What is perhaps distressing about their findings derives from the fact that confidence increased as the *amount of* fallible and irrelevant information increased. Their research shows that the greater the amount and redundancy of fallible and irrelevant information we have, the more confident we feel about the decisions we make based on that information.

INDIFFERENCE TO REGRESSION PHENOMENA   Correct intuitions about regression to the mean are not easily developed despite the fact that we frequently observe such phenomena. Regression phenomena refer to the likelihood that any extreme performance, either high or low, will be followed by a performance closer to the average. Parents usually understand that when their children behave extremely well or extremely badly, neither extreme state will last forever. They can expect their offspring to return to a more typical level of behavior. Teachers likewise understand that average students can perform very well or fail miserably at times only to return to a more typical level of performance. Social workers expect clients in extreme crisis one day to show some improvement the next, even without intervention. Although we observe such occurrences every day, we rarely consider them regression phenomena. More typically, we try to find some extraneous reason for the improvement or deterioration in behavior, for example, the lavish praise we gave our children for their good behavior or the cogent response we made to our client's crisis.

Indeed, Kahneman and Tversky (1982) point out that one of the serious dilemmas of failing to understand the dynamics of regression to the mean is the risk of underestimating the impact of reward and overestimating the impact of punishment. They describe the erroneous conclusions of some experienced flight instructors that verbal rewards have a negative effect on learning and verbal punishments have a positive effect. They based their ideas on the observation that when a trainee achieved a smooth landing and received praise, his next effort typically deteriorated. Similarly, a learner who had a rough landing followed by harsh criticism typically improved. As Kahneman and Tversky point out, "by chance alone, one is most often rewarded for punishing others and most often punished for rewarding them" (p. 11).

Why are intuitions about regression so difficult to develop? As we suggested earlier, we rely heavily on the representativeness heuristic in decision making. We expect that any result of a category or process (output B) will be similar to the dominant characteristics of the category or process (characteristic A). We have difficulty understanding that a characteristic may be unrepresentative whether due to being an extreme value in a distribution or to being heavily influenced by powerful external factors.

Problem Solving, Creativity, and Metacognition

In our discussions of knowledge so far, we have been talking about knowledge of ideas, facts, and objects, or what has been referred to as *declarative knowledge.* In a practicing profession, knowledge about how to do things and how to perform certain tasks, or what is referred to as *procedural knowledge,* is also very important. Procedural knowledge is basically knowledge about how to solve problems. Problem solving is a thinking process directed toward the completion or performance of some intellectually demanding task (Nickerson, Perkins, & Smith, 1985). Clearly, problem solving is fundamental to social work practice.

PROBLEM SOLVING   Researchers of problem solving suggest that inductive reasoning plays a big role in problem solving as individuals pursue goals in complex environments and receive feedback on their success in reaching their goals (Holland, Holyoak, Nisbett, & Thagard, 1986). The fundamental task of problem solving is to determine a series of activities that will enable one to move toward the ultimate achievement of a goal. Three characteristics of problem solving have been identified: (1) it is goal directed, (2) it requires that a goal be broken down into subgoals or subtasks, and (3) it involves identifying an action that will enable one to move toward achievement of a goal (Anderson, 1990). Fundamentally, problem-solving methods are procedures for identifying actions that will allow movement through a series of subgoals to the ultimate goal.

In recent years, computer simulations have been used to develop and test specialized methods for solving specific problems (e.g., for solving quadratic equations), and other methods have been developed that are more general and can be applied to a range of problems. This work has revealed that efforts to delineate a general problem-solving method are increasingly viewed as inadequate and unsatisfactory, particularly when it comes to accounting for expert problem-solving skills (Holland et al., 1986). As discussed earlier, human expertise is critically dependent on specialized representation of knowledge and problem solving procedures in a specific domain of inquiry (e.g., foster care placement, brain cancer diagnosis). Experts solve routine problems by retrieving appropriate "problem schema" and supplementing the schema with relevant information and strategies (Chi, Fillovitch, & Glaser, 1981). The problem schema store information about relevant concepts and specialized solutions that may be applicable. In general, problem solving appears to be a domain-specific process when knowledge is available. Otherwise it appears to rely on general methods of seeking solutions.

One problem with current approaches to understanding problem solving is that they rely on computer simulations that (1) require the problems themselves to be very well defined and (2) fail to incorporate the capacity to learn from experience, that is, to build on and develop problem schemas. The challenge to current research on problem-solving is to describe a problem solving process in which the representation of the problem itself can change and in which varying existing knowledge structures can be used to address novel situations. That is, we need a theoretical model of problem solving that incorporates the benefits of existing and developing knowledge and experience.

John Dewey, whose early work on problem solving significantly influenced social work scholars, articulated the need to learn from experience when he described "the practical work...of modification, of changing, of reconstruction continued without end" (1971, p. 7). More recently Schön, in his effort to develop an epistemology or philosophy of procedural or practice knowledge, emphasized both the importance of problem definition, or problem setting (i.e., adequately representing the problem), and of reflection on practice that "can surface and criticize the tacit understandings that have grown up around the repetitive experiences of a specialized practice, and can make new sense of the situations of uncertainty or uniqueness." Schön (1983) describes the problem solver as a researcher in the practice context. In each instance of problem solving, the practitioner allows himself to experience surprise, puzzlement, confusion in a situation which he finds uncertain or unique. He reflects on the phenomena before him which have been implicit in his behavior. He carries out an experiment which serves to generate both a new understanding of the phenomena and a change in the situation. (p. 68)

Consider the social worker in the following example.

☐   Rita Havens, a social worker in a family agency, is given a referral for family systems treatment for the Garfield family. Rita specializes in family therapy, and she works in an agency that is well known for family interventions; thus, it seems reasonable that the referral would specify family treatment. But Mrs. Garfield shows up for the first appointment alone. She is pale, scared, and apologetic that her husband and kids are not with her. Her husband would not come. In fact, she did not dare ask him. Lately, he is angry all the time, and she wanted to talk without the kids around. Rita feels sorry for Mrs. Garfield and begins to focus on how she might get her husband to come in. She is working earnestly along this track, and Mrs. Garfield follows along. At one point, however, Rita looks at Mrs. Garfield and sees the strain and disappointment in her expression. She says, "Does this really seem like a good idea to you?" Mrs. Garfield responds, "Can't there be some way to get help without my husband?" Rita starts to talk again about the importance of working with the family as a unit, but then stops. "Well," she says, "It seems like there should be some way. Let's try to figure it out." They go on to talk about Mrs. Garfield's fear of her husband, how he threw her across the room last week, and hit her in the face the week before. They share ideas about where Mrs. Garfield and her two preschool children could go for shelter and finally arrive at a plan about how Mrs. Garfield will move in with her brother for the present and how Rita will check into day-care programs for the kids. They decide to meet again in two days. Their contract is to work to keep Mrs. Garfield and her children safe and, over the long term, to help her feel more powerful and supported in pursuing some of her other goals.

Rita could have insisted on a couples or family format. She could have referred Mrs. Garfield to someone else. But because she could see that Mrs. Garfield was sinking, she was moved to think about Mrs. Garfield's problem in another way. She was able to use a different frame of reference—one that allowed her to "throw out a line." She was able to incorporate the context and her practice knowledge and experience to understand the problem differently and more accurately.

CREATIVITY   The addition of creativity, inventiveness, or the ability to look at things in new and unconventional ways, has been cited as a way to improve problem solving. Logical, rational, competent problem solving can be enhanced with the nonrational, alogical thinking processes connoted by the term *creativity*.

Accounts of creativity explain that it is precisely when the informed mind is open and not focused on the problem at hand that bits of previously unconnected, unrepresented information may coalesce to form a creative insight. Because they are novel and unexpected, the associations that constitute a creative breakthrough elude conscious problem solving efforts. Nonetheless, the disciplined search for answers provides the background knowledge and the bits and pieces of information that make creative associations possible.

Two types of research characterize inquiries into the nature of creativity: descriptions of highly original women and men and studies of the process of thinking itself. Analyses of the creative activities of "geniuses" reveal repeatedly that when an individual, after struggling hard with a problem, finally puts it aside, the solution often appears in a flash. This suggests that our brains may work most efficiently when they switch from periods of intense concentration to periods when we attempt to exert very little control over them. There are numerous examples of this process. For example, the mathematician Hadamard wrote that,

> On being very abruptly awakened by an external noise, a solution long searched for appeared to me at once without the slightest instant of reflection on my part— the fact was remarkable enough to have struck me unforgettably—and in a quite different direction from any of those which I had previously tried to follow. (Ghiselin, 1955)

Mozart describes his experience with these processes:

> When I am, as it were, completely myself, entirely alone, and of good cheer—say, travelling in a carriage, or walking after a good meal, or during the night when I cannot sleep; it is on such occasions that my ideas flow best and most abundantly. *Whence* and *how* they come, I know not; nor can I force them. Those pleasures that please me I retain in memory, and am accustomed, as I have been told, to hum them to myself. If I continue in this way, it soon occurs to me how I may turn this or that morsel to account, so as to make a good dish of it, that is to say, agreeably to the rules of counterpoint, to the peculiarities of the various instruments, etc. (Ghiselin, 1955).

Gertrude Stein compares a process she calls creative recognition to the process of giving birth:

> You cannot go into the womb to form the child; it is there and makes itself and comes forth whole—and there it is and you have made it and have felt it, but it has come itself—and that is creative recognition. (Ghiselin, 1952)

Although the blinding insights of social workers have not found a place in the literature on creativity, we know they make productive use of intuitive information. We all can think of times when, having given up trying to figure out how to handle a difficult clinical issue, a good answer came to us—while jogging or driving the car or loading the dishwasher.

The second type of research on mental processes related to creativity helps us understand why the creative process may work in this way. Hogarth (1985) relies on the early work of Campbell (1960) to suggest that the invention of creative solutions rests very simply on the capacity to generate numerous "thought experiments" or analyses of different combinations of factors possibly leading to a solution and a mechanism for selecting, testing, and retaining successful trials. Specifically, Campbell suggests that creativity is enhanced when individuals (1) generate a large number of "thought trials," (2) have a wide experience in life that equips them to generate more hypotheses to test via thought trials, (3) work in an atmosphere conducive to exploratory behavior, and (4) have the capacity to recognize and select the successful solutions that emerge.

As Campbell suggests, several components of creativity can be identified (Nickerson, Perkins, & Smith, 1985). *Ideational fluency,* or the ability to produce large numbers of ideas quickly and easily, contributes to the generation of factors or components that may be useful in identifying novel solutions. *Remote associational ability* is the capacity to retrieve information only remotely associated with the problem at hand. The work habits of Charles Darwin illustrate this latter aspect of the creative process (Gruber, 1981). His notebooks revealed him to be a compulsive note maker who collected lists of ideas, impressions, questions, arguments, images—all of which were organized and reorganized. His notebooks were a chaotic jumble of ideas out of which he constructed order, patterns, and meaning. *Intuition* is another component of creativity and one that is commonly accepted as playing an important role in clinical work. Wescott (1968) defines intuition as the ability to reach sound conclusions with minimal evidence. For example, we say a good clinician has a "feel" for what to do; he or she "senses" when to probe, when to fall back, when to disclose. The clinician cannot explain precisely how he or she knows these things: "it is just intuition." It is taking action based on an emerging coherence of bits of information before the pattern can be explicitly identified. Empathy, or dissociating from one's own experience and associating with the client's, is a form of intuitive response. It gives us information about the client's experience that is relatively direct and proximal and sometimes difficult to symbolize.

Getzels and Csikszentmihalyi (1976) determined that creativity also depends as much on the capacity to select a problem to be solved as the capacity to actually solve it. They call this *problem finding.* Schön (1988) discusses a similar phenomenon, which he calls problem setting.

METACOGNITION   Metacognition is a thinking process that is only beginning to be explored and understood by cognitive psychologists and philosophers (Nickerson, Perkin, & Smith, 1985). Metacognition is essentially thinking about thinking. Specifically, metacognitive knowledge is knowledge about the characteristics and capabilities of human information processing, especially perhaps about our own information-processing capabilities, as well as knowledge about what human beings might be expected to know.

Much of the work in metacognition involves helping individuals achieve greater understanding of their own abilities and limitations and how to compensate for the limitations in a way that maximizes performance. Any skilled performance requires the capacity to determine whether one is moving effectively toward a given goal and to adjust one's performance in order to make the most satisfactory progress. The skills involved in metacognition include those of planning, predicting, checking, monitoring, that is, efforts to control one's performance of intellectually challenging tasks.

Metacognition is particularly relevant to professional work where one must constantly assess one's knowledge and skill and determine whether it is adequate for the demands of practice. This is especially true in clinical work, where knowledge accumulates on a case-by-case basis.

SUMMARY

In this chapter on the thinking processes involved in clinical decision making, we have engaged in a process of metacognition; that is, we have considered the characteristics and capacity of clinicians as human beings dealing with complex information. Highlighting both the strengths and the limitations in our ability to plan, predict, check, monitor and evaluate, we have identified the basic cognitive processes involved. Reasoning, the basic process of figuring something out, operates in every aspect of clinical work. Often our efforts to figure something out rely on shortcuts referred to as heuristics—efficient and familiar strategies that usually, but not always, help us to perceive the right answer. Reasoning is essential to problem solving, the mental process that enables us to move toward and ultimately achieve therapeutic goals. Problem solving itself has long been recognized as a necessary and important aspect of social work practice (Perlman, 1957; Reid & Epstein, 1972). Finally, our problem-solving capabilities are often enhanced by that nonsystematic phenomenon called creativity.

Decision making in social work practice requires recognition of and reliance on knowledge and information—some "hard-wired" or developing mental mechanisms, some available through informal observation or through more systematic data collection procedures—as well as processes for using that information. Understanding the characteristics and capabilities of the relevant information and information processing enables us to consider and conduct our practice with greater insight and effectiveness.

2 INFORMATION FOR ASSESSMENT

2 | Constructing an Understanding: General Issues in Assessment

T his chapter describes the central purposes of assessment and discusses a variety of general issues bearing on the focus of assessment and the nature of the data being sought.

I. Purposes and Characteristics of Assessment
   A. Constructing shared understanding
   B. Assessment over time

II. Issues in Assessment
   A. What should we assess?
      1. People or problems
      2. Dispositions or situations
      3. Strengths or deficits
      4. Person-in-situation
   B. Case example of person-in-situation assessment
   C. The data of assessment: Subjective meanings or objective facts
      1. Personal and communal constructions
      2. Measuring meanings

III. Summary of General Assessment Issues

PURPOSES AND CHARACTERISTICS OF ASSESSMENT

Of all the clinical tasks, none is more central or more constant than assessment. Assessment is a big information-processing job. It consists of selectively attending to and interpreting enormous amounts of information. From the beginning of the clinical encounter to the end, the clinician and the client work to gain a progressively refined and useful understanding of the problem and what can be done about it. In addition, the clinician continually tries to understand the client's situation as a way of connecting with him or her—acknowledging the client and signaling respect.

35

Even though the specifics of the process and content of assessment may vary across situations and settings, diverse assessment endeavors are also shaped by common purposes and considerations. These transcending aspects of assessment are the focus of this chapter.

There are at least two overriding reasons for assessing: (1) to collect and organize information about the client, his or her problem, and its context so that appropriate help can be mobilized, and (2) to use this information as a basis for developing an alliance with the client. These two assessment goals can be separated for purposes of discussion; nonetheless, they are overlapping, mutually influencing, and served by the same information-generating processes.

Constructing Shared Understanding

We sometimes write about assessment as a procedure that the clinician performs on the client (e.g., "I'll ask the questions, you give me the answers."). Actually, both individuals are involved in constructing and reconstructing an understanding. Both are observing, remembering, reflecting, inferring, and sharing information. Certainly the client is assessing the clinician and formulating some opinions about his or her helping potential. Further, both are creating their own explanations of what the problem is about and what help there may be. Each of their explanations is influenced (1) by information given to them by or picked up from the other and (2) by their own perspectives and partialities. The clinician asks the client how he or she understands the current dilemma and what he or she thinks needs to happen in order for things to be better. The clinician processes this information and incorporates his or her translation of the client's story into a beginning formulation. The clinician also influences the client's explanation; this influence is frequently intentional. Often the clinician may want the client to understand the problem in a more accepting, focused, or hopeful way, or in a way that lends itself to a particular intervention approach (Meichenbaum, 1977; Reid & Epstein, 1972). Or the clinician may want the client to enlarge his or her own understanding by further exploring his or her ideas and feelings. Using questions, comments, silences, explanations, and nonverbal expressions and gestures, the clinician tries to nudge the client in the intended direction. The client selectively attends to these communications, encodes them according to his or her cognitive schemas, and incorporates some version of them into his or her own understanding. Over time, as a function of remembering, introspecting, and communicating, the client's and the clinician's respective explanations evolve. They become more elaborate, more complex, and probably more similar.

The client and clinician are engaged in parallel and interactive processes of understanding. How well either understands the client's problem and the pathways out of it is, in some measure, a function of how well the other understands (and communicates about) these issues. By no means is the client simply the supplier of raw data. Optimally, the client is fully involved in exploring and elaborating his or her self-understanding.

Assessment may include a search for classifiable symptom patterns, but it goes beyond usual notions of diagnostic classification. The process of noting symptoms and matching them to a DSM-III-R (American Psychiatric Association [APA], 1987) diagnostic category may contribute to a useful understanding of the nature of the client's dilemma and what to do about it; however, the diagnosis of a disorder does not usually tell us all we need to know about the problem, its context, and the resources for altering it.

Assessment Over Time

Assessment of client problems is not a one-time effort at the beginning of the intervention process. As long as the clinician and client work together, they try to gain a keener understanding of the problem, what seems to maintain it, and what the alternatives or escape routes may be. Although assessment is ongoing, phases can be roughly differentiated according to time and function. Initial assessment is undertaken to build a foundation of knowledge for early intervention and is interwoven with attempts to put the client at ease, orient him or her to the process, and establish the clinician as a respectful, understanding, and competent person. In ongoing assessment of client progress, the clinician uses new information about how the problem and client are responding to interventions in order to (1) build a more complex understanding of the client's problem and his or her resources for change and (2) track the extent to which the problem is changing over time. Ongoing assessment of the change process is related to assessment of progress, but it is distinctive by virtue of its primary focus on how the client actually changes within the context of the therapy (Rice & Saperia, 1984). Each of these phases is discussed in subsequent chapters.

ISSUES IN ASSESSMENT

What Should We Assess?

One of the first questions that arise about assessment is "What exactly should we assess?" For the most part, theorists seem to agree that because thoughts, feelings, behaviors, and social input and responses are central ingredients of personal realities, they all warrant assessment. Clinical theorists agree that these domains are interactive, but provide different explanations of how the interaction actually plays out. According to some versions, one domain—for example, emotion (Zajonc, 1984), environment (Skinner, 1974), cognition (Ellis, 1973), or psychobiological drives (Freud, 1963, 1964)—is granted primacy in a unidirectional chain of influence. In other versions (which we prefer), the domains are conceptualized as reciprocally influential (Bandura, 1986); thus, emotion, behavior, cognition, environment, and physiology each exert influence on all the others. Depending, then, on the view of causality, one assessment domain (or all) is singled out for scrutiny.

There are additional, broad issues that need to be considered when making decisions about the focus of assessment. Should we assess problems or people? Do we focus on dispositions or situations? Should we assess strengths or deficits? What assessment guidelines can we extract from person-in-situation perspectives on clinical practice? And finally, is assessment ultimately concerned with understanding subjective meanings or with tracking the influence of bio-psycho-social "facts"? These overlapping considerations are explored below.

People or Problems

In the simplest terms, most therapeutic models either emphasize changing the person who has the problem or solving the problem. For example, psychodynamic therapies and some forms of cognitive therapy are more likely to ignore the specific problem that prompted the client to seek help in favor of attempting to alter aspects of the client's personal identity and world view. The idea is that the problem—a product of underlying personality deficits or distortions—will subside when the client expands his or her self-understanding and adopts more flexible ways of perceiving, feeling, and acting. At the other end of the continuum are behavior therapies and problem-focused system therapies that formulate client complaints in terms of specific and remediable problems and clear-cut goals. "Instead of trying to reorganize the client's conceptual framework, these approaches aim at helping him to define his goal . . . in specific terms and then to achieve it" (Petony, 1981, p. 36).

We assume that if the clinician's vision is not overly constrained by his or her particular theoretical commitments, the assessments will lead to varying points on the person-problem continuum. For example, sometimes assessments will reveal that a client is beset by an array of problems that have little to do with deep-seated dysfunction, or by problems that can be solved without identity transformation. At other times, assessments will lead the clinician to understand that a client is overwhelmed with problems because there is something fundamentally wrong with the way the client understands himself or herself in relationship to the world, but that the client does not want or cannot tolerate major change in self-understanding. Or it may be that the social worker's assessment will suggest that the client realizes that his or her basic stance toward life is just not productive and is distressed to the point of moving toward more extensive personal change. If the clinician is sufficiently flexible, he or she will be capable of discerning all these possibilities as well as the variations in between. In everyday practice, however, regardless of the focus, assessment and treatment is rarely carried out in a clear-cut, all-or-nothing manner. For instance the road to transformed self-understanding often consists of multitudinous problem-solving steps: confronting dilemmas one after another, understanding them from a perspective that suggests a resolution, and then acting accordingly, that is, acting differently than one has in the past. Further, in trying to solve a problem, one sometimes finds that the client's basic beliefs, emotions, and interpersonal interactions are holding him or her to such a narrow range of functioning that, as long as they are so rigidly in place, the specific problem cannot be solved. In everyday practice, it is not uncommon to move between focusing on specific target problems and focusing on more basic intrapsychic and interpersonal patterns (Ryle, 1982).

Dispositions or Situations

Clinicians' assessment efforts are often limited by what they know how to "fix." For example, if their expertise runs along the lines of helping people to explore their inner turmoil, then they are likely to look for and find complicated intrapsychic dynamics that need to be adjusted and, at the same time, are likely to miss the complicated interpersonal and environmental dynamics that may also be implicated in the problem. Although the reverse imbalance can also occur, clinicians are much less likely to overanalyze environmental contributions to problems while giving personal factors short shrift. As noted in Chapter 1, clinicians' tendency to understand clients' problems by inferring dispositional rather than situational causes probably stems from a variety of factors, including the emphasis of training programs on client dysfunction, feelings of impotence in modifying distressing environmental conditions, the practice of seeing the client in an office where he or she is removed from the situation, and an inherent observer/actor perceptual perspective (Batson, 1972, 1975; Batson & Marz, 1979; Batson, O'Quin, & Pych, 1982; House, 1980; Jones & Nesbitt, 1972; Storms, 1973).

We need to guard against limiting our understanding of problems to what we know how to do or to the resources we are able to offer. It is one thing for the clinician and client to conclude that the roots of a particular problem are environmental and that there is very little either of them can do to change those conditions. It is another to define the problem as a function of personal factors simply because the clinician has greater confidence in his or her ability to manipulate such factors. In this latter case, the clinician is simultaneously blaming the victim, misunderstanding the client's problem, and ensuring that the client will never find or create a solution to what remains a problem.

Strengths or Deficits

In most formal assessments the importance of exploring the client's strengths is usually acknowledged but given relatively little attention. Similarly, we assume that most clinicians undertake more detailed and complicated analysis of deficits than of strengths. Although it is reasonable to look for the factors that are maintaining a problem so that they can be minimized, it is at the same time critical to remember that the client's actual acts of minimization or change come from his or her personal strengths and social resources. The individual in trouble gets out of trouble by drawing on his or her assets: for example, skills, courage, tenacity, creativity, and social supports. As an advocate of positive change, the clinician needs to discover, appreciate, and enhance these positive aspects so that they may be used to address what is problematic.

☐   In sessions, Betty is typically sad, frustrated, guilty, overwhelmed by the burdens
she carries, and angry because she does not receive sufficient support. She goes
back and forth between blaming herself and blaming others for the overall
bleakness of her life. She lists examples of her intolerance, social ineptitude,
and meanspiritedness. According to Betty, her husband, whom she finds "naive
and gutless," is now and always will be a poor provider. Her kids "are all that
keep her going," but their needs, demands, and problems are relentless. She
says that she cannot wait until they are grown and gone. Whatever the cause
of her hopelessness and exhaustion, Betty feels destined for deprivation and
burden.

Recently, Betty gave a lengthy description of several interactions with her
son and daughter. Embedded in her account were details of how she listens to
them, encourages and supports them, backs them up, sets appropriate limits,
shows affection, and gives them sound advice. Betty shared all this information
with no recognition of how good and important and potentially satisfying these
attributes are. What predominated instead were her worries about what could
go wrong and how, if something did go wrong, all the burden would be hers.
But when the social worker said, "You know Betty, your kids are really lucky to
have you," Betty was clearly moved. Something moved. The worker recognized
her as a loving mother and at least for a few moments, Betty saw herself in a
similar way.

Although it is hard beyond belief for a depressed, frustrated, pessimistic woman to
give herself compassionate assistance, a loving, attentive parent may be counted on
to aid in constructive change. Perhaps Betty will be able to build on this newfound
sense of compassion and self-compassion and use it to motivate her efforts to seek
and recognize the support that she wants.

Person-in-Situation

Over the last two decades, social work theorists have emphasized the importance of
focusing assessment and intervention on the interchange between people and their
environments in order to facilitate an adaptive fit or ecological balance (Germain &
Gitterman, 1980; Meyer, 1983). Beyond the notion that social workers should attend
to the personal and social components of individuals' predicaments, the specific
practice implications of person-environment conceptualizations have been hard to
pin down (Brower, 1988). Writing about the ambiguity of social work concepts,
Goldstein (1980) notes that, for her, the idea of focusing on the interface between
people and environments conjures up images of working in cracks. In addition, the
ecological metaphor is problematic because it implies the possibility of some ideal
state of balance—some person-environment fit—that is equally satisfying for all. It
sidesteps issues of competing interests between individuals (between the individual
who is "the person" and the individuals who are his or her social environment),
and it does not address the likelihood of antithetical interpretations about what

is a "good fit" (Gould, 1984). Nonetheless, we do need a way of looking at and understanding the relationships between social realities and personal ones.

There is little doubt that individuals' responses to life circumstances cannot be fully understood by resorting to either social or psychological explanations or by simply summing credits and debits in both the social and personal columns (Bandura, 1986; Brower, 1988; House, 1980; Lazarus & Folkman, 1984; Mischel, 1973). Most simply, there is (1) the environmental situation, which comprises a set of demands, constraints, and resources (e.g., eviction, abusive relationship, unemployment, medication side effects, inadequate housing, bureaucratic requirements, friendship networks, supports and demands from family, available institutional programs); (2) the person who exhibits certain psychological and biological strengths and vulnerabilities (e.g., skills, beliefs, commitments, expectations, physical attractiveness, predispositions, and capacities); and (3) the interaction between the person and the situation (how the environment shapes the individual's beliefs, expectations, and behavioral responses and how the individual acts on, and thus shapes, the environment). An important point in all this is that "person" and "situation" do not stand still—they exist in an ongoing, changing, and mutually influencing relationship. In terms of assessment, this necessitates not only looking at what the situation offers and what the individual is thinking, feeling, or doing about it, but also looking at how these personal responses affect the situation and how this reciprocal influence plays out over time.

Case Example of Person-in-Situation Assessment

☐   Darryl is a 45-year-old man who is recovering from an acute episode of depression. Medication has helped him remobilize to the extent that he is sleeping and eating better, but he is still beset by feelings of weariness, self-doubt, and paralyzing inertia. With a great deal of encouragement and prodding from his estranged wife and his physician, Darryl got himself to the mental health center in the rural county where he lives and asked for counseling to help him with his "mental depression."

   Person. Darryl is a slow-moving, deliberate, self-contained man. Long before the depressive episode, he had trouble "getting going." Then as now, every task that faced him (fixing the roof, calling about a job possibility, taking a load of trash to the dump) was a task to put off. This chronic procrastination seems to be the result of worry that he might not be up to the task, of interpersonal anxiety that makes it hard for him to negotiate or clarify things with people, of feeling overwhelmed by all the other unaccomplished jobs that have reached the crisis stage, and of a low-key, yet impenetrable, interpersonal stubbornness: "I'll do it when I get around to it." It is likely that his recent depression is superimposed on a more chronic state of low mood.

   In terms of personal strengths, Darryl wants to be viewed as a responsible person. Once he gets started, he works hard. He is skilled or semiskilled in a number of areas (carpentry, logging, mechanics, plumbing) and is part of a network of working men from whom he can borrow tools and find out about job openings, and with whom he can "shoot the breeze." He cares about his wife and teenage son and wants them all to be together again. Darryl has modest hopes for himself: "a steady job, a car that runs, getting the house fixed up, having Denise and Raymond come back."

Situation. Eight months ago, Darryl quit his job at an equipment rental firm because he had to drive almost 150 miles a day to get to and from this low-paying job. Since then he has only worked a few weeks in temporary jobs, first as a plumber's helper and then as a car mechanic. He has looked for steady employment but has not been able to find anything. Both the utility and telephone companies are taking him to small claims court for failure to pay his bills. He was recently evicted from the house that he was residing in and maintaining for not taking care of the house. He is now living in a borrowed camping trailer on a ten-acre piece of land that he owns. This wooded land and the uninhabitable house on it are his only assets. Darryl had hoped to log off some of the land and sell the wood. However, the man who was to assist him with this project and supply the equipment seems to have disappeared. When Darryl and Denise married 7 years ago, their plan was to rebuild the house. Darryl has worked on the house off and on, but he has not had enough money, skill, or tenacity to make much progress.

Three months ago, Denise and Raymond (her son from a previous marriage) moved out because Denise was "disgusted with Darryl." At first, Darryl was sure that she would never make it on her own and would have to come back. But now he sees that she is better off without him. Denise and Raymond moved into new, subsidized housing, and Denise was able to increase her hours working as a salesperson in a fabric store from part-time to full-time.

Darryl grew up in a poor family. He was the youngest of four children and the only boy. When times were good, his parents were tenant farmers. When times were bad, his father left the family to work as a farm laborer and his mother went on welfare. Darryl attended school sporadically through the eighth grade, worked on the farm, and at age 17 left home to join the Navy. Darryl was looked after and adored by his older sisters, was relied on by his mother to take over responsibility when his father was away, and was, in his memory, put down and ignored by his father. He could never plow straight enough, get up early enough, or find the stray calves soon enough to please his father.

Current situational resources that Darryl might draw on in digging his way out of his dilemma include his land, the old dilapidated house, the ongoing concern and perhaps affection from his wife and son, and a network of friends who provide him with support, advice, and concrete resources.

PERSON-SITUATION INTERACTION With good reason, Darryl feels insecure about his own ability to make things turn out right. Although he knows much about many things, there is no one area in which he is an expert. He is skilled enough to be able to snag a temporary job when the economy is good but not enough to be kept on when there is a downturn. In part, he is not an expert because he has never kept a job long enough to hone his skills: Darryl often works for people who are also on the margins and therefore cannot guarantee him steady work; he takes whatever job he can get even if it does not suit him; and he lives in a geographic area where steady employment is hard to find. Darryl's situation-based insecurity fuels his hesitancy, plodding manner, and procrastination, which in turn contribute to the probability that others will tell him what to do and he will respond with passive resistance. All of these qualities increase his vulnerability to layoffs, indebtedness, and domestic turmoil.

Although Darryl seeks direction from his wife, he hates the feeling that he is being "led around by the nose." For her part, his wife resents his not following through on the plans they make together. She says she "doesn't mind having to struggle to get by, it is just that Darryl is not much of a struggler."

Darryl's current dilemmas are not simply a function of his slow, plodding, procrastinating ways; nor are they exclusively a matter of inadequate employment opportunities. Although these personal and situational facets both count, we suggest that the interactive pattern—the pattern in which environmental disappointments and deprivations affirm Darryl's sense of himself as a loser whom people try to push around—counts even more. His loser self-concept then inhibits him from fully exploiting the occasional opportunity that does exist, and this perpetuates his problems. The Darryl case is not prototypical of all cases. The relative contributions of personal, environmental, and interactional factors vary from case to case. But that is the point: Assessment needs to be sufficiently free from preconception about where the weight of contributing factors lies in order to detect variations.

The Data of Assessment: Subjective Meanings or Objective Facts

In recent years, several social work authors have argued that efforts to make assessment (and other facets of clinical work) more precise and scientifically rigorous ignore the notion that the "main stuff" of the clinical enterprise is subjective personal meanings, not objective, quantifiable facts. In general, these authors suggest that (1) we live in worlds of social and personal constructions; (2) attempts to define or operationalize these personal and shared understandings precisely are ultimately context-stripping and distorting; and (3) instead of relying so heavily on empirically generated knowledge to inform practice decisions, we should pay closer attention to information from social work's philosophical and value positions (Imre, 1984; Weik, 1987), from a range of qualitative methods that are suited to subjective phenomena and compatible with social work's philosophy and values (Peile, 1988; Rodwell, 1987; Weik, 1987; Witkin, 1991, Witkin & Gottschalk, 1988), and from on-the-spot innovation and creative problem solving (K. M. Wood, 1990). Although we cannot fully examine the complexity of these issues here, we want to consider them briefly in order to forge a perspective that is relevant to the assessment tasks of practice.

PERSONAL AND COMMUNAL CONSTRUCTIONS.   As social work clinicians, much (but not all) of our concern centers on subjective meanings—on how people understand the internal and external events of their lives. In part, this is so because events in the social and physical environment often allow varying ranges of interpretation. Furthermore, altering one's interpretations can make the difference between feeling inured to hope and hopeful action and feeling strong enough and worthy enough to find and make good use of the social resources that seem necessary for a reasonably satisfying life (Wakefield, 1988). Thus, clinicians pay close attention to these personal meanings. We ask our clients to tell us how it is for them, what they want for themselves, how they view their own life chances. We try both to understand these subjective accounts and, ultimately, to shape them into perspectives that allow more flexible, adaptive responses.

Nonetheless, the fact that individuals are active construers of their surroundings does not mean that the environment is entirely neutral and will allow whatever constructions people place on it. The environment also affords meaning—that is, it conveys information with implications for adaptive responses. Environmental cues about how to understand and respond vary along a continuum of ambiguity (Arnkoff, 1980; Bowers, 1984; Neisser, 1980). At the unambiguous and more constraining end, we are offered only a few cues that are universally perceived as meaning the same thing. These are cues that signal key survival events such as physical danger and opportunities for bonding (Bowlby, 1977; Guidano & Liotti, 1983). Although we all encounter some of these events over the course of our lives, many of our clients struggle for survival on a daily basis. Day to day, their lives are threatened by physical violence, abandonment, hunger, or exposure to the elements.

Beyond these unambiguous and universal cues, we are also influenced by a wide range of relatively clear-cut cues whose meanings are set by strong cultural consensus. Many of our ideas about the dimensions of life—love, work, health, worth, and death—are at least partly shared and culturally prescribed.

☐   Jana Lee is 55 years old. She has worked all her life as a waitress and has now been fired from her job because she is older, slower, and more somber than her 19-year-old-replacement. Ms. Lee accurately reads the meaning of her situation: "When you reach your fifties, there's not much out there. I've been everywhere looking for jobs. Waitressing is all I'm good at and they want young girls. It's awful not having anything . . . you lose more pride. I constantly have to ask people for favors not knowing if I can ever pay them back. It gets me very depressed. . . . I've spent the majority of my life keeping the house clean and the kids in line because I thought that's what they were looking for. . . . Now I'm up a creek. I can keep house just great, but nobody pays for that." (Berlin & Jones, 1983, p. 389)

Her understanding is not only a subjective interpretation.

Individuals are active construers of their physical and social environments, and these environments also shape their constructions. This suggests that (1) instead of being entirely subjective and idiosyncratic, a client's constructions usually include some portion of objective understanding—of a universal or social consensus—

about what things mean; and (2) in addition to paying close attention to a client's objective–subjective constructions, practitioners need to assess environmental signals independently. What is the range of meanings *allowed* by the mix of available resources and demands? How can job opportunities, housing alternatives, health care services, safe neighborhoods, and loving friends be found and mobilized in order to signal hope and give cues for initiative and risk taking? In short, practitioners need to concern themselves with personal meanings, social and cultural realities, and the affordances of the material world.

MEASURING MEANINGS   Although the major discussion of measurement issues appears in Chapter 6, a basic discussion of the functions of measurement is also necessary here.

Given that a lot of our clinical attention is necessarily focused on personal constructions, how should we try to understand them? Some argue that using measurement instruments to summarize complex subjective meanings violates these meanings and leaves us with little useful information. According to this line of argument, the importance of an individual's account of his or her sufferings, aspirations, or attempts to find acceptance may not be found in the number of times he or she attempts to make friends or in the relative intensity of his or her loneliness, but rather in the individual's own understanding of what he or she wants, how he or she views the chances of achieving these wants, and what helps and what gets in the way. In these terms, then, in order to apprehend changes in personal meaning, one must look for changes in qualitative patterns and themes as well as for changes in quantitative values of frequency or intensity. Obviously, information about both quantities and qualities of problem-related issues can be informative to the practitioner.

☐   A social worker asks Georgia if she is still feeling trapped about having to care for her mentally ill son. She wants to know if these feelings occur more or less often or with greater or lesser intensity. Georgia says the feelings of being trapped are worse; she feels them even more intensely. Without skipping a beat, the clinician asks, "In what way?" Georgia responds that the reality of having Tom back home is worse than she thought it would be. He is sullen, rude, unkempt, and unwilling to pick up after himself; she is reluctant to confront him for fear he will move out and get into some kind of trouble. She feels guilty for resenting him and worries that her resentful feelings are in some way contributing to his illness. She called Tom's psychiatrist to find out what she should do when Tom doesn't take his medication, but the psychiatrist has not returned Georgia's call. She thinks the psychiatrist views her as one of those "meddling mothers" who have to be "handled."

While the quantitative information provides a shorthand way to convey how this sense of being trapped changes—"It's worse," "It's better," "It's worse again"—the qualitative detail sheds light on concomitant changes in other dimensions of the problem: how the worker and client understand it, how the client experiences it, what supports it, and what might be done about it. If the social worker in this case decides that Georgia's trapped feeling is a central aspect of her dilemma or a good indicator of her overall problem, the worker might routinely ask Georgia to estimate which scaled value (e.g., 1 = none, 2 = a little, 3 = some, 4 = a lot, 5 = a very great deal) best represents how trapped she felt during the past week. It is the assignment of a quantity to a characteristic of interest that is generally referred to as measurement. As Sechrest (1984) points out, "statements of quantity may be as crude as a 'lot of' or 'small,' or ... even ... binary in nature (exists or doesn't exist)" (p. 24).

Even under this liberal definition of measurement, everything of interest is not readily quantifiable. In addition to wanting to know quantitatively how the feeling of being trapped waxes and wanes over time, the worker is even more interested in the shifts in a whole pattern of interacting qualities that seem to compose or form the context for the feeling. Although the clinician relies on the quantitative index for a quick determination of how things are going and as a clear-cut method of communicating about the status of the case, when she really tries to figure things out she focuses on the details that the quantities represent. For example, these details will contain important cues about how to help Georgia untangle herself from the web of constraints operating in her life. As always, the details the worker attends to, interprets, and then recalls and reflects on are only a sample of all the events that have occurred, and those systematically recorded are even more limited.

The central issue raised here concerns measurement adequacy (i.e., determining what is most important to know and then devising a way to apprehend these phenomena in the most bias-free way possible).

Even though the things we want to know about are subjective does not mean that we should not or cannot devise meaningful ways to recognize and describe these phenomena. For example, it is often possible to discern patterns of discourse, affects, and interpersonal processes that can be described, differentiated, reflected on, and recognized when they occur again. Indeed, in recent years social workers, researchers, and others have developed and refined measurement strategies and instruments that focus on interaction patterns, mood states, and various kinds of subjective perceptions. However, there is nothing in these developements that requires us to reduce subjective experiences to indicators that are meaningless and useless. Simply put, the challenge is to find better ways of tracking complex mental phenomena without being excessively reductionistic on the one hand (Weick, 1987), or scattered and amorphous on the other.

☐   Robert Jasper and Reba Goodman had been working together long enough to know a little something about the configuration of feelings, thoughts, behaviors, and responses from others that kept getting in the way of Reba's attempts to feel that she could be a good mother to her kids and give them the sense of safety and security that they needed. With a little prompting and wondering outloud from Robert, Reba wrote down what she thought this pattern was and what she wanted instead. Every week she and Robert worked on finding ways to weaken the old pattern and strengthen her evolving "new self." Every week she wrote down where she thought she was in this process of building new self-concepts. When her definition of the "new self" or the old patterns changed, those changes were easily incorporated into the recording form she used (see Figure 2.1). Both Reba and Robert thought this form was a useful addition to their work together. It helped them keep a focus, stay tuned into Reba's changing sense of what she was working on and what got in the way, and gauge her sense of progress.

Another of Robert's clients, Paul, fills this form out himself (See Figure 2.2). In this case, the recording form has been helpful in prompting Paul to assume more responsibility for figuring out where he is headed and the old responses

---

What Could Happen

Name:_____   Date:_____

Best Possible Self   (Describe here):

12	Some solid and more lasting experiences of the new, improved,
11	unencumbered me.
10	
9	Experience the alternative occasionally.
8	
7	
6	Have a sense of an alternative, but caught in a struggle.
5	
4	
3	See the pattern pretty clearly, but still stuck in it.
2	
1	
0	Entrenched in the pattern—whatever it is.

Dysfunctional Pattern   (Describe here):

*Put a check mark next to the box that best reflects your current state. Add a few words of explanation or self-instruction if you wish. You may modify the description of your dysfunctional patterns and hoped-for alternatives as they become clearer to you.

FIGURE 2.1
What Could Happen Form.

What's Going on Now

Dysfunctional patterns; problematic self (various facets, positive and negative consequences, what triggers the patterns):

What I want instead; best possible self:

What helps and what gets in the way of moving toward what I want:

How close I am to my best self and what I need to do next:

Figure 2.2
What's Going On Now

that deter him. His week-to-week analysis provides a guide for focusing the work and a record of how the change process seems to Paul.

SUMMARY OF GENERAL ASSESSMENT ISSUES

As a result of training, theoretical preferences, and personal and professional experience, most of us take some recognizable position vis-à-vis the assessment issues noted above. Some of us may focus on personality dynamics rather than problem characteristics; to make much of the dispositional facets of personal dilemmas; undertake detailed investigations of deficits while understanding little about clients' strengths; construct complex formulations of psychodynamics with only a a simplistic understanding of psychosocial dynamics. Perhaps we do not take pains to connect our formulations to recognizable occurrences that can be described and differentiated. And whatever they may be, we are perhaps not sufficiently critical of our own impressions.

Given the fact that we each have our own areas of expertise and relative ignorance, the best scenario is one in which our perceptions and abilities naturally match what the client needs and wants. However, all too often they do not match. In these situations we need to move away from the security of what we know and take another tack. Like our clients, we need to draw on our strengths—our flexibility, openness, willingness to risk, commitment to the welfare of the client, awareness of our own biases—to consider perspectives that are less habitual and automatic. We need deliberately to step out of our own professional and intellectual "comfort zone" in order to discern the kind of change that this client is seeking and how he or she is likely to achieve it (Schön, 1987).

3 | Initial Assessment: Purpose and Outline

This chapter describes the purposes of initial assessment and discusses how assessment thinking is influenced by knowledge structures, information, and thinking processes. Particular attention is given to the ways in which common biases may create errors in assessment and how the thoughtful practitioner can take steps to remedy or avoid them.

I. Introduction

II. Purposes and Characteristics of Initial Assessment
    A. What is the matter and what can be done about it?
        1. Specifying the problem.
        2. Setting goals and objectives
        3. Developing a conceptual model
    B. Understanding as intervention

III. Influences of Cognitive Structures, Informational Cues, and Thinking Processes on Initial Assessment
    A. Discerning relevant cues: The influence of schemas and theories
    B. Discerning relevant cues: The influence of availability
    C. Assessing relevant categories of problems: The influence of representativeness

IV. Decision Aids for Assessment

V. Summary

INTRODUCTION

In the initial stage of assessment, the clinician and the client start the process of trying to understand the problem—what it encompasses, obstacles to resolving it, resources for resolving it, and the internal, interpersonal, and situational dynamics that drive it. The clinician tunes into the client's subjective experience to the extent that the client feels a sense of relief at not being alone in her struggle. Through it all, the client is not just a passive supplier of the information that the clinician seeks. Ideally, she is an active partner in determining what needs to be known and evaluating what it all means (Feld & Radin, 1982). Her own efforts to understand gradually contribute to her greater self-knowledge and self-esteem.

PURPOSES AND CHARACTERISTICS OF INITIAL ASSESSMENT

To be more specific, the central and interactive purposes of initial assessment are (1) to learn enough about the client, his problem, and his overall situation to inform early intervention efforts, and (2) to establish a cooperative alliance with him. This latter purpose is accomplished by simultaneously providing the client with cues that signal respect and understanding and that guide him in achieving his therapeutic goals and by giving him "reasons" for feeling a sense of relief and hopefulness through the clinician's understanding, competence, and help in enlarging the client's own understanding. These multiple purposes are all undertaken in the process of generating a reasonably accurate understanding or description of the client's problems and the resources that may be mobilized in resolving them.

What is the Matter and What Can Be Done about It?

Putting aside distracting concerns about being sufficiently profound, fluent, clever, or likable (Strupp & Binder, 1984), the clinician begins the assessment process by asking the client about her difficulties, how she understands them, and how she has tried to handle them. The clinician listens and tries to understand what the problem is and what he and the client can do about it. The clinician hopes that, from all the details of conflicts, worries, mistakes, insults, and uncertainties that the client relates, he will be able to discern patterns in the situation and discover some aspects that can be solved or at least ameliorated. He relies on his prior knowledge of the dimensions of human struggle to focus selectively on the client's account, and he gauges and adjusts the fit of his initial surmises by checking for the client's reactions to the direction he is taking. As Schön (1987) tells us:

> When a practitioner sets a problem, he chooses and names the things he will notice.... Through complementary acts of naming and framing, the practitioner sets things for attention and organizes them, guided by an appreciation of the situation that gives it coherence and sets a direction for action.... Those who hold conflicting frames pay attention to different facts and make different sense of the facts they notice. (pp. 4–5)

We know that there is no one way to locate, define, and analyze a problem—nor even one right way. We also know that some ways are better than others. In the midst of all this ambiguity, we are guided by the dual necessities of building our understanding around the client's view of her predicament and of considering additional ways of understanding the problem, which may in turn suggest different solutions to a client who is not stuck in a solution (Wachtel & Wachtel, 1986). Moreover, to the extent that each of us can construct multiple perspectives of problems, we are more likely to be able to "select the conceptual lenses which best fit the data of the case" (Wood, 1990).

SPECIFYING THE PROBLEM   An adequate understanding and statement of the problem is a basic part of the assessment process. Indeed, a fundamental axiom of problem solving is that the better part of a solution derives from an adequate definition of the problem. Over the course of their work together, the practitioner and client are likely to elaborate or otherwise modify their initial understanding of the problem. Nonetheless, they need a place to start. As we have already discussed the process of coming up with a problem statement that incorporates at least some agreement with the client about what to work on and where to start requires sifting through a significant amount of information in order to identify priorities (i.e. those issues that are most pressing or need to be addressed most immediately.) In addition, the process requires that the practitioner and the client work together from what is typically a vague understanding or broad outline of the client's concerns to a more specific and concrete description or statement.

Guidelines for moving from this vague sense of the client's concerns to a more specific and concrete description include the following:

1. Solicit examples of the problem and consider where, when, and how often the problem occurs.
2. Work with the client to articulate the specific ways in which the problem is manifested. In other words, how does she notice it? What are the parts of the problem that she observes (her private thoughts and feelings), and what do others observe (behaviors, interactions, events, and conditions)?
3. Decide how to keep track of these observable components. It is important to have some systematic way of tracking—of monitoring, documenting, observing, and measuring—the occurrence of the problem. Often thinking in terms of indicators (i.e., ways to measure the occurrence or non-occurrence of the problem) helps to address such concerns, "How will I know when the problem gets better—or worse?" or "How will I know if this intervention effort 'works'?" Thinking about an indicator pushes us to think ahead to what we want to accomplish, to treatment goals and objectives.

It may be the case that some clients have difficulty being specific about what the problem is. In fact, part of what is the matter may be the client's lack of understanding of what is behind her feelings of distress or emptiness. In these instances, confusion about feelings and their causes may be defined as the initial problem. In other situations, the client simply may not be able to find the words to describe her experiences. In this case, the problem–defining process will move more slowly and should focus on helping the client find the words to communicate (to herself and you) about her struggles. Table 3.1 gives examples of ways in which several general concerns may be described more specifically with possible indicators.

TABLE 3.1
Translation of General Concerns into Specific Indicators

Area of Concern	Specific Statement of Problem	Verifying Source
Loneliness	No social interactions outside of work	Client journal entries
Lack of adjustment to nursing home environment	No interaction with other residents; no participation in activities	Staff logs; client self-report
School truancy	Absent from school an average of 3 days per week	School records; teacher report

SETTING GOALS AND OBJECTIVES   Once the specific character of the client's concerns has been identified, identifying treatment goals and objectives is the logical next step. Specifying the problem is one side of the coin; identifying goals and objectives is the other. When we work to specify a problem, we are attempting to understand the nature of existing concerns. When we identify goals and objectives, we are attempting to reach agreement on where we want to go, what we want to accomplish, and what specific changes we seek to achieve in our work with our clients.

In general, the term "goal" refers to the ultimate outcome of our work with our clients, the end point. "Objectives," on the other hand, tend to refer to intermediate goals and steps along the way. These tend to be discrete, manageable tasks that must be completed in order to reach the ultimate goal. Very often we are working on multiple, often interrelated objectives in order to achieve one or more goals.

The process of agreeing on goals and objectives is important for several reasons. First, clear agreement ensures that clients and practitioners have the same initial expectations of purpose and anticipation of outcome. Second, articulating a clear set of goals and objectives specifies the kinds of changes expected or required and establishes standards for evaluating progress and, ultimately, outcome. Advocates of goal-oriented helping strategies describe the dynamic of "target tropism" that results from the simple act of setting a goal. Akin to the phenomenon of phototropism, by which plants move toward a light source, target tropism refers to the tendency for human beings to move toward a relevant and realistic goal once it has been established. Thus, achieving mutual understanding of treatment goals provides a focus and organizing framework for the efforts of workers and clients. At the same time, understanding what the goal is helps to provide a standard for knowing when success has been achieved.

EXPLICATING A CONCEPTUAL MODEL   Whenever we are clear about our understanding and conceptualization of a problem, of its goals and objectives, we are working with an implicit model of our efforts that can be visualized by some adaptation of the one in Figure 3.1. In this representation, we see that we examine information about the client's concerns and problems, individual characteristics (including information about strengths, deficits, and disposition) and situation (including individual/situational interactions) (boxes a, b, c). We translate that into a set of objectives or hoped-for outcomes of our work (box e). We then attempt to identify the intervention (box d), that set of activities that will move the problem from its current state to its hoped-for state.

When we look at the diagram in Figure 3.1, we have to ask how such a simple picture can help us understand the complicated, ambiguous, and often shifting circumstances of our clients. Given the uncertainties and complexities of our client's problems and the interactional nature of our work with them, it may seem appropriate to propose a more elaborate picture, perhaps one with more boxes, circles, or bi-directional arrows. Indeed, such a picture may be closer to the reality of our work. However, we seek here to emphasize that aspect of the picture that helps us be very explicit about how we understand a client's concerns and how we translate these concerns into agreed-upon goals. Even when, or perhaps especially when, there are multiple and interacting problems, multiple goals and multiple intervention activities, an explicit model to guide our efforts is crucial. It will enable us to think more clearly about the set of activities that will move us logically, in accordance with all that we know, toward the accomplishment of our client's goals.

It is important to note that client goals and objectives are not the same as intervention activities. Goals and objectives are a desired state of affairs. Intervention activities are those actions (engaged in by client, practitioner, or others) that can be expected (as according to knowledge available from theory, empirical research, and practice experience) to result in the desired outcome. The task of assessment is that of gathering information related to the first set of boxes (boxes a, b, and c). By being as explicit as possible about that information and about the changes that we seek to accomplish, to articulate an underlying conceptual model that can guide our work. This model will then be systematically tested; this process will improve our understanding of the problem and ways to ameliorate it.

Understanding as Intervention

Along with revealing something about where and how change needs to occur, a conscientious initial assessment also serves therapeutic functions. Optimally, these

FIGURE 3.1
Conceptual model underlying intervention

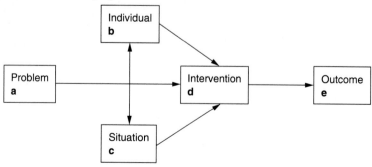

two functions are complementary. The search for clarity and specificity occurs in the context of tuning into the client and helping her understand better her own dilemmas and goals. Consequently, initial assessment can promote a therapeutic alliance. To have someone really listen, to be recognized as having legitimacy, and to interact with someone willing to seek out the complexities behind disturbing behavior and feelings and who is nonetheless able to see the client's personal mistakes: all these are signals to the client that "therapy might work," "the social worker seems to know what he is doing," "it might not be so bad after all," "it's worth a try."

A related potent aspect of understanding as intervention is the experience of being understood by another person. Indeed, the possibility of bringing ignored, forgotten, or devalued aspects of the self into the therapeutic relationship and having them recognized and understood by another is viewed by many theorists as the bedrock of positive change (e.g., Elson, 1986; Jordan, 1984; Strupp & Binder, 1984). Miller (1986) proposes that there are two related reasons that prompt people to seek psychotherapy: feeling inadequate to resolve a current dilemma and feeling alone, unconnected, and not known or understood. She explains that personal growth is most likely to happen within a relationship because being linked up with another person offers the participants access to more resources, energy, and information, and provides an esteem-enhancing sense of recognition and confirmation.

Finally, understanding one's own turmoil can effect powerful feelings of relief and hopefulness. As Hans Selye writes, "Knowing what hurts you has an inherent curative value" (1956, p. 260). This notion is endorsed by several models of therapy (Frank, 1982) and seems intuitively correct. We have all heard people say, "If I only knew what was wrong" or "If I only knew what to expect." Knowing offers relief through predictability, the possibility of adjusting and adapting, and sometimes the opportunity for mastery or control. Even though insight or expanded awareness is not usually a sufficient condition for psychosocial change (Wheelis, 1950, 1973), it can be a major ingredient of change. In these terms, it is important to approach assessment in such a way that the client's own level of understanding is expanded.

In pursuing this purpose, the practitioner prompts the client to generate ideas about what he wants, how things seem to have gone awry, how he thinks and feels about things, and what he does and thinks he might do to make things better. It is the clinician's encouragement of this kind of curiosity and exploration, coupled with her steady, respectful, and empathic attention to the client's expressions, that aids the client in knowing more about himself and his situation and valuing his own feelings and ideas. This increased understanding does not necessarily have to be sophisticated or comprehensive, but it must fit with what the client wants and have some utility (e.g., provide a sense of comfort, hope, or empowerment) for him.

INFLUENCES OF COGNITIVE STRUCTURES, INFORMATIONAL CUES, AND THINKING PROCESSES ON INITIAL ASSESSMENT

As noted above, the clinician's primary task in assessment is to understand and describe the client's problems and the resources that he or she may have for resolving them. The pursuit of this task provides the opportunity or the vehicle for achieving additional assessment purposes: relationship building, and encouraging the client toward self-understanding, confidence and hope. However, the task of assessment requires first and foremost the capacity to discern the most important among the myriad of cues presented and, second, the ability to match these cues to categories or types of problems. This latter categorization process is undertaken in order to consider possible intervention strategies.

These decisions are influenced by the clinician's knowledge structures, the kinds of information that she selects to inform her judgments, and the thinking processes she employs. As suggested in Chapter 1, the clinician's schemas related to professional practice represent her current repertoire for making sense out of a client's problems and for orchestrating assessment activities. Using a variety of thinking processes (e.g. heuristics, logic, creativity), she applies what she knows to the situation at hand. Ideally, through this process she comes to know more.

Discerning Relevant Cues: The Influence of Schemas and Theories

Given the virtually infinite amount of information that we practitioners could use to form a judgment about the nature of a client's problem, we need tools that will help us selectively focus on the information that is most useful. It is well documented that preconceptions (expert theories, personal beliefs and prejudices, and the cognitive structures that underlie them) have a powerful influence on the information we attend to and how we interpret it. This is particularly true when there is some ambiguity in the cues, as is almost always the case in a helping situation.

As practitioners, we know from participating in clinical case conferences that the same client situation can be perceived and interpreted in several different ways. The general phenomenon has been documented repeatedly and we provide one example for illustration. In a study by Temerlin (1968), a video tape was made using a professional actor depicting a healthy and happy man, functioning effectively in his work and his interpersonal relationships. He was depicted as self-confident with reasonable worries, as having had a happy childhood, and with no obvious signs of pathology. One group of participants was casually informed by a senior clinician that the man was a "rare case of a mentally healthy individual"; another group was told that he was an interesting man because "he looks neurotic but is actually quite psychotic." All the members of the first group, who were psychiatrists and psychologists, rated the individual as normal and healthy. In the second group, only 6% rated him as normal (44% rated the actor as psychotic and 50% rated him as neurotic).

Snyder and Thomsen (1988, p. 134) review evidence indicating that therapists differ in the frequency with which they apply particular classifications to randomly assigned clients (Ash, 1949; Borreson, 1965), that their "preferences" for particular types of problems influence intake decisions (Eells & Guppy, 1963), and that therapists with different therapeutic orientations differ in their initial clinical judgments

(Bishop & Richards, 1984; Houts, 1984). Not only do preferences and preconceptions have a powerful influence on judgments, but initial conceptions tend to be formed quickly with minimal information. For example, Breiland (1959) found that adoption workers formed their impressions of prospective parents in the first half of the interview and presumably used the second half to seek evidence to confirm those impressions. Sandifer, Hordern, and Green (1970) showed that 75 percent of the time psychiatrists maintain the diagnostic impressions they made in the first three minutes of a diagnostic interview. Discussing similar findings, Gauron and Dickinson (1969) observe:

> In the very act of reaching a diagnostic decision so rapidly and efficiently, [the psychiatrist] placed himself in the situation of taking a position he felt he must defend until some strikingly better alternative came along. (p. 203)

Further, Snyder and Thomsen (1988) argue that clinicians' preconceptions may act as self-fulfilling prophecies: clinicians may prompt behavioral confirmation from their clients. Behavioral confirmation refers to a process by which one's initial beliefs and expectations about another influence subsequent interactions, with the result that these initial beliefs are confirmed even if based on false stereotypes or far-fetched hypotheses. Given the evidence of behavioral confirmation across a wide variety of largely nonclinical situations, Snyder and Thomsen suggest that this phenomenon is likely to extend to the interactions between clinician and client. In these situations, not only do clinicians interpret their clients' behavior in ways that confirm pre-existing expectations, but they may actually prompt their clients to respond in ways that support these beliefs. The behavioral confirmation model suggests that, during the initial stages of assessment, the clinician quickly forms a working hypothesis about the nature and cause of the client's dilemma and proceeds to probe for the kind of evidence that will make it seem true. Snap judgments about what is wrong are aided both by referral information that contains previous diagnoses and, by the general ease with which certain "preferred" diagnostic classifications come to mind.

Clearly, stereotypes that the clinician holds about characteristics of race, social class, gender, sexual orientation, age, and physical appearance, as well as the theoretical preferences he maintains, may evoke confirming behavior in clients that provides additional examples of these stereotypes and theories. Brodsky (1989), Davis and Proctor (1989), Franklin (1985), and Zymond and Denton (1988), among others, review social science research that documents how perceptions of difference in race, gender, and social class trigger assumptions and expectations about attitudes, beliefs, and behaviors, assumptions that may be detrimental to effective helping. One classic study by Boverman, Boverman, Clarkson, Rosenkranz, and Vogel (1970) revealed the potentially negative influence of gender bias by asking clinicians to rate the characteristics of normal men, normal women, and healthy adults on an adjective checklist. Clinicians found men, but not women, to be similar to gender-unspecified "healthy adults." Since preconceptions based on demographic characteristics are so pervasive and potentially so pernicious in our society, attention to their influence is especially warranted.

Most studies of preconceptions suggest that labels and preconceptions mislead or bias us. Although preconceptions can lead to erroneous and biased conclusions, consider the job of client assessment in their absence. Without sorting and selection tools, every piece of information becomes equally important and must receive equal consideration—an overwhelming prospect. At the same time, remembering and combining particular pieces of information to refine a mutually satisfactory understanding of the problem is impossible in the absence of mental structures.

Let us take the example of the worker whose bruised client reports that her husband, recently released from prison after a conviction for assault, has "started hitting her around a little." Should the worker and client weigh the information about prior violence equally with other information (e.g., that before he went to jail he was a "good provider," that he loves his children, that he wrote home once a week from prison, and that it has been very difficult for his family to survive economically while he was away)? Or should the worker rely on her prior knowledge, her theoretically- and empirically-based preconception that past behavior is a strong predictor of future behavior, and urge the client to consider moving herself and her children to a shelter? Although none of the considerations listed above is trivial and all demand attention, the worker needs some kind of "mental map" that says, in effect, "Here is the critical factor; this is the really crucial consideration."

The practitioner's job is to understand and help each individual client. Clearly, there is no merit in beginning each case with a "blank slate." The worker is probably best served by relying on multiple sources of prior knowledge (theories, research data, personal experiences, intuitions) to construct the most pertinent and plausible understanding of and explanation for the client's situation (Bowers, 1984). Nonetheless, there are risks in relying too heavily on theories and preconceptions (Nesbitt & Ross, 1980). The following situations are particularly questionable: (1) in which a theory is held on poor grounds, (e.g. when the practitioner's theory reinterprets the client's problem in a way that has no meaning or utility for the client); (2) in which a theory is applied uncritically and unconsciously (e.g. for example, when the clinician automatically looks for personal causes of problems without any notion that she is overlooking important social dynamics); and (3) in which a theory preempts examination of data (e.g., in the worst case of behavioral confirmation, in which the clinician prompts the client to offer confirming responses so that neither clinician nor client focuses on the factors that are most salient in influencing the problem). Turning these cautions into guidelines, we can say that preconceptions about the nature of problems and how they can be altered can be helpful if they are (1) held on solid grounds (e.g., have known utility for the kind of problem with which the client is struggling and offer him additional useful ways of understanding and resolving his dilemma); (2) used consciously and with knowledge of their limitation, and (3) evaluated continuously for their utility and their fit with incoming data, the informational cues that the client is providing.

In sum, preconceptions play a major role in refining a meaningful definition of the problem. At the same time, the nature of the information generated by experiences with the client and the way in which it is processed also can and should influence the way the problem is understood.

Discerning Relevant Cues:
The Influence of Availability

Two of the most important influences on our capacity to assess a situation are the salience of specific types of information and the availability of certain types of conclusions. Salience of information derives from characteristics of the data as well as from the way we think about them. We know from Chapter 1 that the cues most likely to catch our attention are vivid, personally meaningful, familiar, and similar to something we have considered or encountered, recently or numerous times.

By far the most readily available data in assessment are the rich anecdotal data provided in interviews with the client as she "tells her story." This type of information, with its capacity to evoke powerful images and emotional responses in the worker, makes it an extremely salient source of understanding. A risk with this type of information is that the worker's own background and experience may have an undue influence on determining the specific aspects of the client's story that assume importance. For example, if a clinician has recently experienced the loss of a loved one, she may be particularly attentive to issues related to loss in her clients. This fundamental observation about therapeutic interactions underscores the importance of a clinician's self-knowledge.

Issues can be salient, both for their familiarity and for their unfamiliarity. Sometimes in an assessment situation we may focus on and remember reported events that startle us because they are unfamiliar. Ross, Greene, and House (1977) provide an example of an availability-mediated influence that leads us to view others' behavior as relatively *uncommon* to the extent that it differs from our own inclinations in similar situations. They asked college undergraduates to engage in a quasi-deviant activity: walking around campus for 30 minutes wearing a sandwich-board with the advertisement, "Eat at Joe's." Students were under no pressure to participate, but it was suggested to them that they could "learn something interesting while helping the research project." To assess the relation between their own decisions and their prediction of *other's* decisions, subjects were asked (1) to decide whether to participate or not, (2) to predict what others would do, and (3) to describe the typical personal characteristics of those who agreed and those who declined to participate. Of those who agreed to participate, 62 percent predicted their peers would do the same; of those who declined, only 33 percent predicted their peers would agree to participate. Participants described nonparticipants as deviants, and nonparticipants described participants as deviants. The implications of the study are clear: our views of deviance and normalcy are heavily influenced by our own choices and experiences. The risk in an assessment situation comes when clients report experiences and beliefs unfamiliar to us and we label these experiences and beliefs as uncommon and therefore problematic or deviant.

Newspapers and other news media shape our views of how frequent or common certain events are. Slovic, Fischoff, and Lichtenstein (1976) discovered a popular belief that more people die from fires than from drowning despite contradictory mortality rates. They explain this by the fact that fires, as compared with drownings, are dramatic and easily captured on film. As a result, we are "overexposed" to fires, or exposed disproportionately to their occurrence. Any aspect of the environment given disproportionate coverage by the news media or through other means—special instructions (Regan & Totten, 1975), seating arrangements (Storms, 1973, Taylor & Fiske, 1975), striking appearance (McArthur & Post, 1977) or "solo" status by virtue of gender or race (Taylor et al., 1979, cited in Nesbitt & Ross, 1980).

Recognizing how powerful salience factors are in influencing judgment helps us to understand why dispositional biases—the tendency to overestimate the influence of individual factors and underestimate the influence of situational factors—are cited as the most frequent, indeed the fundamental, attribution error (Nesbitt & Ross, 1980). As described in Chapter 1, this is particularly true in helping situations, in which the worker's roles of helper and observer lead her to focus on individual rather than situational factors.

Assessing Relevant Categories of Problems: The Influence of Representativeness

We have discussed one basic inferential task of assessment: discerning the relevant cues in order to refine a meaningful definition of the problem. A second major cognitive task in the attempt to define the problem is judging the similarity of the client's difficulty with categories of problems with which we are familiar. Implicit in this task are questions like these: "What is the likelihood that Alison will run away from home? Does her problem belong in the runaway category?" "What is the likelihood that Leslie's minimal attention to her children results from a depression? Should Leslie's problem be classified as depression?" "Will John be able to complete the GED program? Is this a case of underachievement?" This matching aspect of the process of clinical judgment enables us to begin to identify appropriate interventions since interventions are typically related to given problems. In judging the similarity of a given problem to existing categories or processes, we are typically relying on the *representativeness heuristic*.

The risks of relying on the representativeness heuristic in assessment derive from the fact that social workers work with clients on a case-by-case basis. We judge the similarity of our case to a larger class of cases only on the basis of a single case's information. This fact of clinical life leaves our judgments vulnerable to bias because we typically do not have or do not consider other information that is relevant to the assignment of a case to a larger class of cases. For example, we do not always determine how commonly the problem occurs in the larger population and how reliable is the information we use to make these judgments.

In contrast to case-by-case data, survey data or epidemiological data based on larger samples provide more accurate information about the relative frequency of a problem in a specific population group (e.g. use of drugs among teenagers). Further, data from such studies are typically accompanied by information about the validity and reliability of the measuring instruments, thus giving us some sense of how dependable the information is. As we have discussed, although a case may have characteristics that fit a particular class of problems, it is useful to consider whether this class occurs frequently or infrequently both within and outside of our agency or clinical population. If the problem we are diagnosing is relatively rare in either population, then the likelihood that our diagnosis is correct is lower than if the problem is common.

Consider the following example:

☐   Sue is a first-year social work intern in a well respected agency serving the chronically mentally ill. Ron, age 22, has been referred by his family doctor to the agency and Sue has been assigned to be his worker. As she begins assessment, she learns that Ron's isolation from his peers and his fundamental lack of social skills seem to be the primary basis for his referral. In many ways, Ron reminds Sue of the reserved, bookish friends she made in her academically rigorous undergraduate program. Indeed, he is not too dissimilar from her graduate school colleagues who have little time to socialize because of their studies and numerous part-time jobs. Further, Ron communicates to her that he does not believe he belongs in "a place like this." She sees that many of the seriously mentally ill clients in the agency have limited capacity to relate to others and are quite isolated, but she wonders whether social isolation alone is sufficient basis for a diagnosis of mental illness. Her supervisor and other more experienced workers seem not to doubt that Ron "belongs" here.

Sue's recent entry into the field may provide her with easier access to nonclinical comparisons than her more experienced colleagues. As mentioned in Chapter 1 in the discussion of the availability heuristic, particular diagnostic categories are readily accessible to experienced practitioners who work with them every day. It is important to be particularly cautious about our judgments based on information with questionable reliability and validity (e.g., brief interviews, reports from a relatively uninvolved referral source, diagnostic tools of untested reliability and validity). Sue could, hypothetically, formalize and validate her impressions by finding evidence about of social isolation in the general population through population surveys. Although this type of validating information is often difficult to find, her judgment is perceptively informed by the comparisons she is able to make between her client and non-agency populations.

DECISION AIDS FOR ASSESSMENT

To repeat, the two fundamental cognitive tasks in assessment are describing the problem in such a way as to impose meaning on an enormous amount of information, and inferring whether a specific constellation of observations or facts belongs to a larger known category of problems. In completing these tasks, we are vulnerable to some predictable influences. If we are aware of these influences, however, we can seek certain information and adopt certain habits that can help minimize them. These influences and the countervailing decisions aids are discussed here and summarized in Table 3.2.

TABLE 3.2
Assessment Inference Strategies and Related Decision Aids

Assessment Biases and Description	Example	Decision Aids
Theories and pre-conceptions shape what we perceive.	Because theories tend to focus on individual sources of problems, their uncritical application may contribute to dispositional bias.	Hold theory and preconceptions in abeyance. Decide when theory is adequate.
	Race, gender, sexual orientation, and age of our clients may lead to erroneous assumptions and expectations.	Engage in self-exploration to heighten sensitivity to misplaced assumptions and expectations.
Any factor that increases salience of information will receive undue weight in decision making: e.g., concrete, vivid case data dominates abstract, statistical data.	Well-publicized events considered to happen more frequently: observed frequency more important than relative frequency; information on non-occurrence usually not available.	Use information systems to check statistical data and data on non-occurrence.
Problems are defined in terms of personal experience and background.	May see pathology in behavior and events unfamiliar to us.	Use client's experience and definition of problem.

The biases with which we must be concerned include being uncritical of our theories and preconceptions. There are several ways to guard against the misapplication of theory. The simplest is to collect objective information and attempt to understand a situation without immediately applying theoretical concepts to aid understanding. The professor who marks exam papers blind to the identity of the authors is keeping at bay his or her preconceptions about the ability of his or her students. However, as theories can be very helpful for interpreting complex information, it is not sensible to ignore them completely. Once judgments have been made in the absence of theory, a theory-driven interpretation can be compared with the theory-free interpretation. Of course, as we have noted earlier, it is never possible to free ourselves completely from our preconceptions. What we are suggesting here is an approach to gathering and interpreting information that is deliberate in its efforts to identify the theoretical lenses we are using to bring meaning and understanding to information, and then to attempt to achieve some distance from these lenses in order to be able to look at the facts in a "fresh" way. Such a process helps us both to stay in touch with the theoretical tools we rely on, sometimes without conscious thought, and to make room for the possibility of innovation.

Similarly, we need to achieve some distance from the preconceptions that may be triggered by such specific client attributes as race, gender, class, age, and sexual orientation. Robinson (1989) provides a very useful set of questions about race, in this case African American, that the practitioner should address in order to achieve this distance and self-understanding. Questions include: What is my experience with people of color? What did my family teach? How do I exercise authority and relate to authority of others? How do I react in situations in which I observe racist behavior or ideology? As Davis and Proctor (1989) suggest, when clients and practitioners perceive differences in one another, some very natural questions come to mind, such as, Does this person have my best interests at heart? Is this person adequately skilled and trained? Does this person have sufficient understanding of my reality and world view? Robinson's questions (which could be applied to differences in age, gender, class, sexual orientation as well as race) provide a self-exploration exercise that is likely to lead to a level of self-understanding and sensitivity that may help avoid the negative impact of preconceptions and prejudice.

Another factor with which we are concerned is the influence of salient and vivid information. A worker concerned about whether she is overly influenced by readily available information can inform her thinking by examining the frequency of specific types of problems among the agency population as well as the general population. For example, if she learns that the problem she and the client have identified is relatively infrequent in the population, she may wish to double-check for flaws in her reasoning. An aphorism that illustrates the value of taking into account the relative frequency of events is "When you hear hoof beats, think horses not zebras." Similarly, if a worker determines, as in the previous example of Ron, that the "problem" is a common one such as loneliness and social isolation, she may question whether the full weight of the service system should be brought to bear on it. Checking such data informs a decision rather than determines it.

A further concern is the tendency for clinicians to define problems in terms of their own experience, labeling familiar problems as "normal" and unfamiliar problems as "deviant." This tendency contributes to dispositional bias, the well-documented tendency among professional helpers to lodge responsibility for problems primarily with the clients rather than with their situations. This phenomenon could be thought of as a kind of selective perception. The result is that a client's situation may not be properly perceived, with the likely effect that the worker will see the client has having a pathological condition or more serious problems than he or she actually has. To avoid such errors, we identify two "decision aids" that are readily available: our clients and ourselves. Specifically, by taking seriously our client's view of the problem, we are likely to think more broadly and creatively about problems and, ultimately, to reach more accurate conclusions. By being alert and concerned about common cognitive limitations and distortions, we may be more likely to avoid them.

SUMMARY

Perhaps the best decision aid available to us is to approach decision making with a critical stance toward the analytical processes we use. Such an approach would lead us to apply theory with a certain skepticism and to cross-check case-level information with base-rate information from our agency population or general population in order to place our decisions in a broader context. Most importantly, it would lead us to work very hard to understand the client's perspective of the relevant issues. To put it another way, the most important decision aid that we have available is careful habits of mind.

4 | Initial Assessment: A Case Example

T his chapter provides an extended case illustration of initial assessment. By focusing on how the social worker and the client think their way through this process, it provides examples of how multiple sources of information, preconceptions, behavioral confirmations, and biases influence clinical judgments; and how multiple sources of information, reflection, consideration of biases, and openness to additional ways of understanding can enhance the probability of making useful decisions.

Jackie Woods is preparing for an initial interview with the seventh client of her professional career. Jackie is a 29-year-old African-American social work student in her second-year placement at an urban mental health center. Even though she has been through this process six times before, she is still a little anxious. She does not bother to search out the specific reasons behind her nervousness but, in general terms, she is afraid she won't know what to do to be helpful. Jackie does not have an extensive repertoire of formal and experiential knowledge about how to conduct an initial assessment, much less of what to do after that. Her field instructor has tried to reassure her on this matter. He has told Jackie that part of what is required is simple human respect, warmth, curiosity, and problem-solving thinking. She reminds herself that "life experience counts." But both the supervisor and Jackie know there is more to it than that. That is why she is in school—to generate a more complex and solid foundation of conceptual and practical knowledge from which to advance. At some point in the next couple of weeks, Jackie will need to give her client a DSM diagnosis. The agency requires it and so do insurance companies. But Jackie's supervisor has suggested that she get to know her clients in a broader way in the beginning.

"So, okay," Jackie thinks to herself, "what is this assessment business all about?" She reaches into her briefcase and pulls out a beat-up, xeroxed copy of assessment guidelines adapted from the task-centered textbook of Reid and Epstein (1972). Jackie likes this list because it lays out the components of initial assessment in a clear and specific way (see Table 4.1 for an adaptation of the Reid & Epstein model). It provides her with an explicit procedural routine—one that she may eventually incorporate into her own schematic knowledge about assessments and initial interviews.

Jackie reads through this list. It still makes sense. She jots down a few key words on her yellow pad to take into the interview with her. She reminds herself that she does not have to complete all these steps in the initial session or even follow them in exact sequence. "So, okay," she thinks, "I have a place to start, a direction to follow, and I don't have to be too rigid about it all." Jackie's phone rings; her client has arrived.

Jackie introduces herself to Karen Garner, a middle-aged, thin, Caucasian woman, with black, probably tinted, hair. She shows Ms. Garner to her office, makes some friendly remarks along the way, directs her to a chair, and begins. In a questioning tone Jackie says, "I understand that some upsetting things are going on in your life right now." Karen looks extremely pale and strained. Her voice is tremulous as she responds, "I don't know, I just seem to be falling apart." Jackie acknowledges her comment with a slight nod and expression of concern. Karen proceeds to describe how emotionally distraught she has been feeling since her husband's affair. She believes that he ended the affair four months ago, but she is still so mad, weepy, and scared that she feels like her own life is "going down the tube." In response to Jackie's questions about what her own life is like day to day, Karen provides more detail: she is having a hard time concentrating on her work as a real estate broker, she does not feel like seeing friends, she is drinking too much

TABLE 4.1
Initial Assessment Tasks

I.		Identify the problems.
	1.	Ask the client to identify her range of concerns and her main concerns.
II.		Describe and operationalize the problems and goals.
	1.	Ask the client to describe his or her main problems (how he or she experiences and explains them) and his or her main goals.
	2.	Ask for examples and elaborations to get a refined description of the components of the problems and goals (e.g., what behaviors, thoughts, emotions, interpersonal interactions, social situations, person-environment interactions constitute the problems and goals).
III.		Analyze the problems and goals.
	1.	Find out additional information about the personal, interpersonal, and environmental conditions that seem to cause and/or maintain the problems and those that need to be altered in order to achieve the goals.
IV.		Conceptualize the problems and goals.
	1.	Pull together a coherent working explanation of the problems and what needs to happen in order to reach the goals.
	a.	An explanation that builds from the details provided by the client and is, thus, sensible to him or her; one that organizes the information in a way that makes the problem situation more understandable (less chaotic, less amorphous, less abnormal) and that raises realistic hopes that solutions can be found.

(about 3-4 drinks a day), she is smoking too much, she feels constantly on the verge of crying, and she cannot restrain herself from "needling" her husband. Ultimately, she thinks her own inability to cap her anger will drive her husband away.

By now Jackie's preoccupation with her own anxiety and potential inadequacy has largely given way to Ms. Garner and her distress. In the 15 minutes or so that have elapsed, Jackie has already both taken in and necessarily overlooked a great deal of information. Without even thinking the words to herself, she is beginning to focus on some emerging patterns in Karen's account: clinical depression, a "hard" woman who dyes her hair and drinks, overly dependent on an irresponsible man. In these early stages of "naming and framing" she is generating largely dispositional and deficit-oriented problem configurations. These may fit the "facts of the case" or they may reflect Jackie's preconceptions and processes of thinking; possibly both.

In any case, these conclusions are variously influenced by Jackie's observations, personal beliefs (e.g., hard woman, dependent on an irresponsible man), and newly found theoretical knowledge (e.g., clinical depression). She reviews her experiences with other women Ms. Garner's age—mostly friends of her mother's she has known at church—and she wonders whether Ms. Garner will be able to trust her despite their differences in age, experience, and race. For the most part, Jackie's thinking processes are automatic, dominated by the "ready to mind" availability heuristic (e.g., the vividness of Karen's rather stark appearance readily triggers classifications of hard women who frequent bars and dye their hair) and the representativeness heuristic, which matches Karen's descriptions of weepiness and despair to the category of clinical depression. However, Jackie also employs controlled thinking or "mindfulness" as she self-consciously tries to apply what she has learned in her classes about the assessment process and about depressed women.

Karen has also taken in some new information. First, she sees that Jackie is black and relatively young. These observations call upon her schemas about types of people—"young people" and "black people." She is not quite conscious of the exact categories she uses to describe such types, but she experiences the associated feelings. She feels a little dubious about working with Jackie. Nonetheless, she plunges ahead. As she continues to describe her experiences to Jackie, she derives some relief from being able to explain things in an intelligible manner and from Jackie's seeming appreciation of what a mess she is in. She hears herself talking about her tears, drinking, listlessness, and rage and begins to think to herself that she has let things go too far, that she had damn well better get a grip on herself. Although Karen is not aware of exactly where this line of thinking is taking her, she is relying on other networks of abstract knowledge to arrive at the notion that she needs to buck up, control her feelings, and hang on to her husband Tom. These are private and not quite formulated thoughts. She does not share them with Jackie, and Jackie has not discerned any cues that might prompt her to ask about these reactions. Instead, Jackie proceeds by focusing the next portion of the interview on Tom, his affair, and Karen and Tom's marriage.

Karen describes Tom as a big, gruff, fun-loving man who drinks too much. Every evening on his way home from work as a construction contractor he stops by the tavern and spends some hours drinking and regaling "the boys" with jokes and sports stories. As far as Karen is concerned, this habit is only a problem when it becomes excessive, as it often does. In those instances, Tom spends too much time at the bar and neglects her, neglects the kids (two children are out of the home, now young adults; one 16-year-old boy is at home and chronically truant from school), spends too much money, and takes up with other women—"at least one other woman." These topics have been the source of numerous arguments over the course of their 23-year marriage. Karen has been able to handle everything, except Tom's "sneaking around with some conniving bitch." When she first found out about the affair she moved out of the house. However, she moved back two weeks later in response to Tom's remorse. In the months that followed, she felt neglected by Tom and determined to hang on to him. Her strategy was to stay with him all the time in order to ensure that he did not stray again. To have contact and to guard him meant spending a lot of time in the bar drinking with him. Ordinarily, Karen enjoys having a few drinks and then dinner with Tom and other couples one or two nights a week. But now she feels compelled to meet him at the bar every night. This is too much for her.

Jackie's follow-up questions and prompts focus Karen on thinking more about her relationship with Tom and what is wrong with it. What is wrong, she thinks to herself, is that she does not trust him. She also thinks that she will just have to find a way to deal with the mistrust because she does not want to lose him. These thoughts are clearer to her now, as is the anxiety that accompanies them. Still, she does not talk to Jackie about needing Tom, partly because she thinks Jackie might think that she is weak and spineless. This latter thought does not really exist in words; at this point, it is just more of a feeling, a reluctance.

Although Jackie intends to clarify the ways in which Karen feels let down by Tom as a means to solidifying Karen's motivation to expect and get more from this relationship, Karen reads many of these clarifying, underscoring comments as indications that Jackie thinks Tom is awful and that Karen should leave him. What Jackie really thinks is that Tom is not coming through for Karen and that Karen deserves more. As a result of careful observation, Jackie is also aware that Karen now seems slightly more closed and tight as she sits there picking little balls of lint off her sweater.

"I guess you must think I'm nuts, getting into a mess like this," Karen says. "No," replies Jackie, "I don't think you're nuts." Karen looks squarely at Jackie: "Well, what do you think?" For a moment Jackie's mind goes blank and she feels a surge of anxiety. She hates these point-blank questions. She says, "I think you're having a hard time." Karen frowns and Jackie tries again, stammering a little in the process. "I think you are disappointed and hurt and mad that Tom would be disloyal to you when you have been so loyal to him, and I think that you can't quite figure out what would be the best thing to do." Jackie has adapted her conceptualization of Karen's difficulties so that it both fits and extends Karen's own understanding. Karen nods and adds, "But you know, I guess I haven't always been so loyal." Karen goes on to talk about a brief affair she had ten years ago. The other man had been very interested in her, but she broke off the relationship because she couldn't bring herself to leave Tom. She guesses she really is loyal to him. She looks down, picks at her sweater, and then continues, "There's just something about Tom...." She talks about his soft, gentle side that is usually hidden underneath all of the toughness and bluster, his giving her two dozen roses on her birthday, and her feeling that she is the only person who has ever really cared about him. She shakes her head a little and says, "We're quite a pair." On some level, Jackie finally gets it; at least, she thinks she gets it. Her understanding has been importantly filled out and altered by the information Karen has given her. "You feel that the two of you belong together . . . that underneath it all Tom is kind of sweet and needs you to care about him . . . and you . . . ?" Karen shakes her head yes. She goes on: "He's sweet, but he's also a bastard and I can't imagine leaving him!" Jackie waits a few seconds, and then says, "Do you ever imagine it?" Karen's shoulders sag a little and she says, "Yeah, sometimes."

By now Karen and Jackie have even more information. Both of them feel more connected to each other. Karen feels understood, not judged, and is more able to be open; Jackie, too, feels more understanding. Using knowledge largely generated by empathy, observation, and the process of reflection-in-action, Jackie has moved away from her impression of Karen as the hard woman with the dyed hair hanging out in bars. She is viewing Karen from another perspective. Jackie's direct experience of Karen has proved to be dissonant with her "bar floozy" stereotype and caused Jackie to change it. Women who go to bars and dye their hair can be funny, vulnerable, scrappy, and generous. Jackie likes Karen's intensity, her humor, and also her willingness to give Jackie a chance. In addition, something about the way that Karen crumpled at the thought of leaving her husband elicited a surge of compassion in Jackie. Jackie also has a better feel now for how one could get hooked into a relationship with a tough, tender, needy guy. She can imagine it. On the other hand, Karen is now able to focus on the rest of her story—the guy is not always so sweet and tender, and things are a mess between them.

Jackie realizes that their time is almost up. She is a little worried about all the areas they did not explore, and even more overwhelmed by all the information that has been generated. She feels that she somehow needs to pull things together in these closing minutes. She asks if Karen has a sense of what she wants for herself. Karen says, "Well, I guess I need to sort myself out about Tom. I just don't know if I'm up to it." Jackie presses on to get tentative agreement about a focus: "Okay, so even though it's going to be hard, maybe you can figure out how you want things to be with Tom and see if he'll work with you on that." Karen nods. Jackie continues, "And what about just you? How about taking better care of yourself and feeling less distressed on a day-to-day basis?" Karen agrees that she needs to get her own act together. In the last few minutes she and Jackie explore briefly some things she might do in the upcoming week that would be steps toward that: making plans to have dinner out with a woman friend, not following Tom to the bar, cutting back on her own drinking, buying reading material for the evenings she will spend home alone, keeping notes about the difficulties of not tracking Tom. Karen says she is not ready to talk to Tom about coming with her to the mental health center. She is not sure yet that she wants him to and she is sure that he would "snort at the idea." Jackie accepts that. "Not right now, but maybe later." She suggests that in any event, she and Karen need to think through how the two of them can work together, and how the therapy might proceed. These things they can discuss at the next appointment when they will have more time. Karen

agrees to another appointment. Karen and Jackie make a few parting comments, Jackie escorts Karen down the hall, they shake hands at the door, and Karen leaves. Jackie goes back to her office and collapses in her chair: "I don't believe I'm doing this!" Karen walks to her car, gets in, and slumps over the steering wheel: "What have I gotten myself into?"

After a cup of coffee, a brief chat with her supervisor, a few minutes of pacing, and a few more minutes of staring out the window, Jackie sits at her desk to write an assessment summary. This is to be more of a "working assessment" than any final statement. As an exercise in mindful reflection, Jackie pulls together her observations, conclusions, and speculations. She takes time to conscientiously review the details of what happened and thinks more about the key issues: (1) how things are for Karen, (2) the things with which she seems to be struggling, (3) what Karen will need to do in order to feel better and sort things out with Tom, (4) what other information Karen and Jackie will need in order to fill out their understanding of these issues, and (5) what Jackie might have missed, misconstrued, or made up. As she goes through the categories on the assessment form, she writes in what she knows and what she wants to find out, as well as cautions and other notes to herself. Table 4.2 shows her notes for the first category.

As she fills out the other sections of the summary, Jackie will notice and question her largely dispositional understanding of Karen's dilemma. To double-check this formulation, she will reconsider it in the light of Karen's personal and

---

TABLE 4.2
First Assessment Category

Range of concerns and main concerns:
1. Feelings of distress over Tom's infidelity (e.g., frequent crying, anxiety, sniping at Tom, trouble concentrating at work, excessive drinking).
2. Afraid of losing Tom—afraid that he will find someone else or that she will somehow be forced to pull out. Either way, she will be left...bereft, worthless, what?
3. Dissatisfied with other aspects of her relationship with Tom. He drinks too much, spends too much money, neglects kids and her, spends too much time at the bar.

What else?
1. What are her other concerns? What about the kids?
2. What else is a problem in the relationship—what does she want, what is she getting?
3. How much is Tom drinking? How much is this a problem?
4. Does Karen want to fix her marriage, reduce her distress, get over feeling mad at Tom so she does not drive him away? What do I want her to want?
5. Why didn't I pick up more on Karen's anger at Tom? What is it about? Anger may be self-preserving and, ultimately, constructive.
6. Is there anything that I am missing because of our racial differences? Do I feel more constrained because she is white? Would I treat her differently if she were black? How much of the different treatment is appropriate, and how much defensive?

---

situational strengths. She will also wonder if her own inexperience and discomfort in seeing married couples and the fact that she is currently taking a course on women and depression are pushing her toward conceptualizing this problem as an individual, depressive disorder. Jackie will eventually become explicitly aware of her own nervousness about alcohol use, and she will talk with her supervisor about how the drinking might figure into Karen's problems.

Jackie has learned in her class that depression is the most common psychiatric disorder and that at least two-thirds of depressed people are women (Weissman, Meyers, Douglas, & Belanger, 1984; Weissman, Leaf, Holzer, Meyers, & Tischler, 1986). These population data tell Jackie that she is not going against general patterns by viewing Karen as depressed. On the other hand, Jackie knows that population statistics cannot confirm that Karen is depressed. And even if she is, there are still the questions of what is behind the depression: how important is it to Karen's overall dilemma and what to do about it?

What Jackie puts into her summary is her current recollection and reconstruction of the information that she and Karen generated. Inevitably, this reflects only a portion of all the cues available—both those that she picked up but did not consciously notice and those that she selectively attended (Bowers, 1984). The information that she reconstructs in her summary is undergirded by her cognitive structures. It is informed by observation, empathy, intuition, theory, and values. And it is generated by a combination of controlled and automatic thinking processes that occur both at the moment and during later reflection. She sometimes draws inferences based on availability, representativeness, and dispositional characteristics, but part of Jackie's reflection includes identifying and questioning these thinking biases. No doubt Jackie also prompted Karen toward confirming Jackie's hypothesis about what was going on. Here it seems that Karen's confirming responses were based in part on her own experiences. In other words, what Jackie suggested seemed pretty close to Karen's own sense of things.

It is not possible (or necessary) for Jackie to reproduce every nuance of the intial communication and understanding, nor to find the one right way of interpreting these signals. As noted above, the important thing is that Jackie's and Karen's interactive ways of generating and organizing information elicit discernible patterns of a problem that are based on Karen's concerns and that include some solvable or at least diminishable aspects.

From the moment she first laid eyes on Karen, Jackie has been selectively attending and classifying the components of such a pattern. As noted, she has relied on preconceptions, observations, and heuristic thinking. So far, the pattern she has constructed—and now explicitly articulates—is still at the level of a collection of vaguely interconnected parts. Roughly, these parts are: (1) Karen's feeling betrayed, vulnerable, and mad; (2) her idea that she needs to be there understanding Tom as only she can and that this will mean a very great deal to him even though he has a hard time showing it; (3) her losing track of the other aspects of her life (friends, work, health, other interests) as she focuses more on Tom and how to keep him from temptation. This beginning of a discernible pattern is something that Jackie can reflect on, check out with Karen, clarify, modify, and track over the course of the therapeutic encounter. At this stage, Jackie's understanding of problem components or patterns is not in the form of crisply operationalized target problems or a full dynamic formulation. Nonetheless, it has some utility; it gives her a beginning idea of what needs to be worked on and what to keep track of in order to gauge change. The more Jackie fills out this description (i.e., fills out her evolving "Karen schema"), the more elaborate, organized, and resistant to change it will become. This suggests that as Jackie becomes more of an expert about Karen, she will also need to watch even more carefully for flaws in her formulations, and for new information that might expand or even radically alter her growing understanding.

Meanwhile, Karen is also doing some reflecting. She likes Jackie, likes the talk they had. In addition to feeling relieved, she is also very agitated. She is home now, pacing, thinking, and muttering to herself: "I'm not the kind of woman who goes to therapy. And the therapist! The social worker is black and a teenager! God, what am I thinking of?...Well, maybe it will help, but maybe it won't....Sometimes the more you talk about things, the worse they get. Tom would just guffaw...Tom! He's just a two-timing, lecherous drunk...and I'm stuck with him...Am I really going back there?" She pours herself a glass of wine, takes a sip, flings the rest down the sink, curses, and goes to the phone to call her office.

3 ASSESSING PROGRESS AND PROCESS

5 | Ongoing Assessment: Assessing Client Progress

This chapter discusses the reasons for assessing a client's progress over the course of the service contract, at the point of termination, and for a period beyond, and raises a number of considerations that guide the ongoing work of assessment.

I. Purposes and Characteristics of Ongoing Assessment
   A. Understanding the client's problem in the context of remediating change
   B. Evaluating progress and evaluating outcome

II. Fundamental Considerations Guiding Assessment
   A. Documenting treatment and treatment integrity
      1. Treatment activity
      2. Treatment specification
      3. Measuring the implementation of treatment
   B. Documenting change
   C. How will this information be used?
   D. Feasibility considerations

III. Influences of Cognitive Structures, Informational Cues, and Thinking Processes on Evaluating Progress and Outcome
   A. Expectations
   B. Confusing cause and chance
   C. Incomplete information
   D. Hindsight bias

IV. Decision Aids for Evaluating Progress and Outcome
   A. Information systems
   B. Formal monitoring and evaluation

V. Summary

It is common for practitioners to greet clients by asking, "How are you?" or "How are things going?" Even though we may pose this question as a simple pleasantry or conversation starter, once we have started working with a client we really do want to know how he or she is now and how things seem to be going. The client's well-being matters, and in order to move toward positive change we want to continue to fine tune our interventions to what he or she needs. Depending on the current state of the client and the problem, we may, for example, focus on circumventing a further downturn, solidifying a gain, or pushing for further action.

PURPOSES AND CHARACTERISTICS OF ONGOING ASSESSMENT

To reiterate, initial assessment is undertaken to gather information about the client, the problem, and the situation in order to suggest early interventive steps and to give the client a sense of being understood. Without any disjuncture, the practitioner and client proceed to modify and fill out their understanding—to construct a more refined sense of what the problem is, what might constitute help, and to what degree the help is really helping. The major job of ongoing assessment is to understand the client's problem, and to revise that understanding if necessary, while trying to remediate the problem. Working toward this understanding means discerning how and why changes in the client's problem are manifested.

Understanding the Client's Problem in the Context of Remediating Change

From the standpoint of clients, the process of talking and thinking more about their problems and prospects, feeling accepted and challenged by the clinician, and experiencing their own and others' reactions to initial change efforts provides them with new information to synthesize into a more refined and complex understanding. In effect, the client ponders, "Now that I feel more accepted, encouraged, and understood, what do I think is wrong, what do I want, and how do I think I am going to get it?" "Now that I have thought more about all this and talked it over more...." "Now that I know what I'm up against...." "Now that I see what good things might happen...."

As guides, contributors, and witnesses to this process, clinicians also refine and elaborate their own understanding of the problem. They consider what needs to change, how they may assist the client in changing, and the extent to which their current intervention efforts seem helpful or need to be modified. Unlike the researcher undertaking controlled experiments to verify effects, the clinician has an interactional relationship to this investigative process. As Schön (1983) describes:

> The phenomena that he seeks to understand are partly of his own making; he is in the situation that he seeks to understand.... [T]he action by which he tests his hypothesis is also a move by which he tries to effect a desired change in the situation, and a probe by which he explores it. He understands the situation by trying to change it, and considers the resulting changes not as a defect of experimental method but as the essence of its success. (Schön, 1983, p. 151)

Assessing the process, progress, and, ultimately, the outcome of change are overlapping and interdependent endeavors. Details about progress or outcome are most useful when coupled with an understanding of how progress was made. Likewise, information about important therapy processes is incomplete without knowing something about the effects of those processes. For purposes of organization and clarity, we attempt to highlight the distinguishing features of each of these assessment tasks in separate chapters. Nonetheless, as our examples illustrate, we are unable to talk sensibly about any one of these without also bringing in the other two. Thus, in the remainder of this chapter and in the next, we emphasize the tasks of evaluating progress and outcome, but in doing so also focus on the considerable overlap between process and signs of progress.

Evaluating Progress and Evaluating Outcome

Ongoing assessment of progress promotes a more complex self-knowledge in the client. It also provides a basis for more tuned-in understanding in the worker, generates clues about whether the problem is changing and the therapy helping, and yields information about what it is that now needs to be done to assist the process of change. The term "outcome" implies that there is a point in time (usually at the end of the therapy) when all the change efforts come to fruition, a point which can be viewed as the outcome of the intervention work. The truth is that change is not so orderly. For example, processes instigated in therapy may not really effect much change until they interact with a life event at some relatively distant time. Alternatively, the client's end-of-therapy sense of well-being may be washed away by a difficulty that occurs a few days after the final assessment. The unevenness and instability of change is one reason why clinical researchers stress the importance of conducting follow-up evaluations after a lapse of time. On the other hand, it is also reasonable to expect that some positive change will have occurred by the end of the therapeutic encounter. Although the client's progress at this juncture is not the final word, it can be used as one source of information about how the client is doing.

FUNDAMENTAL CONSIDERATIONS GUIDING ASSESSMENT

In putting together an assessment strategy, the fundamental questions are: What do I need to track over the course of the intervention? How will this information be used? and How can I get it in a feasible way? How these questions are answered and the ways in which the clinician actually goes about tracking progress are inevitably influenced by his or her cognitive structures, the kinds of information relied on, and the kinds of thinking processes employed. We provide selected examples of these influences in the pages that follow .

Describing progress requires that we acquire information about the actions and activities of our intervention and the outcomes or results of those activities. Cast in the simplest terms, we can think of our intervention (I) as having some influence on an outcome (O): $I \rightarrow O$ (Greenberg & Pinsoff, 1984). In reality, the large I consists of a great many small is influencing many small os, (and reciprocally, many small os influence many small is), ultimately resulting in an outcome we can think of as O. Thus, the basic requirement for tracking progress is the documentation of treatment, treatment integrity, and change.

Documenting Treatment and Treatment Integrity

TREATMENT ACTIVITY   Perhaps because of the interactive nature of clinical work (the is influencing os influencing is), one of the most difficult tasks for the clinician is to conceptualize and describe the treatment or intervention. The therapeutic process could be understood as defining a problem, determining a set of objectives, and designing strategies for meeting those objectives. The most challenging of these is the last; defining the activities to be engaged in by the clinician and the client that are designed to move the process toward some objective. Often, our intervention repertoire and the language we have to describe it are relatively limited. Nonetheless, in order to document progress we must be able to specify and document the occurrence of various aspects of treatment. In many cases, a simple description of the activities engaged in by clinician, client, and other involved individuals provides a basis for understanding the activities as specific types of intervention (e.g., as instigation, as active listening, as clarification, as reflection of feeling). Of course, the same activities may be conceptualized and labeled differently depending on the theoretical framework being used.

The crucial aspect of documenting progress is sorting out the specific activities that are expected to influence specific outcomes. In the past, studies evaluating treatment as an objective activity have often conceptualized treatment in terms of the professional orientation of the clinician (Orlinsky & Howard, 1975). That is to say, these researchers have determined the treatment approach by asking the clinician to specify his or her professional orientation. Such studies are based on the assumption that there is a direct correspondence between professed orientation and actual clinical behavior. Yet these studies have found actual differences in approach to be minimal (Glass, Mcgaw, & Smith 1981; Luborsky, Singer, & Luborsky, 1975). For example, some research shows that clinicians espousing very different orientations often engage in very similar activities (Goldfried, 1980). A study by Sloane, Staples, Cristol, Yorkston, and Whipple (1975) monitored intervention activities in both analytic and behavioral clinicians and found that both engaged in "interpretation," but behavioral clinicians were found to be more "empathic" than analytic therapists. And not surprisingly, behavioral approaches and analytic approaches both seem to result in similar outcomes. These findings may be explained by other studies showing that there is very little correspondence between theoretical orientation and actual behavior.

TREATMENT SPECIFICATION   Given the inadequacy of using a clinician's professed theoretical orientation to document treatment differences, efforts to specify treatment have increasingly moved to the careful, detailed description of treatment procedures and techniques, often in treatment manuals developed as part of research protocols (Kazdin, 1989). By now, treatment guidelines have been developed that describe explicitly a variety of treatment approaches and strategies: social skills training and cognitive therapy of depressed clients (Beck, Rush, Shaw, & Emery, 1979; Bellack, Hersen, & Himmelhoch, 1980); token economy, milieu therapy, and social skills training for psychiatric clients (Paul & Lentz, 1977); social learning treatment of children with conduct problems (Patterson, Reid, Jones, & Conger, 1975); parent training (Dangel & Polster, 1984); and various methods for working with the elderly and their care givers (Pinkston & Linsk, 1984).

The nature of everyday practice, with its variability in problems and clients, typically precludes the widespread use of treatment manuals. Nonetheless, attempting to be as clear and specific as possible about the ingredients of treatment is important for at least two reasons. First, knowing what is supposed to happen contributes an evaluative standard, a means for guaging the consistency and quality of treatment. Further, a carefully specified treatment can be repeated when it is found to be successful, or revised and modified when it is not totally successful.

One of the difficulties with efforts to specify treatment in manual form is that not all approaches or aspects of a therapeutic intervention are equally specifiable (Kazdin, 1989). Approaches that rely significantly on concrete steps and procedures like behavioral therapies are particularly amenable to documentation. Other approaches, like psychodynamically oriented therapies or Gestalt therapies that rely heavily on interaction processes, are less amenable to detailed treatment specification. A significant amount of psychotherapy research to date has pointed to the importance of specific processes in successful treatment—processes engaged in by client, by clinician, and in client-clinician interactional processes (Stiles, Shapiro, & Elliott, 1986). For example, as Orlinsky and Howard (1975) found, in successful cases, clients "experience a sense of progress in instrumental participation, and see themselves taking active initiative, though being basically accepting in relation to their therapists" (p. 296). Similarly, they found that "in cases with better therapeutic outcome, . . . therapists exhibit active and positive instrumental task behaviors and are warm and respectful toward patients in their interpersonal behavior" (p. 296). However, a significant amount of work also points to the importance of the "therapeutic alliance," or emotional bond and mutual involvement between client and clinician, for successful psychosocial treatment (Bordin, 1979; Luborsky, 1976; Orlinsky & Howard, 1975). Clearly, such processes as these are difficult to describe when trying to articulate the important components in a therapeutic effort.

MEASURING THE IMPLEMENTATION OF TREATMENT   As noted above, one of the advantages of a well-specified treatment is the possibility of monitoring the character and integrity of the treatment offered to assure consistency and quality. Objective, observable treatment procedures and processes can be monitored— sometimes through the use of videotape—to measure implementation. However, the participant's perception of the meaning of the treatment is often as important as the treatment itself, and these subjective meanings can be more difficult to measure.

FIGURE 5.1
Therapy Events

(1) What part(s) of today's session was most helpful to you? Please describe briefly:
    a. What were you and the therapist discussion?

_____

_____

_____

_____

    b. What happened that was helpful?

_____

_____

_____

_____

(2) What part(s) of today's session was not so useful? Please describe briefly:
    a. What were you and the therapist discussing?

_____

_____

_____

_____

    b. What happened that wasn't so useful?

_____

_____

_____

_____

However, measures to address these phenomena have been developed; they typically require clients and practitioners to complete, sometimes after each session, subjective impressions of the progress of treatment. Such measures include the Client Satisfaction Questionnaire developed by Larsen, Atkinson, and Hargreaves (1979) and the Session Evaluation Questionnaire by Stiles and Snow (1984). The Therapy Events form developed by Berlin (1992) is shown in Figure 5.1.

Beyond describing, labeling, and monitoring treatment activities and the perception of treatment activities, it is often useful to consider the amount of treatment provided and received (Yeaton & Sechrest, 1981). When we consider the relative benefits of short- versus long-term treatment, we are considering questions about the optimal amount of treatment (e.g., Reid & Shein, 1960). Similarly, when we consider whether various verbal expressions on the part of the clinician influence outcome, we are concerned with the strength of specific aspects of treatment (e.g., Mullen, 1968). Marsh and Wirick (1991) examined the relative impact of length of treatment (elapsed time from beginning to end) and intensity of treatment (number of client contacts). They found measures of treatment intensity to be more meaningful than those of treatment length in relation to outcome.

Clinicians typically keep track of what is going on in treatment informally, implicitly, impressionistically; they seldom write anything down. Clinicians measure progress by asking themselves questions: "Was I too confrontational?" "Should I spend more time focusing on her strengths?" By noting these thoughts on paper and attempting to translate levels or amounts of certain aspects of intervention into quantitative terms, they may more readily find answers to their questions. At a minimum, such information will provide the basis for detecting patterns and relationships over time between intervention strategies (small *is*) and client responses (small *os*).

The **Working Record**, a structured recording format developed by Berlin (1983), provides a rather detailed way to capture information on treatment amount and integrity. The Working Record is only one form of structured process recording; narrative process recordings are a traditional format in social work, and structuring these recordings has a number of advantages. The case examples in Chapter 8 illustrate the use of the Working Record. Videka-Sherman and Reid (1985) have identified other formats. Fundamentally, structured recording formats are designed to capture information about problems, goals, treatment activities, and the nature of change using qualitative as well as quantitative information.

Documenting Change

As we have discussed, a basic task of assessment is to develop a clear and specific understanding of the client's problems and goals for treatment. Tracking progress requires the specification of realistic and positive indicators of problem reduction and goal achievement. This is the first step in developing adequate and meaningful measures of progress and identifying targets for change. If such measures are to be found, then the clinician must have a well developed understanding of the nature of the problem and the direction the treatment is taking.

Problem reduction and goal achievement represent the most obvious outcome indicators. It is useful to remember that an adequate assessment takes into account clients' perspectives as well as their overt problems, their strengths as well as their deficits. Within these considerations appropriate indicators may be found as well. However, a central concern is to choose measures that are themselves helpful in achieving outcomes identified by the client and others. Keeping this principle in mind enables the clinician to be selective and efficient in his or her choice of data-collection strategies. Examples of targets for change include the following:

- Darryl wants to stop procrastinating.
- Georgia wants to interact with her mentally ill son in a way that is supportive and that protects her own interests and needs.
- Betty wants to feel more satisfaction as a parent.
- Karen wants to clarify what she needs and expects from Tom in their marriage.
- Paul wants to get his children back from foster care.

TABLE 5.1
Purposes of Assessing Progress and Possible Monitoring Procedures

	Purpose	Monitoring Procudures
(1)	Contribute to client's self-understanding and sense of progress	Journals; client self-ratings
(2)	Shape intervention responses	Post-session measures: structured progress notes, observations of interactions during sessions
(3)	Evaluate efficacy of specific inter-cention responses	Outcome measures
(4)	Evaluate overall outcome	Outcome measures

How Will This Information Be Used?

Clinicians may choose to monitor progress systematically for several different reasons: (1) to contribute to the client's self-understanding and sense of progress; (2) to shape intervention responses; (3) to evaluate the efficacy of specific intervention responses; (4) to evaluate the overall outcome of the case; or (5) some combination of these purposes. Discussions of information use in practice often focus on using evidence related to overall outcome, but there are several other possible reasons for collecting assessment information.

The practitioner's central assessment purpose may determine what type of progress information may be most useful. For example, as summarized in Table 5.1, client-generated information (i.e., self-assessments captured in journals or on self-monitoring forms) may be most useful for enhancing client understanding. Rich, detailed, qualitative information of the sort available in process notes or a working record may provide the nuance and complexity that are useful in determining exactly how to intervene. Quantitative indicators collected in a standardized manner over time provide succinct, precise, easily communicated indicators of both ongoing and overall change. By focusing on one (or a combination) of these kinds of information, the clinician can observe the client's progress from week to week (or some other reasonable time interval) for the duration of the contact and for some follow-up period beyond. To keep the process manageable, it may be useful for the clinician to specifically identify a small number of indicators of change (perhaps no more than three) and to track these over time.

Feasibility Considerations

Having made some initial judgments about the kinds of changes sought and having articulated the purposes for tracking change, the clinician is now ready to address an avalanche of other questions: What form should this progress information take? how much information do I need? How often should I get it, and from whom? Can I really trust it? At some point the clinician may begin to wonder if addressing all these questions is worth the effort. Sometimes it is not. Many experienced practitioners have vivid memories about painstaking research efforts (their own or someone else's) that involved enormous amounts of data yet yielded very little useful information.

It is often that case the clinicians automatically evaluate their client's progress without all the complications introduced here. With more or less acuity, they listen for and respond to shifts in their client's communications that signal movement. Like the jazz musician who makes a split-second adjustment to the variation that he hears or anticipates from his fellow musicians or the skier who automatically redistributes her weight when she hits the ice, the clinician does not explicitly think through what the client's communication means or how she will respond; she just responds.

☐   Sonja, the social worker, listens to Joseph, the father, report on an interaction with his foster son that sounds different and better. She moves to strengthen this shift by asking Joseph more about how he saw the interaction. Did it feel better to him? Joseph backs off and denies that anything is different. Sonja acknowledges his dubiousness and asks what he thinks the first step in improving the relationship with his son should be and what it will feel like. After the session, Sonja tries, with some difficulty, to reconstruct and add up all these little moment-to-moment, back and forth shifts to determine whether progress has occurred.

Inasmuch as we cannot avoid incorporating artful, automatic assessment thinking into our clinical repertoires, there is an important role for controlled thinking to play. First, like musicians and athletes, clinicians have to practice to gain proficiency. As students complain to us, this practicing often feels awkward and the sheer number of decisions required often seems overwhelming. The truth is that clinical work involves a lot of complexity. Whenever we "deautomatize" all the considerations and steps in order to learn, we are confronted with an overabundance of steps and details. Nonetheless, it is this very process of plowing through these details that gradually builds a sound basis for relatively automatic response.

Second, no matter how smoothly the process of automatic evaluation seems to flow, we know that our automatic decisions are heavily influenced by information-processing heuristics and the vivid, well rehearsed contents of our memories. At the very least, clinicians need to employ mindfulness or controlled thinking and systematic data collection to articulate and double-check their automatic assumptions; they must also devise explicit plans for collecting information about progress that will supplement the information they retrieve and construct automatically.

Finally, it is also important for the clinician who is thinking his or her way through assessment details to see beyond these details and remember that the essence of these considerations is highly practical; it leads to necessary clinical information. It may be overwhelming, unfeasible, or even counterproductive for the clinician to try to follow all the technical guidelines suggested by the psychometricians and research methodologists on a case-by-case basis. But it is crucial, and not necessarily overwhelming, for him or her to follow the pragmatic spirit of assessment guidelines: that is, to devise ways of getting "good enough" information. Rather than working to transplant traditional social science methods to the clinical enterprise root and branch, the challenge is for practitioners to develop gradually their own specialized investigative and assessment methods.

The basic issue in assessing progress is simply that we need to have ways of keeping track of our client's progress and relating it to interventions that are useful and practical. There is no way around the fact that the clinician needs to invest time, stamina, and creative and intellectual concentration into learning and developing assessment methods. But these methods, ultimately, need to be feasible — they must contribute to, rather than disrupt, the essential features of effective social work. This feasibility consideration often means that the clinician has to adapt or create assessment procedures and tools to fit and enhance a specific clinical process.

INFLUENCES OF COGNITIVE STRUCTURES, INFORMATIONAL CUES, AND THINKING PROCESSES ON EVALUATING PROGRESS AND OUTCOME

Expectations

There are several "extraneous" factors that are likely to influence the clinician's assessment of his or her client's progress. We know that the practitioner's predictions of how much the client will benefit from services are likely to influence the extent to which he or she invests in the helping process and attends to signs of improvement (Snyder & Thomsen, 1988). When prognoses are based more on stable preconceptions (i.e., stereotypes) than on careful case-by-case appraisal of the malleability of circumstances, the resulting expectations for improvement may be unrealistically optimistic or pessimistic. It is well documented that a moderately optimistic bias is functional in that it influences persistence, attention to strengths and improvements and, perhaps, a contagious belief in the client's capacity to grow (Goldstein, 1962). Although a wildly optimistic perspective may generate interventions that are totally unconnected to the perceptions and capabilities of the client, the most pernicious preconceived expectations are pessimistic ones. Essentially, these prognoses say, "Don't waste your efforts and don't expect improvements." Such expectations may be expressed in the following forms: "Clients who are schizophrenic cannot benefit from interpersonal treatment"; "Clients and clinicians from different racial groups are unable to enter into a useful therapeutic alliance"; or "Cocaine-addicted mothers are too immature and self-preoccupied to be drawn into the care of their infants."

One of the strengths new practitioners bring to their work is an enthusiastic expectation that people and conditions will improve. In fact, relatively inexperienced workers are often most successful in stimulating change among groups that tend to be viewed as hopelessly entrenched (Goldstein, 1962).

Confusing Cause and Chance

A second potential source of bias in assessing progress is the clinician's expectation that client progress is the result of intervention. Motivated by a concern both for the welfare of the client and for his or her own competency, the practitioner has a large stake in helping the client. Therefore, if the record of progress shows that the client has achieved his or her goals, the clinician will undoubtedly credit at least some of the improvement to the therapeutic experience. On the other hand, if observations show that minimal change occurred or that the client worsened, the clinician is more likely to place the responsibility for these outcomes on factors external to the therapy (e.g., the client's extreme psychopathology, multiple environmental crises, or absence of family support). In general, human beings are woefully inadequate assessors of whether an outcome should be attributed to their skill or to chance factors. Typically, when it is unclear whether a particular outcome is the result of chance or skill, we tend to attribute our successes to skill and our failures to chance (Langer, 1975). Indeed, even in situations obviously governed by chance mechanisms, such as a coin toss, we tend to attribute success to skill (Hogarth, 1985).

Except for the most disillusioned among us, as clinicians we tend to believe that our services are in some way responsible for positive change. In large part, this general belief in our own efficacy is functional; it keeps us going and primes the energy and optimism that fuel the helping process. It is dysfunctional to the extent that it blinds us to specific shortfalls that, if remedied, could result in better service to clients. Clinicians should go beyond the *belief* that therapy helps and actually document the efficacy of specific interventions. Their assessment of ongoing changes should include observations of the interventions and strategies for determining whether the intervention or some other factor is influencing client change. Such strategies are discussed in the next chapter under the rubric of data collection and research designs.

Incomplete Information

We learn from experience. In general, we pursue strategies that we perceive as successful and avoid those that fail. One difficulty is that we may not be exposed to *all* the consequences of our actions. Suppose that you are working in a family service agency with a large population of time- and energy-stretched single parents. Coming to the agency for appointments is often a major undertaking for members of this group. It is your job to decide which of the clients have enough personal resources to benefit from referral to a new parenting enrichment course offered by the local YMCA but paid for by your agency. Your clients' success in this program will influence your willingness to refer other clients in the future. Naturally, you carefully monitor the success of the clients selected. If 80% of the clients pass an achievement test that serves as your criteria of success, will you count the program as successful? Clearly, you do not have all the relevant information. You could summarize all the relevant information in the following fourfold table (recognizing that under most circumstances you would not have all this information):

	PROGRAM EXPOSURE	
Outcome	Not selected	Selected
Passes test	40 (cell a)	80 (cell b)
Fails test	10 (cell c)	20 (cell d)
Total	50	100

To assess the program adequately, you would want to know the proportion of those selected who passed the test, $b/(b+d)$, compared with the proportion of those not selected who passed the test, $a/(a+c)$. In this example both proportions (40/50 and 80/100) equal .80, even though you expected a larger proportion of those exposed to the program to pass than of those not exposed. However, unless you designed a full-scale experimental analysis of the program, you would not have all this information. Typically, you would only have information on the individuals who participated in the program (in this case 100), and you would only know how many of them were successful. Often you would acquire this information sequentially, as one after another individual participated in the program. Therefore, you would have information that one client succeeded and another failed, but at any one time it would be difficult to judge how many succeeded of those exposed to the program. Most often the situation is as follows: (1) you select individuals for a program according to certain criteria you believe are valid; (2) most of the people in the program are successful; and (3) that evidence convinces you that your judgment is accurate.

Even when all the relevant information is available, we tend not to use it. We tend to focus on the absolute number of successes (cell b) to judge a program and ignore other information. Indeed, the value of formal evaluations of programs is that the research designs used in such efforts force us to consider all the possible consequences of an intervention and all the possible explanations of an outcome. Thus, relying on impressions rather than more formal analyses makes it difficult to learn from experience.

Hindsight Bias

Hindsight is the understanding of an event and the most appropriate course of action related to it *after* it has occurred. Fischoff (1975) studied the phenomenon of "hindsight" by giving subjects descriptions of unfamiliar historical events and asking them to specify the likelihood of various outcomes. He also gave different groups of subjects information about outcomes: actual outcomes, false outcomes, or no outcome information at all. He asked them to specify which aspects of the descriptions were most relevant to their judgments. He found that subjects' predictions were influenced significantly by the outcome information they had received; they judged outcomes that were said to have occurred (whether true outcomes or false) as the ones most likely to have occurred. They also identified pieces of information that *fit* with the given outcomes as the most relevant to their decisions. In other words, knowledge of outcomes seems to affect judgment by making the actual outcomes seem most likely and by highlighting antecedent events congruent with those outcomes as most relevant. Fischoff further documented hindsight bias by asking subjects to predict specific outcomes (e.g., consequences of President Nixon's trip to China) before they occurred and then to recall their predictions after they occurred. He found that subjects recalled larger probabilities for events that had occurred than they had assigned beforehand.

How does hindsight bias work? Consider the difference between foresight and hindsight. When we are looking into the future and trying to predict an outcome, there are several possible outcomes and several different avenues leading to each of them. There are numerous pieces of information related to what might happen, and no foolproof method for sorting among them. Further, there is always the possibility that something unexpected could happen. However, when we assess a situation after some event has occurred, it is much easier to select from the available information those pieces related to the observed outcome and to see this outcome as much more likely.

The implications of hindsight bias are all too familiar to social workers, especially those involved in "life and death" decisions for their clients: for example, whether an elderly client should be placed in a nursing home; whether a child should be returned to her natural parents; whether a mentally ill client with a record of criminal activity should be released from the forensic hospital. One major implication of hindsight bias is that it leads us to judge very harshly decisions with negative outcomes. We assume that a bad outcome necessarily implies a bad decision. Fischoff describes a case of a prisoner with a serious criminal record who escaped from the Oregon State Prison while on an overnight pass. The warden of the prison was criticized by the community, the press, and the governor for giving an individual with a criminal record the opportunity to flee. The fact that the prisoner had a very favorable prison record did not diminish the outcry. Fischoff suggests that, in such a situation, the only adequate way to assess the warden's judgment is to ask several wardens and others to judge whether passes should be issued in this (anonymously presented) case and several others.

Similarly, social workers in many situations would be advised to distinguish between foresight and hindsight and between the quality of a decision and the quality of an outcome. If, as has been previously recommended, they carefully document the evidence or rationale for their decision, then they can defend their decision (without the benefit of hindsight) as adequate even if the outcome is negative. Social workers in such situations would be well positioned to submit their judgment to the type of test suggested by Fischoff.

A second implication of hindsight bias is that it reduces our capacity to learn from experience. Although in most situations it is, no doubt, efficient to restructure our understanding of the world to fit with what we observe, the unconscious and uncritical operation of hindsight bias keeps us from clearly evaluating the relation between antecedents and consequences. We have identified the importance and the difficulty of determining the factors that are causally related to predicted events. The ability to construct causal relations or explanations accurately is crucial to prediction. If we are tempted through hindsight bias to accept apparent, but not necessarily accurate, explanations too readily, we fail to learn from experience what the true relations are.

DECISION AIDS FOR EVALUATING PROGRESS AND OUTCOME
Information Systems

As with other decisions, judgments about the adequacy of intervention efforts can benefit from a good record-keeping system. Fischoff concludes that the best way to reduce hindsight's influence and to learn from our decision-making experience is to record not only the predictions we make but the evidence we used in making them. Then, when the outcome is known, we have some ongoing record of the accuracy of our predictions as well as of the accuracy and adequacy of the information we used to make them.

There are, indeed, numerous ways in which a good record-keeping or information system can aid and improve decision making. Like an insect caught between two window panes, social workers often find themselves trapped in their record-keeping systems, constantly bumping their heads against their requirements as they try to free themselves to do their jobs. They are asked to provide numerous and redundant pieces of information about their clients and their activities without being given the rationale behind the requests and without getting anything in return. It is estimated that 50% of human service agencies now have computerized information management systems, and numerous others have such systems in the planning stages (Finn, 1988). However, few of these systems are designed to aid a practitioner's decision making. In fact, Finn's study shows that only one-third of agencies with computerized information systems report that direct service workers even use the systems. Nonetheless, there are numerous ways in which information systems, computerized systems more specifically, can enhance practitioner performance (Clark, 1988; Gambrill & Butterfield, 1988). The discussion below briefly summarizes the possibilities, if not the realities, of these systems.

Computerized information systems are, fundamentally, an efficient mechanism for storing and organizing client and agency records; that is, they are fancy and flexible file cabinets. A record-keeping or information system implies that each form and each piece of information compliments rather than duplicates the others to provide a coherent picture of the client and his or her situation. As mentioned, many social agencies are making the transition from manual (i.e., file folders and file drawers) to computerized information systems, and many individual practitioners are using agency systems or their own relatively low-cost systems (Clark, 1988). Early uses of management information systems in agencies focused primarily on administrative applications: budgeting, financing, and report generation. Increasingly, however, "integrated" systems that service the decision needs of both direct-service practitioners and managers have been designed and implemented (Benbenishty & Ben Zakem, 1988; Mutschler & Hasenfeld, 1986). The importance of a system that accommodates decisions of both practitioners and managers is straightforward. The information contained in such a system and the decisions it addresses are contained in Table 5.2.

In addition to storing, organizing, and facilitating the use of information collected in assessment, there are other computer applications that aid assessment. First, in addition to collecting specific information for each client in a uniform manner, some applications may store narrative case planning notes for each client. Many psychological tests and outcome measures have been computerized (Hammond & Gottfriedson, 1984; Hudson, 1991) so that the computer can be used to administer and score the test as well to track progress over time. Greist et al. (1983) have even developed an interactive program that "interviews" the client and provides a diagnosis. Ultimately, social workers will no doubt benefit from on-line access to detailed, manualized intervention guidelines such as those described earlier in the chapter. Other on-line services will be helpful as well, particularly those providing access to data bases for quick literature reviews or to reviews of service resources available in the community.

In addition to the assessment purposes described above, computerized record-keeping systems can be designed specifically to counter or provide checks for the types of biases described in this chapter and earlier. For example, a worker concerned about whether she is overly influenced by readily available information (such as vivid case material or her recent participation in particular training programs) can inform her thinking by examining the frequency of specific types of problems among the agency population as well as the general population. For example, if she learns that the problem she and the client have identified is relatively infrequent in the population, she may wish to double-check her rationale for the decision. In most cases, it is inappropriate for population rate data to dominate case data (unless the case data are completely unreliable), but they can provide useful additional information. Similarly, clinical judgments about problem severity can be informed by information about the frequency of the problem in the agency population as well as in the general population.

Additional mechanisms for countering specific biases can be built into computerized record-keeping systems. For example, forms that specifically ask the clinician for the client's definition of the problem remind workers of the centrality of the client's perception. This helps workers to avoid the common mistake of confusing their own perception of what is or should be the problem with the client's. Similarly, forms that solicit information on the client's situation help to check dispositional bias by focusing the worker's attention on these factors; or, as described above, computerized record-keeping systems can be designed to store specific predictions in order to monitor their accuracy later.

Formal Monitoring and Evaluation

Research tools designed for assessing programs and specific interventions are clearly very useful in combatting the particular biases that distort our view of program impact. Evaluation methods, especially those that can be used in clinical settings,

TABLE 5.2
An Information System for Practice Decision Making

Decisions	Data Types	Management Decisions
Initiation, engagement, problem assessment *What is client problem? What is service objective?*	CLIENT DATA - client ID - demographic data - income - presentation of problem - client self-ratings - assessment measures	Program planning *What are service needs of community? What resources will be required to meet these needs?*
Planning, deciding what to do *What are client resources? What are agency resources and constraints? What is most effective?*	TREATMENT PLANNING INFORMATION - on-line access to intervention guidelines for specific problems - agency resources - community resources - client resources	Utilization of staff *How skilled and effective are staff? What are training and resource needs of agency?*
Implementation, monitoring intervention *What service was provided? How much service was provided? What changes need to be made in the service?*	SERVICE DATA - worker ID - client contact date - client contact type - client contact duration - worker progress notes - post-session measures - referral type - referral follow-up - cost data	Service delivery *Which service approaches were used most frequently? What referrals and linkages are used?*
Evaluation and revising intervention *What was outcome?*	TREATMENT PROCESS AND EVALUATION DATA - graphical and statistical analysis of outcome indicators - cost summaries	Monitoring and evaluation *Which service approaches are most effective with which clients? Which approaches are most cost effective?*

TABLE 5.3
Inferential Strategies and Related Decision Aids

Evaluation Bias and Description	Example	Avoiding the Risks
Confusing chance and skill—tendency to attribute success to skill and failure to chance.	Success with case attributed to skill; failure to extraneous circumstances.	Use formal evaluation to assess factors influencing direct change.
Incomplete feedback— often the outcomes we can observe easily do not provide complete information about predictive relationships.	We tend to focus on and remember successes.	Use formal evaluation and records accessible in computerized information systems.
Hindsight bias—once the outcome of a set of circumstances is known, the course of events is seen as obvious and inevitable.	The "I-knew-it-all-along" phenomenon	Maintain records of prediction with reasons for predictions.

have undergone significant development in recent years. Relatively straightforward evaluation strategies are available to the practitioner to aid in assessing intervention outcome. Evaluation methods and information systems that are tools for avoiding bias are given in Table 5.3. Chapter 7 is devoted to a description of evaluation.

SUMMARY

In order to track progress over time, practitioners are challenged to identify key indicators of change by asking themselves (1) what they really need to track over time, (2) how they will use this information, and (3) how they can get it. In the process, their decisions will be improved by their increasing sensitivity to the biasing effects of expectations, of their own tendency to overestimate their skill, and of the failure to consider some critical pieces of evidence. Carefully developed information systems and reliance on formal evaluation strategies can be useful tools for enhancing the accuracy of assessment decisions.

6 | Guidelines and Strategies for Data Collection

$\mathbf{T}$his chapter reviews fundamental guidelines for collecting clinically relevant data and builds on material presented in previous chapters to specify strategies for obtaining quantitative indicators.

I. Guidelines for Data Collection
   A. Specify clearly the client's problems and goals
   B. Collect multiple measures for any one treatment objective
   C. Collect information that is relevant to desired objectives rather than convenient
   D. Collect information early in the course of work with client
   E. Collect some information repeatedly before, during and after intervention
   F. Use good and accurate measures
   G. Organize the data
   H. Obtain the client's cooperation and consent

II. Documenting Change
   A. Interviews
   B. Client-specific measures
      1. Client journal
      2. Monitoring by client
      3. Client-specific rating scales
   C. Standardized measures
   D. Observation
      1. Distinguishing inference from observation
      2. Structured observation: event sampling, time sampling, time point sampling
   E. Institutional records

III. Summary

If the fundamental task of assessment is to gather information about the client, about his or her problem and situation, what information-gathering tools are available to us? We have noted that, ultimately, we are interested in qualitative patterns and themes as well as quantitative indicators and trends. In this chapter we will revisit material from earlier chapters as we focus on ways to obtain quantitative indicators. After reviewing some fundamental guidelines for collecting clinically relevant data, we will focus on specific strategies. For readers with any previous experience in research, this chapter will provide a review.

GUIDELINES FOR DATA COLLECTION

It is useful for clinicians to gain a sophisticated appreciation of clinical measurement issues in order to be well-educated consumers of clinical research and to build a solid foundation of knowledge for personal practice–research endeavors. The process of making sense of various sources of information is like the process of learning all the individual steps of assessment: It gradually creates a foundation for relatively spontaneous and intuitive response. We begin with several fundamental guidelines (adapted from Barlow, Hayes, & Nelson, 1984) for the enhancement of data collection; they are summarized in Table 6.1 and reviewed below.

Specify Clearly the Client's Problems and Goals

As we have stated repeatedly, one major task of assessment is to develop a clear and specific understanding of the client's problems and goals for treatment. The second major task, one essential to tracking progress, is to specify realistic and positive outcomes. This is the first step in developing adequate and meaningful measures of problem reduction and goal achievement. If such measures of progress are to be found, then the clinician must have a well developed understanding of the nature of the problem and the direction the treatment is taking. Although clients may present their problems in vague and general terms, an adequate assessment must strive to refine and clarify problems and treatment objectives so that there are specific, observable indicators attached to each problem or objective. As we have noted, this process of clarification and refinement requires the clinician and the client to construct and reconstruct understanding. For example, the global objective "to help the client take control of her life" could be broken down into subobjectives such as "to exercise three times each week," "to invite a friend for dinner," and

TABLE 6.1
Data Collection Guidelines

---

1. Specify clearly the client's problems and goals.
2. Collect multiple measures for any one treatment objective.
3. Collect information that is relevant to desired objectives rather than convenient.
4. Collect information early in the course of work with client.
5. Collect some information repeatedly before, during, and after intervention.
6. Use good and accurate measures.
7. Organize the data
8. Obtain the client's cooperation and consent.

"to explore and apply for a new job." Attaching observable referents to each objective permits the clinician and the client to document and understand the nature and amount of progress being made.

It is useful to remember that an adequate assessment takes into account clients' perspectives as well as their overt problems, strengths, and their deficits. These considerations may yield appropriate targets for measurement as well. However, a central concern is to choose measures that are themselves helpful in achieving outcomes identified by the client and others. Keeping this principle in mind enables the clinician to be selective and efficient in his or her choice of data-collection strategies.

Collect Multiple Measures
for Any One Treatment Objective

Because client problems are typically multidimensional, treatment objectives are multiple. And because any one measure may not be adequate, it is often important to employ more than one measure to assess progress related to an objective. For example, all measures will vary along a specificity–generality continuum. Specific measures that are very precise and targeted may be sensitive to weekly therapeutic change. However, they may be weak with respect to construct validity; that is, they may not provide the most meaningful measure of overall change. General or global measures typically assess the multidimensional manifestations of a problem or construct. Thus, they may have greater construct validity but less capacity to detect small changes. For example, a client may appear depressed. The clinician may decide to assess the amount of the client's non-work-related activity and the amount of self-criticism as specific molecular indicators of the problem. Although improvement may be detected in these measures on a week-to-week basis, the client's overall feelings of depression may persist. A more general measure such as the Beck Depression Inventory (Beck, Ward, Mendelson, Mock, & Erbaugh, 1961) has greater construct validity. In other words, changes in scores on this measure provide evidence that the client is generally less depressed. It makes sense therefore to collect molecular measures (i.e., targeted, unidimensional measures) on a weekly or biweekly basis and molar (i.e., global) measures on a less frequent basis, perhaps monthly or bimonthly.

Often the distinction between molecular and molar measures is a distinction between client-specific measures and standardized measures. Client-specific measures can be easily tailored to individual clients, problems, and situations. Standardized measures typically indicate general validity, reliability, and norms, or involve published means and standard deviations for specific groups on the measures.

Collect Information that Is Relevant
to Desired Objectives Rather than Convenient

One of the most frequent mistakes that clinicians make is to track something that is not very important. Preoccupied with the technical considerations of assessment (e.g., getting a pretreatment baseline, finding a valid and reliable instrument, or finding an instrument at all), practitioners, especially students, sometimes persuade themselves to reconceptualize the client's problem to fit definitions of a readily available measurement instrument. This strategy has aided many students in squeaking through their research courses, but it is not much help in collecting useful information about client progress. If the clinician is to collect useful information, he or she must look beyond the enticements of easily acquired, but barely relevant, assessment indices and focus on whether the aspects of the problem targeted for change are really changing. If the clinician cannot identify such changes, then he or she has not conceptualized the problem accurately. The clinician must understand the problem well enough to tentatively delineate the major components that are to be assessed in an ongoing way; but must also, at the same time, actively look for ways to fill out, modify, or completely revamp this understanding in the face of new information.

☐ Craig and Mary Beth are social work students in an integrated research and field work course. They are both laboring under the burden of an assignment to conduct ongoing assessments of their cases. Craig is working with a young man named Bob who is on probation for robbery. He is unemployed, isolated, and lonely; he feels hopeless and emotionally distraught; he is struggling with a serious alcohol and marijuana habit. He says that he wants to make something of himself—get a good job, maybe go back to school, have a girlfriend—but he feels too weak and messed up. After listening to Bob describe how down he feels when he is not using drugs (he is often tearful, has difficulty getting out of bed, does not eat, cannot muster the strength to clean up his room, is missing job interviews), Craig decided to use the Beck Depression Inventory (BDI) as a way to assess one component of his problem. Craig now has a record of the changes in Bob's level of depression, measured weekly over a five-month period. Over the weeks, as Craig developed a fuller understanding of Bob's situation, he also used additional ways to assess Bob's progress. Together, these progress markers provided a clear and useful way to understand the extent and nature of the changes Bob was making.

   At about the same time Craig started using the BDI with Bob, Mary Beth was trying to figure out how to measure change with her client Monica. Craig told her about the BDI and Mary Beth decided that it might be just what she was looking for. She thought Monica was a little depressed too. Monica is a single parent of two toddlers. She is beset by financial problems, parenting problems, and problems related to her out-of-control diabetes. As a cause and consequence of these problems, Monica is also frustrated, angry, overwhelmed, and maybe a little depressed. Mary Beth put her efforts into tracking this peripheral aspect of Monica's problems. The results are that Monica feels that Mary Beth does not really understand her or her situation and Mary Beth cannot see what good it is doing her to collect these measures.

Collect Information Early in the Course of Work with Client

Indeed, it is advisable to begin collecting information during the first session with a client. For example, a mother may bring her young son to a clinician at a community mental health center complaining of his behavior problems in school and at home. The clinician may note the number of times during the initial session that the son ignores the mother's requests. As homework, the client may be asked to record specific instances in which the child complied or did not comply with requests or expectations. At the same time, the clinician can make an appointment to see the boy's teacher to collect information about the nature and frequency of classroom problems and perhaps to conduct a structured observation in the classroom.

If data are collected on several problems and treatment objectives, then, as the problem definition and treatment objectives are refined, irrelevant measures can be dropped and relevant measures retained, extended, and added. Further, when data are collected early in the treatment process, baseline or pretreatment information will be available.

Collect Some Information Repeatedly Before, During, and After Intervention

Clinical work lends itself to the repeated collection of information. The same information collected over time is useful in clinical work in that it provides ongoing information about patterns of gradual change. Further, it provides information about the impact of specific therapeutic interventions. This information enables the therapist to make decisions about altering or maintaining particular treatment approaches. From a scientific point of view, having time-series information before and after a specific intervention permits a reasonably strong inference about change and the reasons for change.

If repeated measures are to be compared in a meaningful way, they must be obtained under similar circumstances. Irrelevant influences, such as alterations in the measurement conditions, should be minimized or at least noted. For example, if a teacher is interested in measuring attendance, it will be important for her to have a clear definition of attendance that she can apply consistently. If a full day of attendance is determined by remaining in five out of five classes each day, then attendance at four out of five classes will not count.

Use Good and Accurate Measures

It has been proposed that the clinician use multiple measurement strategies for each of the several objectives identified. We shall see shortly that there are numerous measurement strategies available to the practitioner. What is the basis for choosing among them?

Criteria that are useful in judging the adequacy of differen᷊ ment instruments include: relevance, sensitivity to change, reliabi᷊ A measure that is directly *relevant* to targeted client outcomes ultiᵢ the most helpful information. Although this seems obvious, it is eas᷊ of this point. For example, when working with an adolescent client fᴄ᷊ treatment goal is more regular school attendance, the clinician may be ᷊pted to measure the client's self-esteem if the clinician's theoretical model suggests to her that her client skips school because he does not feel good about himself there. Many of her interventions are aimed at helping him gain more self-respect; it is natural for her to focus on this outcome. However, since the ultimate aim of the client, his parents, and his teachers is to improve his attendance, tracking changes in this behavior (perhaps in addition to measurements of self-esteem) keeps the enterprise on target.

Many measures of individual characteristics and behaviors that seem appropriate for clinical settings have not, in fact, been designed to measure change and are thus not *sensitive to change*. It is often difficult to judge whether a given measure will be sensitive to change. Several considerations are helpful. One of the best indicators is a measure's track record of detecting change. If you have used a measure in the past that did not detect change when other measures did, the evidence suggests that the measure is not sensitive. Second, measures that are directly related to specific behaviors targeted for change are generally more sensitive than more global measures of personality characteristics. Molar, or global, measures of characteristics are multidimensional and address concepts at a higher level of abstraction. Molecular measures, more unidimensional and targeted to specific aspects of a concept, tend to be more sensitive to change.

Reliability refers to the extent to which measures are repeatable. Every type of measure involves some kind of error, and the measure is reliable to the extent that the error is minimal. There are several possible sources of error. First, there would be variation because different items on a measurement instrument would result in slightly different scores. Second, human factors such as fatigue, misreading, and guessing can result in variation between different administrations of an instrument. There are three basic ways to assess the reliability of a measure: (1) by examining the extent to which individual items on an instrument relate to one another *(internal consistency reliability)*; (2) by examining the extent to which the same result is achieved when the same instrument is administered at two different points in time *(test–retest reliability);* and (3) by dividing an instrument in half and assessing the extent to which the same result is achieved on each half *(split-half reliability).*

The *validity* of a measure refers to the extent to which an instrument measures what it purports to measure. The validity of a measure can be assessed by determining, as based on superficial examination, the extent to which the measure appears to focus on the relevant concepts *(face validity);* the extent to which the measure correlates positively with a different measure of the same construct *(construct validity);* the extent to which the instrument adequately samples an entire domain of content representative of a construct *(content validity);* and the extent to which a measure is related to performance in some criterion of behavior *(predictive validity).*

⌐rganize the Data

If a clinician were to follow all the guidelines for data collection, he or she ultimately would secure an enormous amount of recorded information. To be interpreted, the data must be organized. For example, time-series data can be graphed conveniently by placing units of time along the horizontal axis and relevant units of the target measure on the vertical axis. The clinician is advised to obtain several measures relevant to the same problem. For example, when a school social worker works on a student's school adjustment, it would be useful to have measures related to academic performance and to social adjustment. It is often desirable to place all of the measures on the same graph. This permits the clinician to look at all the relevant information simultaneously and to observe any covariation among measures. In other words, the clinician can assess whether different measures of the problem vary in the same direction or different directions in response to the intervention efforts.

Obtain the Client's Cooperation and Consent

All the measurement strategies discussed above depend on the complete cooperation and consent of the client. Using the information collected in a spirit of discovery enhances the value and validity of the data.

DOCUMENTING CHANGE

There are a variety of data-collection strategies and instruments available: data derived from interviews, whether live or recorded on videotape, audiotape, or transcript; self-report data collected by the client and others; observational data; and institutional records. Each approach brings with it specific strengths and liabilities, some of which are summarized in Table 6.2 and discussed below.

Interviews

Social workers gather and use information from a variety of sources, but interviews represent the backbone of information-gathering strategies. Interviews with the client and individuals in the client's life are conducted for many different reasons: to collect information about problems and about progress, to establish rapport with the client, to provide support, to influence change, to reach a decision. Interviews are particularly efficient means to gather information because they permit the clinician to collect information directly and indirectly. That is, the interviewer can gather information in response to a specific question and, at the same time, informally attend to such nonverbal cues as physical appearance, mood, and consistency of information and affect. Therefore, a significant amount of information can be collected in a relatively short period of time. Interviews also permit the interviewer to check the validity of reports by comparing the congruence of information and affect. They are particularly useful for gathering information about complex and emotionally laden events. They can be conducted in a supportive, nonthreatening atmosphere that facilitates self-disclosure. Furthermore, they are flexible; that is, they permit the interviewer to pursue several different lines of inquiry, to repeat and rephrase questions to make sure they are understood, and to clarify the meaning of a response.

The limitations of interviews are, of course, that they rely heavily on the client's report. The practitioner often has not observed the events being discussed. The accuracy and completeness of the report can be promoted both by the client's ability and willingness to provide the information and by the skill of the interviewer in making the client feel comfortable and in eliciting clear, well defined responses.

Client-Specific Measures

Interviews provide a basis for acquiring a significant amount of information, both directly and indirectly. In addition, they set the stage for obtaining systematically recorded information about problem-related issues. This systematically recorded information can be in the form of narratives in client journals, monitoring and rating scales, or, when available, standardized measures relevant to the problem.

CLIENT JOURNAL   Narrative accounts of a client's ongoing activities, thoughts, and feelings provide rich descriptive information that can be useful in understanding the nature of a problem and the situational factors contributing to it. The process of keeping a journal can be very informative for the client as well as the clinician. An open-ended format reveals events that have the most salience for the client and his or her perception of them. A prestructured format permits the client to record particularly relevant information. For example, it may be useful to track the antecedents and consequences, or the feelings and thoughts, surrounding the occurrence of a specific event.

MONITORING BY CLIENT   Monitoring, or the recording of events or behaviors as they occur in the natural environment, is a very useful clinical tool. For assessment, information derived from monitoring provides evidence of the magnitude of the problem; that is, how often it occurs, how long it lasts, and—to the extent that they are recorded—the subjective states and physical circumstances surrounding the occurrence. If clients themselves are engaged in the recording, they have complete access to information about the frequency and nature of the occurrences of the behavior, even when covert emotional or cognitive events are being recorded. If significant others are involved, they may be restricted to observing and tracking more public, observable events.

In order for monitoring to be successful, the monitor must both notice and record events. *Frequency,* or the number of times an event happens within a given time period, is the monitoring information most often completed. Many ingenious mechanisms have been devised for obtaining frequency counts that are efficient

TABLE 6.2
Some Advantages and Limitations of Various Data Collection Strategies

Advantages	Limitations
INTERVIEWS	
1. Interviews are efficient means of gathering information about a problem: information is available both directly and indirectly by checking the consistency of information and the congruence of information and affect.	1. Interviews place heavy reliance on client self-report. The client must be able and willing to engage in verbal interaction.
2. The interview provides the optimum means for collecting complex and emotionally-laden information since the interviewer can create a supportive environment.	2. The conditions of the interview and the verbal skill of the interviewer as well as the client can bias the completeness and accuracy of the information e.g., an anxious or overly active interviewer can reduce information received.
3. The interview is useful for gathering complex information since the interviewer can repeat or rephrase questions to make sure they are understood or to clarify the meaning of a response.	

**IDIOSYNCRATIC SELF-REPORT MEASURES:
JOURNALS, MONITORING STRATEGIES, AND RATING SCALES**

Advantages	Limitations
1. Self-report measures provide an opportunity to obtain information about events that cannot be observed: e.g., thoughts, feelings, dreams, preferences, perceptions.	1. Self-report measures may be vulnerable to a range of biases related to a desire to minimize or exaggerate a problem to please the worker.
2. Self-report measure provide an opportunity to focus the informaion that has greatest salience for the client.	2. Self-report measures may themselves influence the outcome of an intervention.
3. Self-report measures can be structured with standard format and instructions that ensure uniformity across measurement circumstances.	3. Reliability and validity cannot be readily assessed.
4. Temporary freedom from cues or consequences provided by an interviewer may enable the respondent to be more candid in some circumstances.	
5. Self-report measures are efficient, requiring minimal investment of time for completion.	

TABLE 6.2 (*continued*)

Advantages	Limitations

STANDARDIZED MEASURES

1. Standardized measures are relatively inexpensive and easy to use.

2. It is possible to determine the general adequacy of a measure's reliability and validity.

3. Standardized measures can obtain specific kinds of information across clients and situations providing comparative information when that is useful.

1. Standardized measures appropriate for the specific situation may not be available.

2. Most standardized measures focus on problems; many fewer measures have been developed to measure client strengths and resources or situations.

3. For the most part, indicators of a measure's quality have been determined for groups and may not hold for the specific situation.

OBSERVATION

1. Observational techniques provide information about individuals who may be unable or unwilling to provide descriptions of their behavior (e.g., children).

2. The validity of information derived from observation is very high since events are recorded as they occur in the natural environment.

3. Observers can be trained to a high level of reliability.

4. Many reaserchers believe that individuals adjust to the presence of observers so that the observer's presence has little biasing influence.

1. Observational strategies are time- and resource-intensive.

2. Observational strategies are restricted to public events and information; access to private events, e.g., thoughts, feelings precluded.

3. Observational techniques are vulnerable to extraneous influences: e.g., it is impossible to conduct a classroom observation during a fire drill.

INSTITUTIONAL RECORDS

1. Institutional records provide historical information.

2. Information from institutional records can be obtained relatively inexpensively.

3. Accuracy of information does not depend on client recall and respondents have no reason to bias responses.

1. Definitions and data collection methods may shift over time, thus biasing information.

2. Data may be missing.

3. Original reason for collecting information may have built-in biases.

and easy, including making tally marks on a sheet of paper, using a golf counter, or making indentations in a piece of soap (in one's pocket) with a fingernail. *Duration,* or the length of time a behavior persists, can also be recorded easily.

CLIENT-SPECIFIC RATING SCALES   During assessment, as clients identify the specific problems and goals that will be the focus of the intervention, idiosyncratic rating scales can be developed. Rating scales specify a feeling, thought, or event and ask the rater to place it on a predetermined scale. Rating scales have been described as the "all-purpose" measurement procedure (Bloom, 1982, & Fischer, 1982, p. 167) because the practitioner and client must develop their own scales for measuring whatever they have identified as the focus of intervention. An advantage of rating scales is that they can focus on problems or events that other measures cannot. Specifically, rating scales can be used to measure the thoughts and feelings (e.g., feelings of depression, exhilaration, anger, loneliness) that may be a focus for the worker and client, or the level of intensity of such thoughts and feelings. A client working on feelings of anger and control might develop the following scales:

	FEELING ANGRY AND FRUSTRATED					
Livid	1	2	3	4	5	Not at all
	FEELING TRAPPED WITHOUT OPTIONS					
Feeling trapped	1	2	3	4	5	Feeling as if there are choices

Rating scales have high face validity since they are designed to measure individual, idiosyncratic events. Because they often measure things that only the client can report on, they can be expected to be the most accurate representation available of those events. However, the reliability of these measures typically cannot be assessed since they are designed for use with one individual. Although some have questioned the construct validity of self-report rating scales, there is no evidence that these measures are more or less valid or reliable than other measures. Concerns arise due to the potentially reactive nature of these scales: the process of completing the scales may itself change the client's responses to them. However, in many cases, it is the changed perceptions themselves that are of interest regardless of the reason for the change.

Developing the scale requires some straightforward considerations. The scale determines the level of intensity of the response to an item; for example, strongly agree—agree—undecided—disagree—strongly disagree. A scale can contain any number of positions, although five positions is common. The scale should be constructed so that intervals between points are consistent. Further, it is important that the scale measure only one feeling. It is often tempting to place opposites such as "anxious" and "calm" at the ends of a scale. However, because it is possible to feel both simultaneously, it is better to be completely unambiguous and to measure only one dimension at a time (e.g., a scale measuring only degrees of anxiety). It is also useful to anchor the scales at both ends with concrete examples that describe a specific condition or state. Often clients can identify meaningful examples for end points.

The advantage of rating scales is that they can be used as repeated measures because they are easy and quick to complete. Results can be transferred to a graph for visual tracking over time. They also can be completed by the client, the clinician, or a significant other; thus they have a range of applications.

All written self-report mechanisms, whether tailored to the client or standardized, carry with them certain benefits and liabilities. As was pointed out previously, these instruments are efficient to use. They can be completed in a variety of different settings with minimal investment of time. They provide access to information about events that are not observable, such as perceptions, dreams, thoughts, and feelings. The standard, uniform format they require ensures consistency of information across time and context. The limitations of these instruments are related to their validity. They may be highly reactive. Because the observer is also the observed, the responses are vulnerable to bias deriving from a desire to please the clinician or to minimize the nature of the problem. Furthermore, the simple act of recording and reporting information may influence the nature of the problem.

Standardized Measures

When we think of measurement and data collection, a standardized paper-and-pencil test is often the first image that springs to mind. And, indeed, there are a large number of such measures that are relevant to clinical assessment. The advantage of standardized measures is that they are readily available and, typically, have been evaluated in terms of their quality.

A standardized measure is one developed with uniform administration and scoring procedures that is accompanied by some information about its adequacy: typically, specific information about the reliability, validity, and norms for the measure. In other words, a standardized measure is one that has gone through a process of development so that its adequacy could be tested and enhanced. Norms refer to average scores for different groups, which provide a standard of comparison for any individual score. If research has shown that individuals who score above or below a certain point can be distinguished from other groups with respect to certain characteristics, then *cutting points* may be provided. For example, Hudson (1982) provides points at which scores may begin to indicate a clinically significant problem. These cutting points are, of course, meant to be used with some flexibility.

There are numerous collections of standardized measures that could be useful in clinical assessment. Some of these are listed in Table 6.3. Collections that are particularly useful in clinical social work include: *The Clinical Measurement Package* (Hudson, 1982); "Rapid assessment instruments for practice" (Levitt & Reid, 1981); *Measures for Clinical Practice: A Sourcebook* (Fischer & Corcoran, 1987); and *Measures of Social Psychological Attitudes* (Robinson & Shaver, 1973).

TABLE 6.3
Collections of Measures for Clinical Practice

Beere, C. A. (1979). *Women and women's issues: A handbook of tests and measures*. San Francisco, CA: Jossey-Bass.

Chun, K., Cobb, S., & French, J. (1975). *Measures for psychological assessment*. Ann Arbor, MI: Institute for Social Research.

Edelson, Jeffrey. (1985). Rapid-assessment instruments for evaluating practice with children and youth. *Journal of Social Service Research, 8*(3), 17–31.

Filsinger, E. E. (Ed.). (1983). *Marriage and family assessment: A sourcebook for family therapy*. Beverly Hills: Sage.

Fischer, J. & Corcoran, K. (1987). *Measures for clinical practice*. New York: The Free Press.

Fredman, N., & Sherman, R. (1987). Handbook of measurements for marriage and family therapy. New York: Brunner/Mazel.

Hudson, W. W. (1982). *The clinical measurement package*. Homewood, IL: Dorsey Press.

Hudson, W. W., & Harrison, D. F. (1986). Conceptual issues in measuring and assessing family problems. *Family Therapy, 13*(1), 85–94.

Johnson, O. (1976). Tests and measurements for child development. San Francisco: Jossey-Bass.

Kent, R. N., & Foster, S. L. (1977). Direct observational procedures: Methodological issues in naturalistic settings. In A. R. Cim in ero K. S. Calhoun, & H. E. Adams (Eds.), *Handbook of behavioral assessment*, (pp. 279–329). New York: John Wiley and Sons.

Levitt, J., & Reid, W. R. (1981). Rapid assessment instruments for practice. *Social Work Research and Abstracts, 17*(1), 13–19.

Robinson, J. P., & Shaver, P. R. (1973). *Measures of social psychological attitudes*. Ann Arbor, MI: Institute for Social Research.

Collections of measurement instruments are most frequently organized according to type of problem (e.g., alcoholism, assertiveness, stress) or by population group (adults, children, couples, families). Ciarlo, Brown, Edward, Kiresuk, Newman (1986) suggest an organization according to (1) substantive focus (individual, interpersonal, or community), (2) assessment approach (idiosyncratic, partially standardized, or standardized), and (3) respondent (client, collateral, therapist, or other). We have suggested that, although measurement of problems often provides the most direct indicators of outcome, useful assessment information may be provided by the clients' perspectives of goals as well as their overt problems, by their situations as well as their dispositions, and by their strengths as well as their deficits. The "law of the instrument" suggests that these domains are ignored frequently because there is no convenient way to measure them. To the end of identifying ways to measure these domains, we list in Table 6.4 specific measures addressing these issues as well as measures frequently used to understand problems and goals.

TABLE 6.4
Frequently Used Measurement Instruments

Measures of client perspectives
Problems and goals
Derived from Battle, C., Imber, S. D., Hoen-Saric, R., Stoone, A. R., Nash, E. H., & Frank, J. D. (1966). Target complaints as criteria of improvement. *American Journal of Psychotherapy, 20,* 184–192.

RELIABILITY: Information not available for adapted from.
VALIDITY: Information not available for adapted form.

Striving
Cantril, H. (1965). *The pattern of human concerns.* New Brunswick, NJ: Rutgers University Press.

RELIABILITY: Information not available.
VALIDITY: Information not available.

Measures of client situation
The Home Observation for Measurement of the Environment (HOME)
Betty M. Caldwell, Center for Child Development and Education, University of Arkansas at Little Rock, 33rd and University Avenue, Little Rock, Arkansas 72204.

RELIABILITY: Some support for reliability.
VALIDITY: Some support for validity.

Family Environment Scale
Moos, R. H., & Moos, B. S. (1983). Clinical applications of the Family Environment Scale. In E. E. Filsinger (Ed.), *Marriage and family assessment: A sourcebook for family therapy.* Beverly Hills: Sage.

RELIABILITY: Internal consistency of subscales range from .61–.78; test-retest ranging from .68–.86.
VALIDITY: No information

Stressful Situations Questionnaire
Hodges, W. F., & Felling F. P. (1970). Types of stressful situations and their relation to trait anxiety and sex. *Journal of Consulting and Clinical Psychology, 34,* 333–337.

RELIABILITY: No information available.
VALIDITY: Some support for construct validity reported.

Measures of client strengths
Pleasant Events Schedule
McPhillamy, D. J., & Lewisohn, P. M. (1982). The Pleasant Events Schedule: Studies on reliability, validity and scale intercorrelations. *Journal of Consulting and Clinical Psychology, 50,* 363–380

RELIABILITY: Test-retest ranging from .69–.88.
VALIDITY: Some support for construct validity.

Family Adaptability and Cohesion Scale
Olson, D. H., Portner, J., & Lavee, Y. (1985). FACES-III, Family Social Science, University of Minnesota, 290 NcNeal Hall, St. Paul, Minnesota 55108.

RELIABILITY: Internal consistency ranging from .68–.77; test-retest ranging from .80–.83
VALIDITY: Good face validity reported.

TABLE 6.4 (*continued*)

Problem-Solving Inventory (PSI)	
Heppner, P. P., & Peterson, C. H. (1982). The development and implications of a personal problem-solving inventory. *Journal of Counseling Psychology, 29,* 66–75.	RELIABILITY: Internal consistency ranging from .72–.85; test-retest ranging from .83–.89. VALIDITY: Good construct validity reported.
Self-Efficacy Scale	
Sherer, M., Maddox, J. E., Mercandante, B., Prentice-Dunn, S., Jacobs, B., & Rogers, R. W. (1982). The self-efficacy scale: Construction and validation. *Psychology Reports, 51,* 663–671.	RELIABILITY: internal consistency ranging from .71–.86. VALIDITY: Some construct validity reported.

Observation

The practical job of the observer is to understand what is seen by assigning particular behaviors to categories. Observations can be highly unstructured or very tightly structured. Narrative descriptions represent the most unstructured approaches to observation. The social work tool of process recording in which a set of interactions is recorded in depth and detail is an example of a highly unstructured approach to observation. As Patton (1990) points out, unstructured observations are not unscientific observations. The use of observational methods requires "disciplined training and rigorous preparation." (p. 200) Such training and preparation includes learning how to write descriptively, learning how to separate detail from trivia, and using rigorous methods to validate observations and inferences. Inferences drawn from observations documented in process recordings are typically validated through conversations with a supervisor. The supervisor helps the practitioner determine whether the inferences logically follow from the observations, and whether they are consistent with theory and with practice experience.

DISTINGUISHING INFERENCE FROM OBSERVATION   To distinguish between observations and inferences is a very important skill for any practitioner. Observations are descriptions that can be related to actual conditions whereas inferences are conclusions, interpretations, or global summaries of those conditions or events. A great deal of valuable information can be lost if the practitioner moves too quickly from observation to inference. Practitioners who characterize a client as "hostile" or "anxious" should, for their own understanding and for that of those with whom they communicate, be able to link these interpretations to their physical, behavioral referents. For example, a client may be described as communicating in monosyllables and avoiding eye contact, behavior that could be interpreted by one practitioner as hostile and by another as anxious. Because we live in a society in which psychological terminology has become a part of everyday discourse, it is extremely important for professionals to use language precisely.

Unstructured observations may also benefit from "sensitizing concepts", that is, ideas or categories that enable us to break complex reality into distinguishable, manageable, and understandable parts (Patton, 1988). An observation becomes more structured when predetermined categories are imposed on it. It is nearly impossible to avoid some sensitizing concepts, since formal and informal theoretical frameworks certainly shape our understanding. During assessment, concepts and categories such as problems, goals, strengths, and weaknesses guide our impressions. Overall, categories can be general and natural or small and easily observed. Broader, naturally occurring categories are typically high in face validity but interobserver reliability may be harder to achieve. More specific categories are more reliable, but sometimes at the cost of validity. Broader categories rely on observer inference to a much greater degree than narrow categories.

Observational schemes of varying structure have been developed to serve a variety of purposes. General-purpose schemes are represented by Bales (1950). More specific observational codes have also been developed; a comprehensive list of observational schemes used in family settings, institutions, schools, and communities is available in Hayes and Wilson (1979).

STRUCTURED OBSERVATION   A practitioner who seeks accurate and detailed information about a behavior as it occurs in a natural environment can benefit from conducting his or her own structured observation; for example, information about parent–child interaction or student–teacher interaction. Deciding how to sample behaviors is the fundamental question in conducting a structured observation. Two approaches to sampling are possible: *event sampling* and *time sampling.* In *event sampling,* a particular event is selected for observation. Such an approach is particularly useful for discrete events that occur at a relatively low rate, since it requires recording only when the event occurs. Monitoring, as discussed previously, is event sampling; frequency counts for specific behaviors are gathered for particular periods of time. The advantage of this approach is that naturally occurring events that are targeted for observation possess an inherent validity and continuity.

Time sampling requires the selection of specific units of time, either intervals or discrete points, during which the occurrence or nonoccurrence of a specific behavior is recorded. Time-interval sampling is useful for events that occur continuously or frequently. It requires that a period of time be divided into smaller intervals. The occurrence or nonoccurrence of the target behavior during the smaller interval is then recorded. Neither the duration of the behavior nor multiple occurrences of the behavior is recorded. The length of the observation interval is determined in part by the frequency of the behavior—intervals may need to be shorter if the behavior happens more frequently. For example, if a classroom behavior is to be observed, a class session of 30 minutes could be divided into 30 one-minute intervals in which the observer records the occurrence or nonoccurrence of a behavior during the last 10 seconds of every minute. The observer would not record for 50 seconds, then observe whether or not the behavior occurred during the next 10 seconds, relax for 50 seconds, then observe in the next 10 seconds, and so on. In this way, 30 observations would be made.

Interval recording requires the establishment of a definition of a behavior to be recorded and rules for recording its occurrence; that is, what to record and how

(Budd, Rogers, & Schelmoeller, 1972). For example, suppose you are working with an elementary school child and her teacher and parents are concerned about her ability to concentrate on her work in class. You want an accurate assessment of the problem, so you decide to conduct a structured observation. To do this, you might determine upon the following definition of the target behavior and recording rules:

DEFINITION OF ON-TASK BEHAVIOR

Child is looking at work on the desk or presented by the teacher.

RULES FOR RECORDING

1. On-task behavior is recorded on the top horizontal row of the grid.
2. The occurrence of the behavior is recorded by placing a check on the grid in the one-minute interval in which it occurs.
3. On-task behavior may be recorded only once in a single interval, although it may occur more than once during that time.
4. On-task behavior that begins in one interval and extends into subsequent intervals is recorded once in each interval.
5. If the child remains off-task for the entire interval, a dot is placed in the interval on the grid.

Such a definition of behavior and rules for recording are together called the *observational code*. The observational code is developed by the practitioner for each case and involves a description of the behavior, examples of its occurrence, and exclusions to the definition, that is, related behaviors that do not fit within the definition. Behaviors are recorded on data sheets made up of grids. Each horizontal row of boxes is used to record *one class of behavior* and each vertical column corresponds to one *time interval*. A complete grid that incorporates several behaviors of interest might look like the one below. It is filled in only for on-task behavior.

On-task	√	.	√	√	.	√
Talking appropriately						
Talking inappropriately						

Reliability of the observational code can be assessed when two observers use the code to record behaviors and then make an interval-by-interval comparison of agreement between themselves. A simple formula for checking reliability is the following:

$$\text{Reliability} = \frac{\text{Number of intervals with agreement}}{\text{Total number of intervals recorded}}$$

Using this formula on the grids below, you would calculate a .50 level of reliability.

	OS	√	■	√	■	√	■
Observer 1	C						
	T						

	OS	√	√	■	■	√	√
Observer 2	C						
	T						

Time point sampling is another approach to time sampling in which particular points of time are specified and the occurrence or nonoccurrence of a behavior at these points is recorded. This approach is particularly useful for recording ongoing behavior, such as the time an adolescent spends in his or her room, or the time an elementary child spends watching television. Although equal time intervals can be set, it is possible to use kitchen timers and wristwatch timers to determine random intervals.

One particular type of *time interval* sampling that is useful for assessing groups is *placheck* (planned activity check), used by Linsk, Howe, and Pinkston (1975) to assess the sociability of older individuals in a residential setting. The approach requires the observer to define the behavior he or she wishes to record. Then, at given intervals, the observer counts the individuals engaged in the activity and records the total. The observer then counts the total number of individuals present in the area of the activity and calculates the ratio of those involved to those present.

Institutional Records

Institutional records can provide a very useful source of assessment information, especially if they are available over a period of time. Records of school attendance and grades are particularly useful for work with children. Work and health records and records of the use of health and mental health services can provide valuable evidence of functioning.

The advantage of institutional records is that they typically have been collected over long periods of time and thus provide information from the past that is not otherwise accessible. Further, the information has been collected for institutional purposes and is therefore not vulnerable to such biases as the client's desire to please the worker, or the worker's desire to see progress. With institutional cooperation, information can be obtained easily and economically.

The disadvantages of institutional records are not unrelated to the advantages. Because they are collected over a long period of time, changes in the definitions used or the data collection methods employed may affect the applicability of the

data. For example, a school social worker may note a significant increase in police reports of gang activity near her school in a given year. It may be the case that there has been a change in gang activity, or perhaps the police have simply begun to classify certain kinds of juvenile crimes in a different way. Further, the specific institutional purposes for the data may create bias. For example, if school funding is determined by a formula that is based on the number of students in attendance, there may be a tendency for schools to underreport absences.

SUMMARY

Collecting information that is useful in clinical work requires keeping in mind some fundamental ideas. First, good and useful information derives completely from a full understanding of the client's perspective of the problem and his or her goals. The client's consent to and cooperation in the process of collecting data not only add to the quality of the data but may be instrumental in achieving the client's objectives. Further, more than one source of information collected over time may be relevant to the measurement of any treatment objective. There are many possible data-collection strategies, each with its distinct benefits and limitations. The treatment objectives should be the key in identifying and selecting available strategies and measures; the strategies and measures should not drive the treatment process. In other words, data collected will be most useful when the social worker focuses on finding the most relevant, rather than the most readily available, measure. Finally, in order to be maximally useful, the worker will have to work with it, organize it, and perhaps reorganize it—in other words *use* it to think about problems and progress.

7 | Organizing and Analyzing Data

I n order to make sense of the significant amount of clinically relevant data available, the practitioner must identify ways to organize it so that important patterns and trends become apparent. This chapter provides specific strategies for organizing and exploring both qualitative and quantitative data. Included in the discussion are approaches for distilling important data from structured and unstructured case recordings, guidelines for constructiong visual displays, and the use of time-series statistical techniques in confirmatory data analysis.

I. Organizing and Displaying Data: Exploratory Data Analysis
   A. Techniques for Organizing Qualitative Data
      1. Selected empirical summaries
      2. Logical analysis of effects
      3. Informative events or critical incidences
      4. Summary
   B. Visual Display of Quantitative Data
      1. An effective display avoids distortion by (1) showing variation yet displaying numbers in proportion to quantity; (2) clear labeling; (3) eliminating *chartjunk*
      2. A good visual display encourages comparison
      3. An effective graph reveals different level of detail

II. Analysis of Time-Series Data
   A. Times-Series Designs
      1. Selecting single-case, time-series designs
      2. Logic of single-case, time-series designs
      3. Drawing valid inferences
   B. Clinical Questions Addressed by Time-Series Designs
      1. Is the intervention working? The A-B and B designs
      2. Is the intervention causing the change? The A-B-A, A-B-A-B, B-A-B, muliple-baseline, and multiple target designs
      3. What aspects of the intervention are most important? Construction and deconstruction designs

III. Interpreting Time-Series Data: Variability, Trend and Level
   A. Variability
   B. Trend and Level

IV. Assessing the Statistical Significance of Clinical Time-Series Data
   A. Checking the Assumption of Independence
   B. When Observations are not Independent: Transforming the Data

V. Summary

Because of the nature of interpersonal exchange, the clinician necessarily processes a great deal of detail: bits of information about how the client looked and acted in the session, what he or she said, and what the practitioner felt, thought, and said. If the practitioner's intent is how to find implications for intervention in this flow of information, he needs some way to organize it. The statistician John Tukey has suggested that a basic problem with any body of data is how to make it more easily and effectively "handleable by minds" (Tukey, 1977, p.v.). Any strategy that results in a simpler description or that organizes information so that main ideas or trends can be identified helps to make it more "handleable." Tukey points out in his book *Exploratory Data Analysis* that for much of their history statisticians and data analysts have been concerned primarily with description, with the organization and presentation of details of a phenomenon. More recently, emphasis has been placed on confirmation; that is, determining whether a statistically significant relationship exists between two variables or sets of variables. Tukey urges us to consider exploration and confirmation as mutually reinforcing activities. In his view, the best way to understand where the interesting and important information may be is to explore, to try many approaches to organizing information, anticipating that some, even most, will not be fruitful.

   In this chapter, we discuss specific strategies whereby both qualitative and quantitative data may be organized and explored. We provide specific guidelines for good visual displays and their interpretation. Finally, we discuss fundamental elements of confirmatory analysis in clinical research, specifically with respect to time-series research designs and statistics.

ORGANIZING AND DISPLAYING DATA: EXPLORATORY DATA ANALYSIS

Techniques for Organizing Qualitative Data

There are several *information synthesizing* strategies that provide guidelines for systematically organizing the detail available in such rich qualitative data as are recorded in the Working Record. These strategies facilitate incremental improvements in practice approaches rather than definitive tests of effectiveness (Reid & Davis, 1987). They are consistent with developmental research and formative evaluation efforts.

SELECTED EMPIRICAL SUMMARIES   The first strategy in an empirical summary consists of identifying and documenting selected elements of a case. This is a type of structured recording, although it is more focused than the Working Record. Indeed, the Working Record (or some other type of process notes) could provide the basis for empirical summaries. As can be seen in the example in Figure 7.1, an effort is made to use clear language and to define any ambiguous concepts with specific indicators from the case. Such summaries can be viewed as a type of qualitative time-series data, where the same type of information is gathered and organized over time as a basis for analyzing change and patterns of change.

In these distillations of the pattern of Georgia's problem (presented in Chapter 7), the worker has found a way to assess Georgia's progress. She arrived at this assessment strategy by making a few decisions. Essentially, she asked herself, "Out of all the available information about Georgia and her problem, out of all the varieties of content, patterns, and summary indicators that I might focus on, which will provide me with the most useful, meaningful, and readily available cues about her progress?"

LOGICAL ANALYSIS OF EFFECTS   As we have noted several times, developing and evaluating a "working" conceptual model with logical causal links is one of the ongoing phases of progress monitoring. Adapting the work of Miles and Huberman (1984), Reid and Davis (1987) describe a technique called logical analysis for establishing links among problem, context of the problem, intervention, and change. Logical analysis is an effort to document the relationship between intervention and change in order to provide a specific basis for inferences about what caused the change. Clearly, these inferences are strengthened when (1) the evidence of

FIGURE 7.1
Empirical summary, problem patterns, G case

Session-to-session review of problem change:

Session 2. Summary of Problem Pattern: Georgia doesn't know what to do about Tom's offensive behavior and so suffers it, feels resentful, and feels guilty about resentment. Psychiatrist and other mental health professionals are not forthcoming about how to deal with Tom.

Session 3. Summary of Problem Pattern: Georgia still submits to Tom's offensive behavior; resents his encroachment on her time, house, and peace of mind; feels less guilty about resentment and is focused more on her own needs and Tom's responsibilities; fuming about unresponsiveness of the psychiatrist.

Session 4. Summary of Problem Pattern: Georgia confronted Tom in angry, blaming, highly critical way; feels very guilty, trapped, and helpless; feels criticized by psychiatrist for creating negative emotional atmosphere.

---

intervention and its effects is specific and detailed, (2) the inferences are consistent with a particular theoretical perspective, and (3) other possible explanations are unavailable.

In Figure 7.2, we provide a logical analysis for the Donna case (presented in detail in chapter 8). We have attempted to provide the links among the problem, problem context, intervention, and change that illustrate the presumed causal relationships. Key elements of the case are selected, organized, and displayed so that the strength and quality of the inference can be carefully analyzed. The logical analysis can be viewed as a way to build on and elaborate the conceptual model described in Chapter 3. In the example provided here, the chain of relations assumed to be causal is identified. The chain begins with contextual factors causing the problem, which then influence a series of interventions designed to ameliorate the problem. The diagram includes indicators of level of confidence about the causal inferences.

INFORMATIVE EVENTS OR CRITICAL INCIDENCES   It is often the case that, in thinking about work with a client, practitioners can identify specific events that seemed to mark a turning point. Reid and Davis (1987) suggest a strategy for capturing such events more systematically. They suggest that the worker record "informative events"; that is, any incidence that may have informational value, offer valuable insights, or enhance understanding. They suggest categorizing events in a way that is meaningful for practice improvement or model development. They use the following categories: (1) model limitation; (2) promising innovation; (3) skilled or unskilled application; (4) practitioner noncompliance; (5) instructive success; (6) instructive failure; (7) theory-related occurrence. Such categories are best constructed in the context of specific practice questions; that is, in the context of what the practitioner is trying to understand about his or her practice. Task analysis, another strategy for understanding the causal mechanism in a change-inducing interaction, is discussed in greater detail in Chapter 9.

The goal in monitoring progress is to improve practice and effectiveness in an ongoing way. Information-synthesizing strategies enable the practitioner to bring some order to the rich information available in ongoing practice.

SUMMARY   As noted, ongoing assessment of client progress is undertaken in order to understand the client and his or her problems more fully, not least whether the problems are improving. Thus, assessing progress means moving along two intersecting tracks: assessing progress in terms of the client's understanding of the nature of the problem, and assessing progress in terms of the client's doing better, feeling better, getting along with others better, procuring needed resources, or taking a more adaptive perspective. Even for the expert, there is a lot of information to track and reflect on, and it is useful to have a system in order to do that. The social worker in the Donna case relied on the Working Record to prompt her to collect, track, and reflect on a wide range of information relevant to Donna's progress and the overall management of the case. Information-synthesizing strategies presented in this section that use information from the Working Record are designed to help the clinician to (1) figure out what it is that he or she needs to know in order to be most helpful, and (2) systematically organize and explore such information.

FIGURE 7.2
Logical analysis of intervention effects

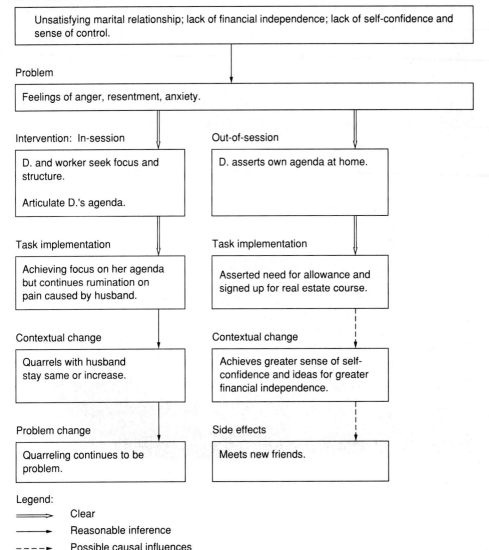

Contextual factors

Unsatisfying marital relationship; lack of financial independence; lack of self-confidence and sense of control.

Problem

Feelings of anger, resentment, anxiety.

Intervention: In-session

D. and worker seek focus and structure.

Articulate D.'s agenda.

Out-of-session

D. asserts own agenda at home.

Task implementation

Achieving focus on her agenda but continues rumination on pain caused by husband.

Task implementation

Asserted need for allowance and signed up for real estate course.

Contextual change

Quarrels with husband stay same or increase.

Contextual change

Achieves greater sense of self-confidence and ideas for greater financial independence.

Problem change

Quarreling continues to be problem.

Side effects

Meets new friends.

Legend:
⟹   Clear
—➤   Reasonable inference
- - -➤   Possible causal influences

Visual Display of Quantitative Data

"The greatest value of a picture," writes John Tukey, "is when it forces us to notice what we never expected to see" (Tukey, 1977, p. vi). Pictures in the form of plots and graphs of quantitative information can organize information and enhance understanding. The use of plots and graphs in the analysis of clinical data has the additional advantage of keeping the practitioner and the client in direct, ongoing contact with indicators of progress. When key indicators are graphed at regular intervals (e.g., after each session), shifts and trends can be detected immediately and programs modified accordingly.

Principles governing the design of good pictures or visual displays are not well articulated in the social science and social work literature. Tufte, however, in his books *The Visual Display of Quantitative Information* (1984) and *Envisioning Information* (1990), provides a good starting place. Through numerous powerful pictorial examples, he shows how a good visual display can communicate with clarity, efficiency, and precision. A good display has the following characteristics: it avoids distortion, (i.e., it tells the truth); it encourages comparison; and it reveals different levels of detail. Each of these characteristics is discussed below.

AN EFFECTIVE VISUAL DISPLAY AVOIDS DISTORTION   We translate information into pictures or images in order to document, to communicate, or to reason about knowledge. It is important, then, that our pictures "tell the truth." Three principles provide guidelines for achieving visual integrity (Tufte, 1990):

(1) A graph should be designed to show variation in the data yet represent numbers in direct proportion to their quantity. In clinical practice, data are often collected and organized to determine changes over time, with the x-axis used to document time and the y-axis documenting a scale for the progress or outcome variable. When the y-axis scale divisions are much larger (or smaller) than the x-axis scale divisions, any changes will appear exaggerated. It may be appropriate to emphasize a clinically significant change, but it is also appropriate to alert the viewer to attenuated or elongated scales. For example, in Figure 7.3a below the y-axis does not begin at the origin or zero position and the scale divisions on the x-axis are much smaller than those on the y-axis. This has the effect of exaggerating the amount of change within each phase as can be seen when Figure 7.3a is compared with Figures 7.3b and 7.3c. Figure 7.3b represents the data with the entire scale beginning at zero. Figure 7.3c shows the same data with reduced scale intervals on the y-axis. This has the effect of attenuating the appearance of change both within and between phases. In Figure 7.4 we see a visual distortion in the column length achieved by placing the x-axis well below the origin. In general, graphs such as these "tell the truth" when the x-and y-axes are clearly labeled, when they begin at the origin (unless otherwise indicated), and when they rely on meaningful scales.

(2) Clear, detailed labeling of the major dimension on the graph should be provided. Important events should be labeled and any explanations should be written on the graph. Because we are often concerned with the relation between specific interventions and progress or outcome or between specific types of outcome, it is particularly important that phases of treatment or the use of different intervention strategies be clearly labeled and the experimental design used in the study be carefully documented.

(3) *Chartjunk* should be avoided. Tufte uses the term chartjunk to refer to unnecessary material: for example, lines, grids, or decorative patterns that may be added to a graph but that convey no information. The growing availability of computer graphics with numerous "chartjunk options" increases the temptation.

FIGURE 7.3
(a) Visual distortion produced by attenuated y-axis; (b) Identical data on an undistorted graph; (c) effects of reducing y-axis scale. (*Source:* B. S. Parsonson and D. M. Baer. (1978). The analysis and presentation of graphic data. In T. R. Krotochwill (Ed.), *Single-subject research: Strategies for evaluating change.* New York: Academic Press.)

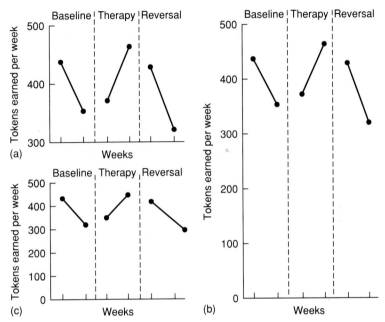

FIGURE 7.4
Visual distortion of column length on a bar graph by displacing x-axis well below the zero line. (*Source:* B. S. Parsonson and D. M. Baer. (1978). The analysis and presentation of graphic data. In T. R. Krotochwill (Ed.), *Single-subject research: Strategies for evaluating change.* New York: Academic Press.)

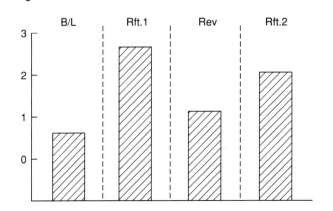

FIGURE 7.5
Chartjunk

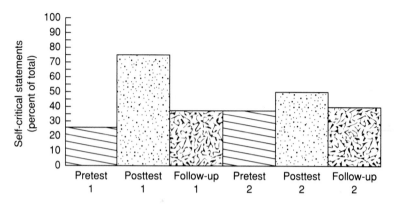

Figure 7.5 is an example of a graph filled with chartjunk. The designs within each bar carry no information about treatment type or measurement period.

A GOOD VISUAL DISPLAY ENCOURAGES COMPARISON   Fundamental to reasoning about quantitative information is the question, "Compared to what?" Graphics are an efficient means to reveal change over time; difference among phases, series, categories, or groups; and alternative options. Comparisons can be facilitated through *visual stratification*, or the use of size, color, value (i.e., light and dark), and texture. Figure 7.6 shows the data for a husband and wife on Moos' Family Environment Scale. Plotting the data in this way invites comparison of two individuals for the assessment of areas of convergence and divergence across sereral different categories of family environment.

AN EFFECTIVE GRAPH REVEALS DIFFERENT LEVELS OF DETAIL   Tufte recommends adhering to the *micro/macro principle*; that is, attempting in one graph to depict the overall trends without losing specific detail. His examples include several isometric maps, such as that of the University of Chicago (Figure 7.7), which reveal the details of individual buildings and plantings while providing a coherent perspective and "feeling" for the campus. Carefully arranging detailed and complex information makes that information appear clear and simple.

ANALYSIS OF TIMES-SERIES DATA

Time-series Designs

So far, we have discussed in this chapter various strategies for organizing information to increase understanding. Research designs are also strategies for collecting and organizing data; they enhance the validity of the interpretations we can draw from a data set. In this section, we focus on clinical time-series designs, designs that allow multiple observations of individual cases across time.

There are several basic elements of the single-case, time-series design: (1) identification of relevant feasible measures with known reliability and validity;

FIGURE 7.6

Pretherapy family environment for the Cartwright family. (*Source:* R. H. Moos and B. S. Moos. (1982). Clinical appreciations of the family environmental scale. In Erik E. Filsinger (Ed.), *Marriage and family assessment: A sourcebook for family therapy.* Beverly Hills, CA: Sage.)

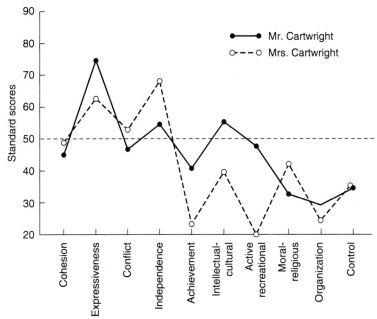

FIGURE 7.7

Isometric map of University of Chicago

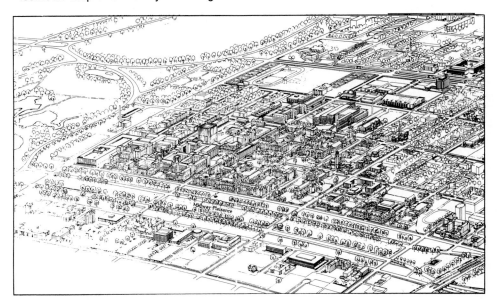

(2) specification of intervention procedures; (3) repeated measurement during various phases of intervention; and (4) frequent graphing of results. Basic and detailed discussions of the use of these designs in clinical practice are available elsewhere (Bloom & Fischer, 1982; Hersen & Barlow, 1976; Jayaratne & Levy, 1979). Discussions of the application of single-case designs in a service context reveal that they are not without their difficulties and dilemmas (Thomas, 1978). Constraints in the service setting may prevent long and stable baselines or block the opportunity to withdraw interventions to establish behavioral control. However, these designs do help organize information in practice, with the result that progress is continuously monitored and intervention decisions are made on the basis of what is happening.

SELECTING SINGLE-CASE, TIME-SERIES DESIGNS   There are numerous types of single-case designs. However, the types that are likely to be used in an ongoing way in practice are more limited. The selection of a particular design depends first on the questions you are attempting to answer and, second, on the type of information available. Often it is impossible to determine the appropriate design until well into the assessment process. The fact that you do not have a design does not mean that you are not collecting relevant baseline information. Indeed, the baseline information you collect often helps determine the appropriate design.

There are three questions that can be addressed with single-case designs: (1) Is the intervention working? (That is, have the treatment objectives been addressed?) (2) Is the intervention causing the change? (3) What aspect of the intervention is causing the change? The discussion of designs is organized by these questions.

LOGIC OF SINGLE-CASE, TIME-SERIES DESIGNS   The basic purpose of research designs is to guide the collection of data so that the conclusions drawn from the study are unambiguous and valid. Treatment studies typically compare data collected under treatment conditions to data collected in the absence of a treatment. In experimental group designs, individual subjects are randomly assigned either to a treatment group or to a "no treatment" control group. Then the performance of these two groups is compared to assess the effectiveness of the intervention.

In single-case designs, observations over time of one individual during a preintervention, "no treatment," or baseline phase are compared with observations over time during an intervention phase. These two phases are then compared to assess whether there is a difference or improvement in the intervention phase and whether the difference can be attributed to the intervention.

In the tradition of single-case research, phases are designated with letters of the alphabet, with A designating the baseline phase, B designating the first intervention phase, C designating a third phase and so on. In the purest application of single-system designs, each letter stands for a single intervention strategy. However, clinicians rarely use a single strategy. Bloom and Fischer (1982) indicate that, in reality, the letters indicating phases can represent an intervention that is a single technique (a procedure), several procedures (a package), or several packages (which they refer to as a program).

DRAWING VALID INFERENCES   Inferences that can be drawn from single-case designs are strengthened when the clinician adheres to the following guidelines. First, it is advisable in any one phase to collect sufficient data to ascertain a stable pattern. Not all data series will provide a stable pattern, but the phase should be long enough for natural patterns of variability to emerge. When baseline data are stable, it is much easier to use visual analysis to detect changes in pattern in the intervention phase. Second, whenever possible, the lengths of phases should be approximately equal, so that whatever external factors are influencing the data will have equal opportunity to influence each phase. Finally, comparisons should only be made between adjacent phases; for example, A-B or B-C in an A-B-C design. Comparisons of nonadjacent phases (e.g., A-C) does not permit the clinician to account for the impact of an intervening phase, which could be responsible for any change that occurred in C. The comparison A-C would require the implementation of an A-B-A-C design.

Visual and statistical criteria can be applied to answer the first of two major evaluation questions, whether there is a difference between two phases. The second question, whether the difference can be attributed to the intervention, is essentially a determination of whether the intervention *caused* the outcome. Three criteria can be used to assess whether a causal relation exists: appropriate sequence in time, concomitant variation, and the elimination of plausible rival hypotheses. Appropriate sequence in time refers to the fact that, in a causal relation where phenomenon X causes phenomenon Y, we expect that a change in X will be followed by a change in Y and not vice-versa. Concomitant variation refers to the fact that X and Y will co-vary, or change together in a causal relationship. If they are positively related, a positive change in X will result in a positive change in Y. Finally, the elimination of plausible rival hypotheses refers to a process of seeking alternative explanations for the outcomes observed. Campbell and Stanley (1963) made a significant contribution to the study of such causal relationships by categorizing the primary alternative explanations for the effects of treatment; that is, reasons other than the treatment that could account for the results. Their categories provide a useful guide for clinical work as well. The alternative explanations, or threats to the validity of causal inference, that are particularly problematic in clinical work are set out briefly here.

(1) *History*. History is an alternative explanation when an event occuring simultaneously with the treatment could possibly affect outcome. For example, if during treatment a strongly positive or negative event occurs in the client's life (such as falling in love or losing a loved one), it will be very difficult to determine whether the treatment or this event was responsible for any observed effect.

(2) *Maturation*. The client's maturation could also be an alternative explanation of outcome. The multiple measures required in single-case designs help rule out this rival hypothesis because trends due to maturation should be identifiable in the baseline phase.

(3) *Instrumentation*. Some aspect of the measurement strategy or instrument could affect the outcome measure. For example, observational measures are vulnerable to the effects of "observational drift," in which two observers maintain interobserver reliability or consistency while simultaneously, unknowingly changing the metric of the code. Or, if a measure requires a great deal of effort on the part of the client, there may be a tendency for the client to reduce the time and effort devoted to completing a measure in a way that changes the character and accuracy of the responses.

(4) *Statistical regression.* This is a threat that operates particularly when the baseline consists of one or two extreme scores. As discussed in Chapter 1, extreme scores tend to be followed by less extreme scores. If it is impossible to obtain a relatively stable baseline, then the change from an extreme score to a more moderate score could be attributed erroneously to the treatment.

In a previous section, we discussed the idea of validity in terms of measurement instruments: "Is our measure actually and adequately measuring what it is supposed to be measuring?" When we examine alternative explanations for the results of our intervention, we are examining the *internal validity* of our causal inferences: "How confident can we be that our intervention was responsible for the changes we observe?" Research designs are mechanisms for reducing or removing the influence of extraneous factors so that we can attribute with some confidence any changes we observe to our intervention. Campbell and Stanley (1963) distinguish between internal validity and external validity. *External validity* refers to the extent to which our findings can be applied to other populations and environments. In a broad setting, external validity is strengthened to the extent that results are based on a large random sample from the population about which we wish to generalize. Because single-case, time-series designs are based on a single case, they are criticized for weak external validity. In a clinical setting, external validity is strengthened whenever the clinician can pursue a clinical replication; that is, the repeated application of the same intervention package by the same clinician in the same setting to similar clients with a similar constellation of problems resulting in similar results.

Clinical Questions Addressed with Time-series Designs

An analysis of published clinical time-series studies shows that most clinical researchers rely primarily on the A-B, the A-B-A-B, or the multiple baseline designs (Marsh & Shibano 1982). However, the utility of clinical research designs can be discussed in terms of their capacity to address three basic clinical research questions: (1) Is the intervention working? (2) Is the intervention causing the change? and (3) What aspects of the intervention are most important? We use these questions to organize our discussion of these research designs below. A summary of the designs is provided in Figure 7.8.

IS THE INTERVENTION WORKING? THE A-B AND B DESIGNS   Without question, of the designs we will discuss, the A-B design has been applied most frequently in service settings. It is characterized by repeated measurement in a baseline or nonintervention period (the A phase) followed by repeated measurement during the period of intervention (the B phase). It is assumed that the baseline reflects a naturally occurring pattern that would continue if not interrupted by an intervention. As such, the intervention phase can be compared with it to determine whether any changes have occurred. Determinations of change are unequivocal when the baseline is stable and the intervention has a sharply accelerating or decelerating trend (as in Figure 7.9a) or when the intervention phase has a trend that is in the opposite direction of the baseline phase (as in Figure 7.9b or c). Changes in the trend and level of data between baseline and treatment phases are the primary

FIGURE 7.8
Summary of clinical time-series designs

Clinical research question	Design
Is the intervention working? (Are treatment objectives being met?)	A-B B
Is the intervention causing the change?	A-B-A A-B-A-B B-A-B
	Multiple baseline: $A_1B_1B_1B_1$ $A_2A_2B_2B_2$ $A_3A_3A_3B_3$
	Multiple target: A_1B_1 A_2B_2 A_3B_3
What aspects of the intervention are most important?	Deconstruction: A-BC-A-B-A-C
	Construction: A-B-A-C-A-BC

Notation: A = baseline, A_1, A_2 = baseline for different target behaviors (same intervention)
            B = intervention, B_1, B_2 = same intervention for different target behaviors
            BC = concurrent presence of different interventions B, C

bases for attributing change to the treatment. The strongest attribution is based on a shift in trend and in level in the improved direction. Clearly, however, there are many possible combinations. The most likely are shown in Figure 7.9 in order of decreasing interpretability.

The value of the A-B design is in its consistency with normal practice procedure; that is, an assessment or data-gathering phase followed by an intervention phase. Further, the A-B design enables the practitioner to monitor and assess progress on an ongoing basis. The comparison between the baseline and intervention phases provides very useful evidence on whether the intervention is working. It should be clear, however, that this design cannot provide evidence about whether the intervention itself causes the change. Further, if the intervention is complex, this design does not permit the clinician to unravel which aspects are most important.

FIGURE 7.9
Possible configurations of change in baseline and treatment phases

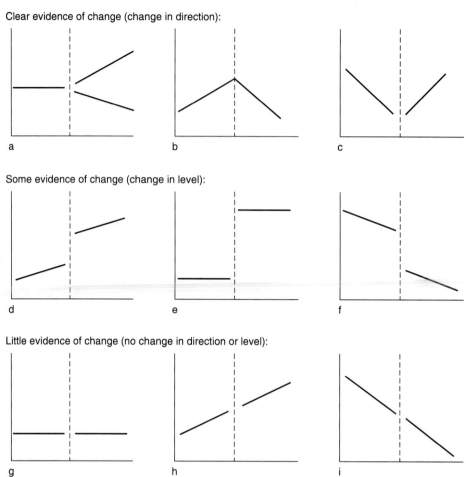

Clear evidence of change (change in direction):

a   b   c

Some evidence of change (change in level):

d   e   f

Little evidence of change (no change in direction or level):

g   h   i

   The limitations of the design result from the fact that it does not enable the clinician to eliminate alternative explanations for any change observed; it does not permit the worker to attribute the change automatically to the intervention. Campbell and Stanley (1963) (see also Cook & Campbell, 1979) provide a useful and comprehensive discussion of these and other drawbacks of this design.
   A useful A-B design requires a clear and accurate description of the intervention. It is necessary to specify when the intervention begins and exactly what program or aspect of the program is being evaluated. The effect of any type of intervention can be measured in the B phase. An intervention can be global, such as supportive listening, or specific, such as a behavioral reinforcement program, but as we discussed in Chapter 5, it is necessary to specify what the intervention is.

For example, consider the case of Mr. Palmer, a frail 84-year-old man who lives alone and receives several kinds of in-home assistance from a local community-based agency serving the elderly. He recently has asked the agency for assistance in managing his health insurance. His doctor has advised him to change from his HMO to Medicare and a supplemental health insurance policy. Mr. Palmer also has several hospital bills that he does not understand. He has been making frequent calls to the agency (three to four calls each day) expressing great anxiety. The student social worker who has been assigned to Mr. Palmer as her first case decides to focus on straightening out his bills to determine if this will alleviate his anxiety. She uses the number of telephone calls to the agency as a measure of anxiety. She can use agency records to determine the number of times he called in the week prior to her intervention and then continue to monitor the number of calls subsequently. The results shown in Figure 7.10 reveal that achieving some order in his personal affairs signficantly reduced the number of calls to the agency.

B-designs are useful when it is necessary to intervene immediately (e.g., in a crisis situation) without gathering baseline information, even retrospective baseline information. B-designs are less desirable than A-B designs because they lack preintervention comparison data. However, they serve as useful guides for gathering information about progress over time and provide absolute evidence relevant to

FIGURE 7.10
Example of A-B design: Number of telephone calls to agency before and after intervention

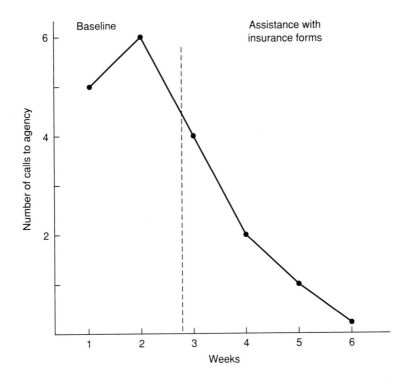

whether treatment goals have been achieved. Further, sometimes the initial B-phase will be followed by a C- or D-phase; that is, other interventions. In such cases, the B-phase can provide comparison data, albeit not "no treatment" comparison data. These designs can help organize data collection, can provide evidence of whether treatment goals are reached, and can provide evidence of the nature or pattern of change (e.g., whether rapid or gradual, with high or low variability). But they provide no hint as to whether the pattern observed is any different from the preintervention pattern.

Consider the case of Mrs. Jones, a 68-year-old woman who was referred to the medical social worker for "supportive counseling." Mrs. Jones, a widow, had recently retired from a successful career as an advertising agency executive. She had maintained an independent life focused primarily on her career, and had regular contact with her three grown children. Although she had had no history of heart problems, she was hospitalized for triple bypass surgery followed by an amputation of her right leg above the knee. Mrs. Jones responded to the loss of her leg and mobility, and the temporary loss of her independence, by responding minimally in any interaction, particularly any discussion of her physical condition and related sense of loss.

Because Mrs. Jones refused to discuss these issues with her family, the social worker determined to use her visits with Mrs. Jones to encourage her to talk about her condition, her feelings about it, and her plans for adapting and regaining as much mobility as possible. Because the intervention, which consisted of the social worker's warm and concerned presence, began immediately, the social worker determined that she would use a B-design to collect data on the amount of time Mrs. Jones spent discussing topics relevant to her condition. The data the worker collected (see Figure 7.11) show that after four days she made progress in helping Mrs. Jones begin to think and talk about the implications of the loss of her leg.

IS THE INTERVENTION CAUSING THE CHANGE? A-B-A, A-B-A-B, B-A-B, MULTIPLE BASELINE AND MULTIPLE TARGET DESIGNS   To attribute a change to an intervention, not only is it necessary to demonstrate *temporal contiguity*, (i.e., the introduction of the intervention is followed by shift in the pattern observed in the baseline phase), but also *concomitant variation* (i.e., eliminating the intervention eliminates the effect).

In the *A-B-A-B design*, the first B-phase is followed by a withdrawal of the intervention (a second A-phase), which may be followed by a reintroduction of the intervention (a second B-phase). To the extent that the treatment effect appears and disappears with the introduction and withdrawal of the intervention, the evidence of concomitant variation suggests a *causal* relation between the intervention and the outcome. On the basis of such evidence, especially when supported by efforts to eliminate plausible rival hypotheses, observed change can be attributed to the intervention. The A-B-A-B design is a strong and useful tool for determining whether an intervention caused an observed change.

The implementation of this design is not without difficulties. Having overcome the barriers to achieving positive change, workers and clients are often reluctant to withdraw the intervention and to return to baseline conditions associated with the problem. However, a short-term return to baseline can provide information about

FIGURE 7.11
Example of B-design: Frequency of Mrs. Jones's willingness to discuss her condition

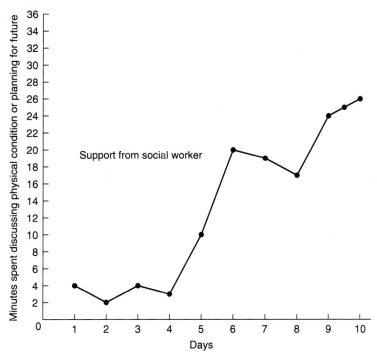

conditions contributing to the problem that can be very useful in the long term. Gambrill and Barth (1980) have noted that natural withdrawals are often brought about by vacations, illnesses, or other interruptions in the treatment process. When workers and clients are clear about the information that can be gained from withdrawals, implementation becomes easier.

Information about causal relations can be obscured in these designs if the outcomes measured fail to return to baseline levels during the return-to-baseline phase. This may happen when the target behavior becomes part of a repertoire of behaviors that are difficult to "unlearn." It also can happen if it becomes naturally reinforcing. For example, a child's reinforcement schedule, designed to improve school behavior, may be difficult to reverse if the child's improvement has led to positive interactions with teachers and other students in the school.

Consider the school social worker who is working with Jon and his family to improve his school attendance and performance. Jon had been attending, on average, 3.5 (out of 7) classes per day when he was referred and, although he was an intellectually able eighth grader, his absences interfered with his performance. The intervention consisted of a class card that Jon carried with him to each of his classes. He was required to have his teachers initial the card at the end of each class. When they did so, they also made a point of writing a positive comment on the card about his performance and generally interacting positively with him. Jon and the social worker went over the cards and comments. In the middle of their work together, the social worker went on vacation for one week, bringing about a "return to baseline" condition (in the sense that she was no longer monitoring attendance on a daily basis). As shown in Figure 7.12, the close scrutiny and positive interactions afforded by the card seemed to be effective in improving Jon's attendance. There was some decrease in attendance when the social worker was not there, but Jon's performance returned to earlier positive levels when she returned.

The *B-A-B design* is basically a variation of the B-design in which baseline and intervention phases are introduced following an initial intervention phase. Such a design has the same advantages as the A-B-A-B design in terms of potentially offering strong information about the causal relation between the intervention and the outcome. However, here too the interpretation of such designs can be difficult when behaviors fail to return to baseline levels.

A *multiple baseline* design is achieved when more than one behavior is monitored over time and then an intervention is applied successively to each behavior, resulting in a longer baseline phase for each behavior. The design is typically depicted as:

$$A_1B_1B_1B_1$$

$$A_2A_2B_2B_2$$

$$A_3A_3A_3B_3$$

FIGURE 7.12

Example of A-B-A-B design: Jon's school attendance and performance

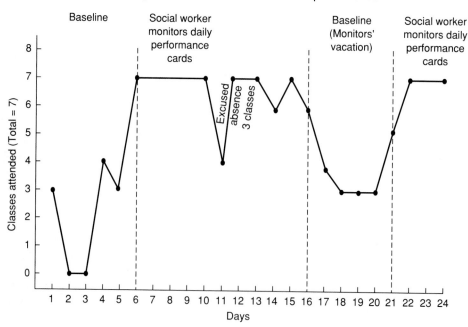

This notation indicates the successively longer baselines. A multiple-baseline design may be applied across behaviors, people, or situations. That is, the three different behaviors of one person may be monitored (across behaviors); the same behavior of three different people in the same setting may be monitored (across people); or the same behavior may be monitored across three different settings (across situations). Like the A-B-A-B design, this design permits one to draw inferences about whether any changes observed can be attributed to the intervention. Although the design can be thought of as a series of A-B designs, it is stronger than an A-B design because comparisons can be made across behaviors (or people or situations) as well as between the baseline and intervention phases. If a treatment effect is observed following an introduction of an intervention in three different behaviors at three different times, then the evidence for a causal relation is strengthened significantly. Therefore, the multiple baseline provides useful evidence about whether an observed change should be attributed to an intervention without requiring withdrawal of the intervention.

Consider the example of the social worker in the University Counseling Center whose client, Joanne, came to the counseling center in her first term in her graduate program in biology. She complained of extreme feelings of anxiety in the classroom, in the library, and in weekly meetings with her advisor. Her anxiety level was interferring with participation in class, completion of her work, and her overall progress in graduate school. The worker helped Joanne learn and practice simple relaxation techniques. She also devised with Joanne a self-rating form to record her perceived tension level. The objective was to provide Joanne with an active coping strategy for reducing tension in anxiety-producing situations. Using a multiple baseline strategy, Joanne first employed the relaxation techniques before she entered the classroom. After two weeks, she used them as well just before she entered the library to study. And after an additional two weeks, she used them just before meeting with her advisor. As shown in Figure 7.13, the relaxation techniques were very helpful in reducing the anxiety she felt in those situations.

The *multiple-target design* is a variation on the multiple-baseline design that is useful when it is impossible to apply interventions sequentially (i.e., at different times) to different behaviors, settings, or individuals. It is useful for documenting the impact of an intervention on several different target behaviors at the same time. Because history remains a viable threat to the validity of causal inferences in such cases, the design may not permit inferences that are as strong as those available with the multiple-baseline design. The design can be depicted as:

$A_1 \, B_1$

$A_2 \, B_2$

$A_3 \, B_3$

An example of the application of the multiple-target design is provided by the case of Helen, an active, healthy, 30-year-old woman who came to the social worker because she wanted to stop smoking after being addicted for 12 years. She was concerned that past efforts to stop smoking had resulted in dramatic increases in carbohydrate and alcohol consumption. She was particularly concerned about

FIGURE 7.13

Example of multiple baseline design: Impact of relaxation techniques on graduate student anxiety levels

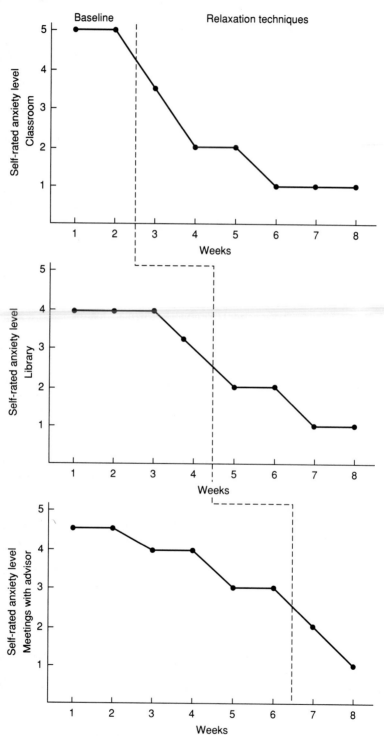

the latter since her father died of complications related to alcohol just one year earlier. She also reported feelings of depression during past efforts to stop smoking. The social worker entered Helen in a smoking cessation program and developed a log in which Helen monitored her alcohol and calorie consumption, along with the number of cigarettes smoked. In addition, she had Helen complete the Beck Depression Scale at three points during their work together. The results of the work are shown in Figure 7.14. Helen's concerns about alcohol and calorie consumption were validated but, after an initial increase, they returned to their preintervention level. The data also revealed some increase in depression.

What Aspects of the Intervention Are Most Important?

For most problems, we do not have a refined understanding of the specific intervention that will result in specific outcomes. Indeed, research seems to suggest that most problems are determined by multiple factors, which suggests in turn that effective interventions have multiple components. Very often, as we work with a client on a complicated problem or set of problems, we engage in more than one strategy simultaneously. But at some point we may wish to unravel which aspects of the intervention are most important. There is a single-case design, called the deconstruction design, that enables one to evaluate individual components of an intervention.

This design can be denoted as an A-BC-A-B-A-C. In this design, the practitioner begins with an intervention consisting of two elements (BC) and then systematically attempts to identify the most effective element. The practitioner does so by withdrawing the two elements together and then reintroducing each element separately. Whatever is determined to be the most effective element (B,C, or BC) is then reintroduced and allowed to stay in place. A related design, the construction design, begins with each element introduced individually and builds toward the combined element A-B-A-C-A-BC. Here too the most effective element will be reintroduced as the final component. By adding or subtracting components in the context of returning to baseline each time, the clinician obtains a reasonably clear view of the relative contributions of each component.

Take the example of the social worker who attempted to reduce his own reliance on cigarettes through a program that combined a point system and physical exercise. He could redeem points he earned—by reducing the number of cigarettes smoked each day—in "dates" for a movie or dinner with his wife. As the data in Figure 7.15 show, the program was very successful. However, keeping track of points turned out to be cumbersome and he was eager to determine whether that part of the program was essential. Therefore, adhering to the tenets of deconstruction design, he returned to baseline for one week. Then he implemented only the exercise aspect of the program. This turned out to be very successful as well but, to understand fully the impact of the point system, he returned to baseline again and subsequently implemented only the point system. This turned out to be not as successful as exercise alone so he returned finally to the jogging without the point system.

FIGURE 7.14

Example of multiple-target design: Levels of cigarette, calorie, and alcohol consumption and depression during participation in smoking cessation program

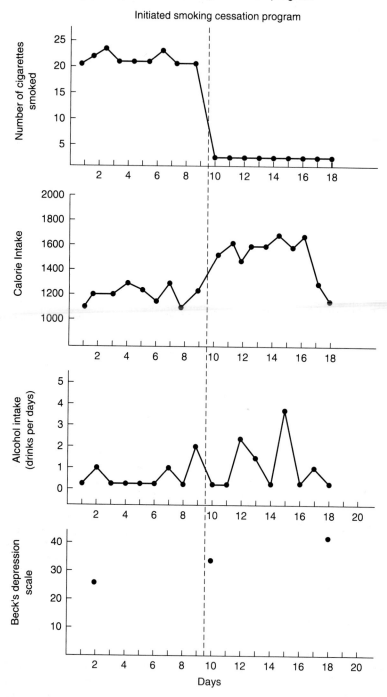

FIGURE 7.15
Example of deconstruction design: Impact of a point system and jogging on consumption
of cigarettes

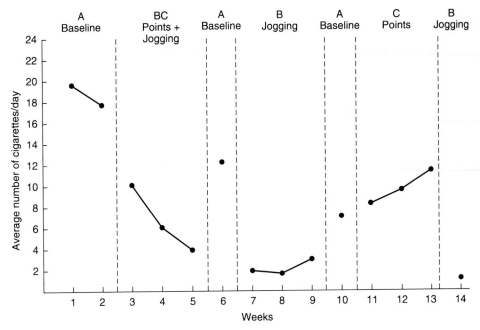

Pre- and Postchange

As we discussed in the measurement section, some types of measures, like counts
or observations, readily lend themselves to repeated application over time. Others
(e.g., the interview, which typically requires the practitioner to fill out a goal at-
tainment scale or the somewhat lengthy target complaint measure [Battle, 1966])
lend themselves to less frequent administration—typically once before, once after,
and once at the follow-up to the intervention. Such pre- and postmeasures, while
useful in themselves, should be used in conjunction with ongoing time-series measures since pre- and postmeasures are vulnerable to regression effects whenever an
intervention follows a single and possibly extreme measure.

VISUAL ANALYSIS OF TIME-SERIES DATA:
VARIABILITY, TREND, AND LEVEL

Time-series data graphed continuously in a clinical setting lend themselves to visual analysis. Several authors (Glass, Wilson, & Gottman, 1975; Jones, Weinrott,
& Vaught, 1978; Kazdin, 1976) have specified the properties of time-series data
necessary for inspection; we set them out briefly here.

Variability

The logic of single-case designs requires comparisons between phases; multiple-baseline designs require comparisons between phases and series. The baseline, or "no treatment" phase, provides the standard for assessing the impact of treatment. A stable baseline, one that has no visible trend and does not vary excessively about its average, provides the strongest basis for determining whether a change has occurred. Conversely, a baseline drifting in the direction of improvement provides minimal basis for attributing improvement to treatment.

Variability in a series very often occurs immediately after an intervention is implemented. If it continues within a specific treatment phase, it may indicate that some event in the environment is influencing the pattern. If a series continues long enough to detect systematic or cyclical patterns in the data, these patterns may provide evidence about external factors. For example, a child's phobic behavior toward school may prove to be related to course scheduling (e.g., if phobia is greatest on days when physical education is scheduled). The strongest evidence of an intervention effect derives from a distinct change in level and increased stability in the treatment phase following a variable baseline. When baseline and treatment data are both variable and changes in level are small, the overlap in the scores makes interpretation much more ambiguous. As a general rule, the greater the variability in a phase the more data points needed to interpret the data adequately.

Trend and Level

Changes in the trend and level of data between baseline and treatment phases are the primary bases for attributing change to the treatment. The strongest attribution is based on a shift in trend and in level in the improved direction. Clearly, however, there are many possible combinations. The most likely are shown in Figure 7.9 in order of decreasing interpretability.

ASSESSING THE STATISTICAL SIGNIFICANCE OF CLINICAL TIME-SERIES DATA

Although visual analysis of a clinical data series can convey significant information, additional information can be gained through statistical analysis. Statistical analysis can augment visual analysis in several different ways. In environments in which social workers work and collect information—homes, schools, communities—there are numerous influences that may compete with or dampen the impact of the intervention. This can result in subtle intervention effects that may not be obvious visually. Statistical methods can increase whatever control can be achieved through experimental design. The clinical research literature in social work is filled with discussions of the merits of various time-series designs for improving experimental control. As discussed above, more complete experimental control has the advantage of increasing the likelihood of detecting an effect and allowing appropriate causal inferences to be made through the elimination of plausible rival hypotheses. This control can be enhanced through statistical procedures for eliminating the effects of nuisance variables as well as through design control. Statistical techniques may be used to allocate contributions to the total variance so that an existing effect may be detected. In addition, conditions that are considered requirements for unambiguous interpretation in visual analysis are unnecessary in statistical analysis. For example, the stable, trendless baseline required for visual analysis is unncessary for statisical analysis because statisical analyses can account for influences that cause trends in the baseline.

As a result of these considerations, statistical techniques appropriate for the analysis of clinical time-series data have been developed and used with increasing frequency. Motivated by the work of Box and Jenkins (1970) and Box and Tiao (1975), several authors have developed procedures for interrupted time-series analyses. Box and Jenkins developed the autoregressive integrated moving average (ARIMA) model for analyzing time-series data. Others have adapted these models and developed others for use in practice settings (Gottman, 1981; Horne, Yang, & Ware, 1982; Hudson, 1977; Marsh and Shibano, 1982; Tyron, 1982).

Practice settings present particular challenges for the application of statistical time-series methods. In particular, as Marsh and Shibano (1984) note, less is known about clinical time-series data than about other types of time-series data. Information about patterns and trends that might be expected in certain situations is not available and, as a result, interpretation is more difficult. Further, in a practice context, the number and frequency of observations are determined by practice and ethical considerations. Consequently, a relatively small number of observations may be collected. In the review of over 70 time-series studies in clinical settings conducted by Marsh and Shibano (1984), many had no more than 10 observations in a single phase. Time-series analysis procedures based on the Box and Jenkins ARIMA model are recommended only for series with at least 20 observations per phase and, therefore, are inappropriate in many practice situations. However, several strategies have been developed for analyzing shorter series. For example, approaches developed by Gottman and Leiblum (1974), Hudson (1977), and Jayaratne (1978) are limited to uncorrelated series. The approach developed by Tyron (1982) handles uncorrelated data but is problematic because the results are determined to some extent by the size of the sample. Gottman (1981) and Marsh and Shibano (1982) recommend autoregressive models in these situations. The estimation procedure in autoregressive models requires solving linear equations rather than the nonlinear equations required in ARIMA models. For a more complete discussion of these methods, the reader is directed to Gottman (1981) and Marsh and Shibano (1982).

Here we present a straightforward approach originally adapted from industrial settings by Gottman and Leiblum (1974) called the Shewart Chart or the Two-Standard Deviation approach. This approach has several advantages. The procedure can be completed easily with a hand calculator, it can accommodate both independent and autocorrelated data series, and it can be completed even with "short" baselines (i.e., when there are fewer than ten points in the baseline).

Two assumptions are inherent in the approach. First, that the observations are independent; that is, that they vary randomly around some constant value. Second, that a standard deviation (a statistical measure of variability that defines that area of a normal distribution on either side of the mean where approximately two-thirds of the observations will fall) can help define "significant" or important change. The procedure requires the following steps:

1. Time-series data are plotted graphically with the preintervention or baseline period and the post-intervention period clearly designated. The mean and standard deviation are calculated for the baseline period only.
2. A two-standard deviation band is drawn above and below the baseline mean for the entire intervention period.
3. Evidence for statistically significant change is provided by the drift of two successive observations outside the band. This rule of thumb is based on the idea that in a set of observations that are independent and normally distributed, one would expect only 5 out of 100 observations to fall outside the two-standard deviation band.

   Suppose you are working in a preschool classroom with teachers and a 6-year-old boy who has frequent altercations with other children. These result in chaos in the classroom and tears and bad feelings on the part of the child and the teachers. For a baseline period of 10 days, the teachers track these incidences. The teachers calculate the mean and standard deviation for these days and draw a two-standard deviation band above and below the mean. They intervene by removing the boy from the situation for five minutes each time he has a difficult interaction. When he returns, they give him a positive activity and praise all appropriate behavior. Negative behavior decreases markedly until there were two successive points outside the standard deviation line. The data are presented in Figure 7.16. Steps for computing the Two-Standard Deviation Approach are presented in Table 7.1.

FIGURE 7.16
Impact of time out on negative behavior of 6-year-old

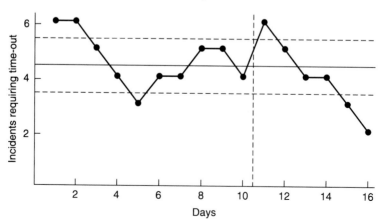

TABLE 7.1
Steps for Computing Two-Standard Deviation Band Approach

Computational steps	Data

1. Record baseline observations.

x

6
6
5
4
3

2. Sum (Σ) these scores.   4

3. Calculate mean:
divide sum by n where n is the number
of scores in baseline phase.

$$\left(\text{Mean} = \bar{x} = \frac{\Sigma x_i}{n}\right)$$

4
5
5
4

$46/10 = 4.6 = \text{mean} = \bar{x}$

4. Calculate standard deviation:
find $(x - \bar{x})$ for all scores, then $(x - \bar{x})^2$,
then sum and divide by $(n - 1)$.
Find the square root.

$$\left(\text{Standard Deviation} = \sqrt{\frac{\Sigma(x - \bar{x})^2}{n - 1}}\right)$$

x	$(x - \bar{x})$	$(x - \bar{x})^2$
6	1.4	1.96
6	1.4	1.96
5	.4	.16
4	−.6	.36
3	−1.6	2.56
4	−.6	.36
4	−.6	.36
5	.4	.16
5	.4	.16
4	−.6	.36
46	0	8.40/9 = .93

$\sqrt{.93} = .96$

5. Form the two standard deviation band
by doubling the standard deviation,
adding it to the mean for the upper
band and subtracting it from the mean
for the lower band.

$2 \times .96 = 1.92$
$4.6 + 1.92 = \textbf{6.5}$
$4.6 - 1.92 = \textbf{2.7}$

6. Plot the upper and lower bands around
the mean.

7. If two consecutive data points during
the intervention phase drift outside
the standard deviation line, there is
evidence for a statistically significant
shift.

Checking the Assumption of Independence

It is not unusual for some time-series data to be autocorrelated, meaning that an observation in the future is related to or predictable from an observation in the past. We would expect that whatever factors influenced a behavior at one point in time would also influence the behavior at a second point in time. Evidence indicates that autocorrelation occurs relatively infrequently in clinical time-seres data (Marsh & Shibano, 1984). However, in order to use the procedure described above, we need to know whether a particular time-series is autocorrelated, and if it is, to transform or work with the data in order to remove the dependency or autocorrelation.

Autocorrelations can occur among observations that are one time unit apart (lag-1 autocorrelations), two time units apart (lag-2 autocorrelations), three time units apart (lag-3 autocorrelations), and so forth. The specific pairs of observations that are examined in lag-1, lag-2, and lag-3 correlations are shown below. The notation we use allows us to think of any observation as occurring at time t. The next observation is then described as occurring at time $t+1$. The observation two time units apart occurs at time $t+2$; and the observation occurring three time units apart or with a lag of 3 is denoted as $t+3$. Calculating a first-order autocorrelation requires pairing the following observations: t, $t+1$. Similarly, calculating a second-order autocorrelation requires pairing these observations: t, $t+2$.

Table 7.2 shows how we can assess the relation between pairs of observations of lag-1 autocorrelation using the equation for the correlation coefficient r_1. The general equation for the correlation coefficient of lag-k is $r_k = \sum_{t=1}^{N-k}(x_t - \bar{x})(x_{t+k} - \bar{x})/\sum_{t=1}^{N}(x_t - \bar{x})^2$.

In order to determine whether an autocorrelation coefficient is significantly different from zero, Gottman and Leiblum (1974) suggest using Bartlett's test (1946), which requires us to compare r_k to $2/\sqrt{N}$, where N is the number of observations. When r_k does not exceed this value, it is not significantly different from zero, and we can proceed with the two–standard deviation procedure with confidence that our observations are independent.

When Observations Are Not Independent: Transforming the Data

If the calculation of r_k shows it to be greater than $2/\sqrt{N}$, then it becomes necessary to transform or manipulate the data in a way that removes the relation between observations. Two useful approaches with time-series data are the first-differences transformation and the moving-average transformation. Complete explanations of these transformations can be found in Gottman and Leiblum (1974) and Gottman (1981).

Each time a data transformation is performed, r_k can be calculated and Bartlett's set divided by test performed. When there is no longer evidence of autocorrelation, that is, when $r_k < 2/\sqrt{N}$, then is possible to proceed with the two-standard deviation procedure.

TABLE 7.2
Steps for Assessing Autocorrelation

**Computational steps for lag-1
autocorrelation, r_1**

$$r_1 = \frac{\sum(x_1 - \bar{x})(x_2 - \bar{x}_1) + \cdots + (x_{n-1} - \bar{x}_{n-2})(x_n - \bar{x}_{n-1})}{(x_1 - x)^2 + (x_2 - x)^2 + \cdots + (x_n - x)^2}$$

1. Calculate mean of scores from baseline.

2. Calculate deviations from mean.

3. Multiply first difference $(x_1 - \bar{x})$ by second $(x_2 - \bar{x})$, second $(x_2 - \bar{x})$ by third $(x_3 - \bar{x})$, etc. and sum.

4. Square each difference value $(x_i - \bar{x})^2$ and sum.

5. Divide results of step 3 by step 4.

6. Perform Bartlett's test, i.e., compare

$$r_k \text{ with } 2\sqrt{n} = 2/3.15 = .63$$

If r does not exceed this value, it is not significantly larger than zero. Proceed with 2 s.d. procedure. If r does exceed value, transform data to remove autocorrelation. See Gottman & Lieberman (1974).

Data

Time point	x	$(x - \bar{x})$	$(x - \bar{x})^2$
t	6	1.4	1.96
$t + 1$	6	1.4	1.96
$t + 2$	5	.4	.16
$t + 3$	4	−.6	.36
$t + 4$	3	−1.6	2.56
$t + 5$	4	−.6	.36
$t + 6$	4	−.6	.36
$t + 7$	5	.4	.16
$t + 8$	5	.4	.16
$t + 9$	4	−.6	.36
	46	0	

SUMMARY

The understanding and insight that can be derived from quantitative data are significantly enhanced by applying various tools for synthesizing, organizing, and displaying data. In this chapter, we have discussed information synthesis strategies that facilitate the summary and organization of rich qualitative data. We have also discussed approaches to visual display of data that maintain the integrity of the data while perhaps permitting us to see the unanticipated. In the final sections of the chapter, we have discussed single-case research designs of particular relevance to practice, with special attention to visual and statistical analysis of data derived from these designs. Each of these approaches to information organization and display are aimed at making rich practice information more manageable and meaningful.

8 | Tracking Progress in Everyday Life: A Case Example

T his chapter provides an example of how practitioners can develop and use a system for organizing information about clients' progress. By first specifying the kind of information that is most useful in assessing progress and then attempting to obtain and organize that information in a useful way, practitioners can develop formats for managing what often seems like overwhelming detail. The Working Record, a case recording format, is offered as one example of a way to keep track of the client's progress.

By the time they have met with clients a few times, practitioners are already handling huge amounts of information. They have already absorbed a great deal of detail about strengths and troubles, started to hone in on a problem area, and begun to try some interventions to see how the problem might be diminished. They clearly need some way of managing everything they know, figuring out what they do not know, and deciding what information is most important (in this instance, most important in terms of understanding the client's progress and the implications of progress, or lack of progress, for subsequent work).

Agency recording requirements necessarily influence the kinds of information that social workers get and use. Agency guidelines are often useful and cannot be ignored; however, practitioners need to determine how to meet (or change) agency requirements while simultaneously obtaining the kind of information that is most useful to them. Donna's social worker did just that. She developed a recording format that reminded her to seek out and organize the information both she and the agency required. This record-keeping form, the Working Record (Berlin, 1983), asks for week-to-week assessments of qualitative and quantitative aspects of the client's problems and descriptions of what the clinician and client do to reach the client's goals.

Specifically, the Working Record consists of five elements. The *Initial Summary* sums up early impressions and gives a general description of the client, her situation, and her problem. The next section, *What Needs to Happen*, is completed prior to each session and provides a means for the practitioner to plan each session. In the *Content and Process of Session* section, the session focus, the strategies used by the practitioner, and the client's presentation and responses are described in detail. The next section, *Recurring Patterns*, prompts the practitioner to note themes and patterns in the content and process of the session and how patterns change from week to week. The *Tasks Completed, Tasks Assigned* section provides a place to monitor homework tasks that are assigned and completed. Quantitative assessments of progress are recorded in the *Problem Level* section. Finally, *Notes for Next Time* is used to record insights and plans that the practitioner wants to incorporate into the next session.

The example that follows provides excerpts from the Working Record for the client Donna and shows how the record shaped both the information considered and the way it entered into the clinical decision-making process. The example illustrates how the Working Record prompted the practitioner to routinely define, track, and think about how to respond to the main characteristics of Donna's problems as they changed over time.

☐ **WORKING RECORD: INITIAL SUMMARY**

Donna is a 52-year-old woman who requested therapy because she has been feeling anxious, angry, and desperate. She attributes her distress to having recently stopped smoking, menopause, and dissatisfaction with her relationship with her second husband. Her first husband died when she was in her early 30s and pregnant with their third child. When she remarried 8 years ago, she gave up a responsible job, sold her home, and moved in with Vernon (also a widower) and his four children. Over the past years, she has not felt comfortable in her husband's home or with his children, who continue to let Donna know that she is the interloper. She complains that Vernon is closed and withholding in emotional as well as financial matters. Over the course of this marriage she feels that she lost her financial independence and her self-confidence. She wants them back. Even though Donna feels demoralized, fragmented, and out of control, it is still apparent that she is an articulate, energetic, forceful woman. She has clear-cut preferences and notions of what she wants for herself.

WORKING RECORD: PROGRESS NOTES

Client __*D.H.*__   Date __*5-5-88*__
Session __*2*__

I. What Needs to Happen: Immediate and Evolving Treatment Plan
(complete prior to session)

- *Get more information re: D's goals and strengths and the supports D. can rely on to reach goals.*
- *Review tasks. Involve D. more in generating new ones.*
- *Check out idea of formulating problems and goals in terms of "resentful compliance" (problem) vs. "laying cards on table" (goal).*
- *Stay more focused.*

II. CONTENT AND PROCESS OF SESSION (MAIN FOCUS, STRATEGIES, CLIENT PRESENTATION AND RESPONSE)

- D. looked more relaxed, has been sleeping better; interrupting her own ruminations during the past week helped, took time for herself.
- She thought she talked too much last time—too diffuse and rambling. Didn't want to do that again. Still, took a lot of interrupting and focusing to help D. complete a train of thought. She's fragmented and tangential—seems hard for her to talk about current issues without going back to the beginning.
- Gave detailed account of recent blow-up with Vernon. She wanted to cancel weekend visit from his kids because she was feeling too stressed from quitting smoking and ??? He said no. She raged, wheedled, begged. Still, no dice. I tried to focus D. on what she wanted from V. in that interaction and more generally. She wants him to support her—show that he cares about her. Sharon: "How might he do that?" D.: "I've never asked him to turn his back on his children... but I'm sick of them always coming first. When I first moved in the house..." D. proceeded to recount numerous incidents in which she felt snubbed by V's kids and unsupported by V.
- Began to explore the notion that D. might think about saying and doing what she wanted with respect to the upcoming weekend—even if V. didn't fully agree. Got as far as: D. would like to reduce visit from two nights to one; buy deli food for picnic instead of cooking; be unavailable as babysitter for rambunctious grandchildren. Idea of presenting position of what she is willing and unwilling to do seemed a bit alien.
- Hard for D. to pursue this track—deflected by associations to V's current and past unfairness. D. also introduced issue of "Catholic guilt" around selfishness. Brought up with intensity, but dropped rather quickly in response to fairly gentle counter. Overall, she doesn't seem quite ready to "solve the problem." Feels too bad about what she's lost, not gotten, etc. I need to acknowledge that more clearly—but not get us stuck there. At several points, threw her head into arms and sobbed heavily—as if she's really got to be in a lot of pain to get attended to.
- Despite the above, D. seemed to be at least somewhat intrigued with the idea of defining and pursuing her own agenda. (Grabbed my hand, "Thank God someone finally understands.") She thought Problems and Goals Scales (see p. 149 for description) captured central issues. She made suggestions for a few changes in my wording of her problems and goals.

III. RECURRING CONTENT AND PROCESS PATTERNS AND PATTERN CHANGES

- Donna is variously complying, appeasing, begging, and resenting in order to get Vernon to attend to her—agree with her, give her more money, compliment her, spend more time with her, ally himself with her in response to his children.
- D's resentment further fuels V's withdrawal, which, in turn, adds to D's feeling that she has lost of all her power, resources, confidence.
- Needs to develop and act on notion that her power does not come from V.—that she can find and communicate her position without insisting that he agree.

IV. TASKS COMPLETED TASKS ASSIGNED

- Engaged in pleasurable and distracting activities: movie, library, walk
- Successfully refocused away from ruminations 50% of time

- Fill out Striving Scale (see p. 151)
- Monitor attempts for assertion and internally-directed action
- Continue pleasurable activities and add to activities list

V. PROBLEM LEVEL

Blame scale = 1   In-session emotional stress 0 _ _ _ _ _ _ _ x _ _ 10
Complying Scale = 1

VI. NOTES FOR NEXT TIME

- Try engaging D. in setting the agenda for sessions. Maybe just ask her if she wants to tell everything as it comes to mind—or if she'd like me to keep a particular focus. Focus and structure will probably help reduce her anxiety.
- Think more about the high drama aspects of D's presentation (Check Millon book on personality disorders & DSM-III re: histrionic disorder).
- Probably need to see Vernon. Raise possibility.
- Hear her concerns re: menopause.
- Still need to get to D's hopes for herself. Question is, can she generate those while she's still so preoccupied with everything that's the matter? Or would trying to do so pull her out of the despair a little more? See if you can engage her re: the particulars of what she wants.

In this second session, the clinician is working along three major fronts: (1) developing a further sense of what Donna's big issues are; (2) trying to figure out how Donna is most likely to think about and make changes; and (3) trying to develop a working alliance with Donna. Coming into this session, the clinician had already synthesized information she gleaned from initial assessment observations as well as organized theory (e.g., cognitive theory, interpersonal theory, self-in-relation theory) and personal beliefs into a tentative hypothesis about the nature of Donna's problems. The social worker's notion was that Donna's difficulties centered around interpersonal patterns of resentfully complying with the demands of others instead of taking initiative and acting from her own internal standards, and of trying to regain some of what she wanted by blaming and browbeating others to admit guilt, agree with her, and come through for her rather than clearly expressing her wants, opinions, and preference (Benjamin, 1982). The clinician's expectations for Donna's improvement were moderately high.

Although other reasonable perspectives could be taken in understanding Donna's problems,[1] the one devised by the worker is reasonable. It fits with Donna's sense of things, offers some ideas about remediation, and is flexibly held. In general, it is a good idea to articulate and organize one's initial impressions so that they can be examined, reflected upon, and consciously used to provide a necessary sense of direction for early intervention work. Although the clinician acts on these early impressions as if they were true, it is also important that she frame them as *working hypotheses* that need to be tested, modified, or discarded. We know from earlier chapters that even when beliefs or intuitions are framed as tentative, it is possible to structure and selectively attend to the client-clinician interaction in a way that promotes behavioral confirmation of even dubious or stereotypic hypotheses (Snyder & Thomsen, 1988). This phenomenon makes it doubly important to consciously look for cues related to setting the focus of intervention, prognosis, and improvement that fall outside one's expectations.

The social worker in this case used the Working Record as a reminder to be explicit about her working hypotheses. She viewed them as tentative, consciously directing herself to consider additional pieces of information beyond the problematic pattern she identified (e.g., what Vernon does to prompt these responses; the contributions of hormonal changes). Even so, the worker was most attentive to the parts of Donna's ongoing account that readily supported her initial formulation. This tendency is not necessarily bad—so long as the initial formulation seems to fit, prompts useful interventions, and does not obviate consideration of additional factors. It is the social worker's job to continuously double-check to make sure he or she is meeting these conditions.

As suggested in Chapter 5, clinicians double-check the validity and utility of their working hypotheses by (1) carefully watching and listening for information that is not explained by, or runs counter to, their conceptualizations; (2) considering whether alternative ways of understanding the problem might give them a more effective range of therapeutic options; and (3) making sure that they are taking

---

[1]For example, it seems reasonable to consider putting more emphasis on her social isolation, her low work-related self-esteem, the interactions of the entire family, or intrapsychic conflicts.

account of their clients' views. This last way of checking the validity of one's conceptualization and strategy (staying attuned to what the client wants) is a major value
position of social work and other human services professions. Not only is it strategic
and pragmatic to give serious weight to the client's own goals; the profession says
it is *right*. This kind of value knowledge should implicitly or explicitly figure into
the positions taken by practitioners. Once practitioners have tentatively identified
what seem to be meaningful dimensions of their clients' situations, they can begin looking for signs of progress within those situations. Necessarily, the ways that
clients and problem situations are understood influence the ways in which change
is observed. By extension, as social workers alter their understanding or working
hypotheses to account for new information, they also alter how they define and
track their clients' progress.

As noted, Donna's social worker is primarily zeroing in on and tracking changes
in the "resentfully complying and blaming" pattern. Specifically, she records her interpretations of Donna's expressions of *qualities* of the pattern (see Working Record
for Recurring Patterns and Pattern Change) and Donna's estimates of *quantities* of
this pattern on the "problems and goals" form (see Working Record for Problem
Level). Rather than tilting her assessment of Donna's improvements to conform
to her own hopefulness, predictions from theory, or personal experience, the social worker attempted to systematically collect observations about the changes in
Donna's problem situation that were meaningful, reliable, and valid. The worker
sought this information because (1) she was looking for additional cues about how
to make the intervention more effective and (2) she wanted to know if Donna was
getting better.

ASSESSING THE QUALITIES OF PROGRESS   In order to assess qualitative changes,
the worker (1) attended to Donna's in-session account with an ear tuned toward
a pattern of problematic beliefs and interactions and (2) noted variations in the
pattern—instances that confirmed it, and deviated from it. Sometimes the social
worker made brief notes of what Donna actually said so that she could later accurately reconstruct Donna's descriptions. For the most part, this is just regular
clinical work. We always attend and encode incoming information according to preconceptions of what is important. The difference here is that the worker makes
some of her preconceptions explicit. In effect, she said to herself, "Donna feels she
has to 'knuckle under' or coerce the agreement of others in order to get what she
wants, and this is central to her feeling upset and 'stuck'; I am going to track her
accounts of these kinds of interactions as a way to gauge progress." During and after the session, the clinician understood Donna's communications using Benjamin's
(1992) Structural Analysis of Social Behavior. This instrument provides guidelines
for coding interpersonal communications according to the degrees of affiliation
and control they convey. Although she used Benjamin's system (see Chapter 9) in
a relatively casual way, it provided her with a theoretical and empirical basis for
classifying Donna's problematic communications. She classified the communications Donna made to others as primarily "complying," "blaming," and she classified
those Donna made to herself, as "lacking confidence," and "feeling powerless." The
clinician classified Donna's goals as primarily "initiating," "allowing differences,"
and "feeling able and secure."

...he social worker's qualitative indicators seemed useful. They reflected ...s in interactions and beliefs that were central to the client's struggle, provided the practitioner with some cues about how to proceed, and were feasible to collect. Although it is difficult to know the extent to which these indicators were influenced by extraneous factors (e.g., the worker's wish to see change, her dispositional bias, the client's wish to please the worker), the practitioner took pains to maintain accuracy and consistency in her observations by grounding them in specific examples of Donna's interpersonal interactions. Even though her qualitative assessment necessitated reducing available information into summary form, the form captured relatively meaningful patterns rather than "decontextualized" bits.

With respect to obtaining information in context, it is important to remember that Donna's account was given within the context of the therapy; it was a story she told the therapist—an interpersonal communication to her—and to some extent, it was influenced by the therapist's return communication. Whenever we track qualitative changes in the client's account of the problem, we are coding the story that the client wants us to hear or has been prompted to tell. Although the client's view, as cocreated by the clinician, provides relevant information, like all other single perspectives (e.g., observations of behaviors, reports from family members), it is not the whole story. Nonetheless, if we track the central characteristics of this view in an explicit, systematic way, they can provide us with useful details about how things are going, whether therapy is helping, and what we might try next.

ASSESSING QUANTITIES OF PROGRESS   In order to provide an even more compressed account of change, the clinician asked Donna to use a 13-point scale to indicate the degree to which she experienced specific aspects of her problem and a related goal. Each week she checked the scale value that indicated how close she felt to being "stuck" with the problem or achieving the goal. She also gave a brief written explanation of what the number represented to her. Tables 8.1 and 8.2 show these "problems and goals" instruments as they were adapted to reflect Donna's particular problems and goals. As a result of a long-term effort to locate an instrument that was brief, simple to complete, useful to the task of assessing progress, and both individualized and standardized, the clinician developed and refined this measure by putting together and modifying what seemed to be the best features of several related instruments (Battle et al., 1966; Ryle, 1979, 1982; Benjamin, 1982).

The problems and goals measures that the social worker used meet at least some of the "good indicator" criteria listed in Chapter 6. The measures were easy to complete, seemed sensitive to change, reflected phenomena central to Donna's view of her problem, and suggested productive avenues for intervention. Even though there are no formal data on either the construct or predictive validity of this hybrid instrument, there is a modest amount of information on the concurrent validity of target-complaint measures like this one. These data suggest a relatively strong association between ratings on target complaints and an overall improvement factor (cf. Mintz & Kiesler, 1982). Again, it is difficult to know whether the problem and goals measures provided reliable information. Aside from possible influences of extraneous factors on the scores, the extent to which Donna made varying interpretations about the meaning of scale points from one measurement occasion to the next is a particular cause for concern—and usually is in situations in which

TABLE 8.1
Target Problems and Goals

Client _Donna_   Date _May 5_

Problem: *Complying resentfully*

Goal: *Acting according to internal standards — considering my own wishes*

12	Solid, substantial improvement
11	
10	
9	Clear, moderate improvement; have made some real gains
8	
7	
6	Problem and goal stalemate
5	
4	
3	Problem still bothers me a lot
2	
✔1	
0	Problem couldn't be worse; feel really stuck

Put a check in the box that best indicates the level of your problem or goal now. Add a few words of explanation or self-instruction if you wish.

measurement scales are applied to varying configurations of subjective personal states. Luckily, these varying meanings can be obtained simply by asking the client what a given response stands for, for example, what experiences are behind the "7" or the "2." There is some minimal information on the reliability of the "generic" target-complaints scale that suggests adequate test-retest reliability, content stability, and a mixed picture regarding interjudge reliability (cf. Mintz and Kiesler, 1982).

Because Donna tended to be quite distressed in the sessions and because the worker was implicitly using information about Donna's emotional state to make judgments about her problem and progress, the clinician decided to make her observations more systematic and explicit. She used a 0–10 scale to help her rank the intensity of Donna's distress. Although this scale is very easy to use and provides a way to keep a record of one's impressions about how an aspect of the client's difficulties is changing from session to session, the meaning of a score (its implications for intervention and a deeper understanding) can be discerned only in the context

.uDlems and Goals

Client __Donna__   Date __May 5__

Problem: *Trying to get control of the situation by blaming others for not coming through*

Goal: *Laying cards on the table, clearly expressing preferences, expressing own*
           views without exacting admission of wrong-doing; allowing differences to
           exist

12	Solid, substantial improvement
11	
10	
9	Clear, moderate improvement; have made some real gains
8	
7	
6	Problem and goal stalemate
5	
4	
3	Problem still bothers me a lot
2	
✓1	
0	Problem couldn't be worse; feel really stuck

Put a check in the box that best indicates the level of your problem or goal now. Add a
few words of explanation or self-instruction if you wish.

---

of other information. For example, a high distress rating might have meant that
Donna was upset because she realized that her familiar, but dysfunctional, ways of
operating were no longer working and she was struggling to replace them, or that
she was completely caught up by these dysfunctional patterns and suffering from
their consequences. In addition, the worker was undoubtedly inconsistent in the
way she applied the ratings. Therefore, she did not assume that her numbers were
any more than rough indicators.

The "striving scale," which was assigned to Donna as homework, is an adaptation of a set of survey questions designed by Cantril (1965) and is another version
of an individualized rating scale. According to the instructions for this scale, Donna
first defined the characteristics of herself or her life that she would possess in the
best and worst possible futures: "regain control of my life in every way possible"
and "total insecurity—old, alone, poor, displaced from any sense of belonging." With

TABLE 8.3
Striving Scale

1. We all want certain things from life. When you think about what really matters in your own life, what are your wishes and hopes for the future? In other words, if you imagine your future in the *best* possible light, what would your life look like if you were to be happy? Take your time in answering; such things aren't easy to put into words. Write out your answer next to number 10 on the ladder. Please try to be specific.
2. Now consider the other side of the picture. What are your fears and worries about the future? In other words, if you imagine your future in the *worst* possible light, what would your life look like? Again, take your time in answering. Write out your answer next to 0 on the ladder. Please be specific.
3. Where on the ladder do you feel you personally stand at the *present* time? Step number ___3___.
4. Where on the ladder would you say you stood *five years ago*? Step number ___7___.
5. And where do you think you will be on the ladder *five years from now*? Step number ___8___.

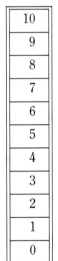

←Specific characteristics of your life in the best possible future—what you need to be, do, or have in order to be happy (list here): *Regain control of my life in every way possible.*

←Specific characteristics of your life in the worst possible future—what are your worst worries and fears about how you and your life might turn out (list here): *Total insecurity— old, alone, poor, displaced from any sense of belonging.*

Reprinted by permission from H. Cantril, *Patterns of Human Concerns.* Copyright 1965 by Rutgers, The State University.

the positive outcome anchoring the upper end of the 0–10 scale and the negative outcome, the bottom, Donna then estimated her current position relative to these possible scenarios, her position 5 years ago, and her projected position 5 years into the future (see Table 8.3). In order not to overload Donna with measures, and assuming that her sense of herself vis-á-vis long-range goals would not change rapidly, the clinician asked Donna to complete this measure every 3 weeks. Cantril does not

formation about the reliability or validity of this measure, but it was
was feasible, made sense to Donna, seemed sensitive, and reminded her
.. she needed to take some initiative in order to "regain control." And once again,
it was Donna's explanations for her ratings of the experiences that provided the cues
for intervention.

☐ WORKING RECORD: PROGRESS NOTES

Client _D.H._   Date _9-21-88_
Session _____7_____

I. What Needs to Happen: Immediate and Evolving Treatment Plan
(complete prior to session).

- *Prompt D. to think through issues, e.g., best outcomes in her struggles with V. over his son, the will, etc. You're doing all the searching and formulating for her. Cut it out.*
- *Review and assign tasks. Complete P&G + Striving Scale*
- *Find out where resistance to V's participating in therapy is coming from.*

II. CONTENT AND PROCESS OF SESSION (MAIN FOCUS, STRATEGIES, CLIENT
PRESENTATION AND RESPONSE).

- *Reported some progress: 1) Signed up for real estate courses at community college. Seemed only mildly pleased at accomplishment and prospect. 2) Reported several instances of "laying cards on table." 3) Allowance negotiations underway.*
- *Re: Allowance: Donna asked and Vernon agreed to give her a set amount of money each month for her personal expenses (hair salon, gifts, gas, lunch). V. considering whether it would be better to give D. a check each month or pay credit card bill. I suggested D. might also consider her preference. Decided she wants $100.00 cash plus her own credit card.*
- *Recognized her progress and made a small point about D. giving over the details of her life to V. as if she expected him to take better care of her than she could. Response was self-criticism and criticism of V. I stopped action for a moment. S: "What else might you take from what I said besides feeling put-down for having needs and wanting to blast V. for not meeting them?" D: "I'm trying." S: "I know you are.... So, what about the idea of being a more active player in your own life? Does that have some appeal... or is it second best to getting V. to take better care of you?" D: "It does, but Vernon comes through better for Neal than he does for me. Neal is home from college now and he's moved in... V. is buying him a car... they watch TV together all evening... N. never picks up his clothes... V. expects me to keep*

quiet and not raise a row in front of him... I love V. but I hate N.'s father... when it comes to Neal, Vernon is unfair and a cheat." S: "What has he cheated you out of?" "What have you lost?" D: "I don't know... everything... me." S: "V. hasn't paid good attention to what you want and so...?" D: "And so I'm nothing, I don't count."

- *By way of wrapping up, suggested that maybe D. was trying to move down two divergent paths at the same time—one was to expose how much pain she felt because V. hadn't come through for her in the way she wanted (like her father hadn't) and the other was to reclaim what she lost. "They are related paths, they cross over each other, but then they go in separate ways...." D. said she got it.*

- *Also suggested we needed to be talking to V. about some of these things. D. has mentioned the possibility to him, but in context of an argument. Briefly explored her concerns re: couple's sessions. Main issue is that I would take V.'s side. "What if I didn't take anyone's side against the other?" D. said it would be hard for her. Said that was pretty much the position I take now—I'm for her and not against V. D. said she would ask V. to call me this week, if she felt ready. In any event, we agreed to talk more about it.*

III. RECURRING CONTENT AND PROCESS PATTERNS AND PATTERN CHANGES

- *Donna continues to report instances of having successfully asked for, taken, asserted what she wanted. But she still gets pulled back into intense feelings of having been cheated. She's furious—in the first instance, that her father acted like such a good guy, gave her mother responsibility for all the disappointments, discipline, etc., but turned out to be very disapproving and controlling; in the second instance, that her "nice" first husband died; and in the third, that V., who was supposed to look out for her during her later years, is not forthcoming.*

- *D. is still caught between staging a protest (that V. can effectively shut out) and reclaiming what she wants. She ventures outside the more futile position a little more often, but she still feels precarious and vulnerable when she's just saying or doing what she wants. She feels more powerful when she is angry and blaming. Maybe she can transfer the power of anger to the position of asserting her own wants? The issue is not to become more independent so much as it is being more direct and effective in getting her needs for closeness and support taken care of.*

IV. TASKS COMPLETED TASKS ASSIGNED

- *Negotiated with U. re: about allowance*
- *Found out about real estate class (signed up)*
- *Attended clinic educational mtg. on menopause (helpful, will go back for 2nd session)*

- *If ready, raise issue of couple's sessions with U.*
- *List things about Neal's moving in that bother her; consider some solutions*
- *Follow up on $ negotiations*

V. PROBLEM LEVEL

Blame scale = 5
Complying scale = 9
Striving scale = 6

In-session emotional distress

0 _ _ _ _ _ _ x _ _ 10

VI. NOTES FOR NEXT TIME

- *Still think I am trying to move too fast. In part, because I don't think D. is interested in "long haul" therapy. (Why should she be?) Need to talk about the time frame we both have in our heads. Also, I'm impatient and uncomfortable with her fury. Keep catching myself hurrying her to do something constructive with anger . . . partly because she gets disorganized and fragmented when she is so mad. Moving in right direction, but I need to slow down. Let her have her anger—recognize it, wonder about it, maybe trace it to earlier contexts, and then move on to thinking about what else . . . nice and slow and easy. Look more at "feeling cheated" by father and first husband. Keep track of idea of somehow using anger to promote feelings of powerfulness and to drive self-direction rather than blame, but don't try to make it happen too fast. Make sure D. understands that my goal is not for her to give up on wanting care from U. The idea is to find a way to both exhibit self-respect and to recruit care and attention from U.*
- *Be careful around bringing U. in. D. is ready to feel displaced. Could do important work re: getting good attention, feeling cheated, etc., around this issue.*

The Working Record from the seventh session shows that the worker was still attending to qualitative and quantitative indicators of Donna's progress in taking a more initiating, direct, nonblaming, and self-respecting stance in her interaction with others. The worker's optimistic prognosis kept her especially attentive to signs of progress and provided her with an extra sense of commitment, persistence, and confidence. These qualities contributed to the interpersonal working environment for Donna. Presumably they contributed the extra boost she needed to find and develop other parts of herself.

Although the clinician's qualitative observations suggest that Donna was making progress in looking after her own interests more directly, at the same time, it was also evident that the practitioner's (and presumably Donna's) understanding of the problematic pattern had become sharper and more complex. As a part of this altered working hypothesis, the worker had framed a dilemma in which Donna was torn between (a) wanting to make people admit they had cheated her and to make them mend their ways and (b) taking the most direct, likely-to-succeed avenue to generating self-respect and respect and care from others.

Aside from practice theory and observations, the worker's personal reactions also contributed to her understanding of Donna's dilemmas and her progress through them. The clinician was aware of her discomfort at Donna's anger and wondered if it resulted in some counterproductive moves. This awareness also contributed to a fuller realization that even though Donna wanted and needed care and attention from others, she pushed them away. More generally, her empathic attention prompted a kind of gut sense of just how vulnerable and hurt Donna felt and moved the practitioner to a clearer sense that she deserved better care; "independence" was not really the goal.

Both the blame scale and the complying scale show that Donna saw herself operating in an interpersonal range that was closer to her goals. Similarly, her in-session distress score was lower.

Over the course of 14 sessions, the Working Record showed that Donna made moderate progress. Ratings of in-session emotional distress moved from initially high levels (9, 7, 8 in first three sessions) to more variable levels (high to moderate) in the middle phase and relatively low levels (3, 4, 3) in the last three sessions. As shown in Figure 8.1, Donna also showed progress on the individualized problems and goals scales. On the 13-point scale anchored by the problem, "*complying resentfully*," at the low end of the scale and the goal, "*acting according to internal standards*," at the high end, Donna's self-ratings moved from early "upwardly mobile" ratings (1, 4, 7, 6) to ratings of mostly 8s and 9s for the remaining sessions. Similarly, on the scale anchored by the problem, "*trying to get control of the situation by blaming others for not coming through*," and the goal, "*clearly expressing my preferences and views without exacting admissions of wrong-doing from others—taking care of myself and allowing differences to exist*," Donna also rated herself as moving away from her habit of coercion toward a new pattern of more direct communication and action (1, 3, 6 in the beginning sessions to ratings between 7 and 9 in the middle phase to consistent 9s in the final weeks).

Donna's ratings on the striving scale also showed some positive movement. As noted earlier, she first defined her best and worst possible futures: "Take control of life" and "Old, alone, displaced—overwhelmed with insecurity," respectively. With the positive description anchoring the upper end of the 0–10 scale and the negative description at the bottom, Donna rated her perceptions of current, past, and future positions on four occasions (approximately once monthly) during the therapy

FIGURE 8.1
Changes Over Time in Complying and Blaming.

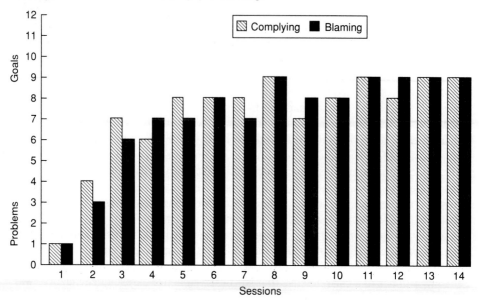

TABLE 8.4
Striving Scale Scores

	Five years ago	Present	Five years into future
Session 3	7	3	8
Session 7	6	6	10
Session 10	8	5	9
Session 14	5	6	9

(see Table 8.4). As these numbers indicate, her estimate of her current and future status increased from the first to the second month of treatment and thereafter remained relatively static. Her memory of her position in the past fluctuated moderately. Donna's final estimate suggests that she sees herself as doing slightly better now than 5 years ago and is relatively optimistic about her future.

SUMMARY

As noted in Chapter 5, ongoing assessment of client progress is undertaken in order to understand the client and his or her problems more fully, including whether the problems are improving. In other words, at the same time that the client and clinician are developing a more refined understanding of what the problem is, they are also interested in knowing whether the problem is getting better. In these terms, assessing progress means assessing progress along two interacting tracks: assessing progress in understanding the nature of the problem as well as assessing progress in doing better, feeling better, getting along with others better, procuring needed resources, or taking a more adaptive perspective. Optimally, this complicated process is fueled by a variety of information, each kind having a somewhat specialized role in filling out the picture of change. In addition, the process requires that the worker possess both flexibility and precision, clarity of thought and a tolerance for ambiguity, and an ability to challenge her or his own assumptions and perceptions. As clinicians accumulate more experience in working their way through this assessment process, many of the considerations and strategies become more reflexive and take up less cognitive capacity. But even for the expert, there is too much information to keep track of and to reflect on without assistance. It is necessary to adopt some kind of a system for doing that. In this case, the social worker relied on the Working Record to prompt her to collect, track, and reflect on a wide range of information relevant to Donna's progress and the overall management of the case. The Working Record may not be the best system for every situation, but it is offered as an example of how clinicians can determine what it is they need to know in order to be most helpful and then systematically seek such information.

9 | Ongoing Assessment: Assessing Therapy Process

T his chapter focuses on the importance of understanding how change is occurring over the course of clinical work. It discusses the kinds of information and thinking processes practitioners commonly use to explain change and emphasizes the utility of new tools emerging from psychotherapy process research to augment these approaches.

I. Purposes and Characteristics of Assessing Process

II. Contributions of Knowledge Structures and Informational Cues to Understanding Change
   A. Theoretical knowledge about change
   B. The role of empathic knowledge in understanding and assessing change

III. Strategies for Understanding and Assessing Change: The Role of Psychotherapy Process Research
   A. Trends in psychotherapy process research
   B. Clinical process assessment
   C. Conceptualizing change and focusing assessment
      1. Changes in therapy and in life
      2. Locus of the change
      3. Meaningful chunks of change
      4. Change within episodes
   D. Tools for assessing processes of change
      1. Observational coding systems
      2. Process measures and report forms

IV. Summary

PURPOSES AND CHARACTERISTICS
OF ASSESSING PROCESS

The central purpose of assessing the process of therapy is to increase understanding about how changes in the client's problems actually occur. Assessment of progress and outcome focuses on discerning changes in quantitative and qualitative attributes of the problem to determine whether, and what kind of, change has occurred; in contrast, assessment of process focuses on the things the worker, client, or others do that result in change. As noted in previous chapters, assessments of progress and process are closely interconnected endeavors. When progress is detected in small increments of change, the distinction between the client's progress and his or her change process all but disappears. At some point, the client's "mini-outcomes" or signs of progress (e.g., the first dawning of a new recognition, an assertive response, an expression of emotion) are exactly the processes that contribute to subsequent and more substantial change (Greenberg & Pinsoff, 1986a).

Identifying the processes that add up to or influence change is important because it gives us relatively direct information about how to assist those processes—about how to intervene. If we know the sequence of steps a person takes in resolving a debilitating intrapsychic conflict, learning a new skill, or finding and using environmental resources; if we know what extra-therapy environmental and interpersonal conditions assist the client in taking those steps; and if we know which of our own communications aid the client and mobilize the environmental supports, then we have some informed ideas about how to be helpful.

In short, we need some procedures to help us track how the client is changing and in what therapy or extra-therapy context so that we can better help the process along. Although the worker in the Donna case (see Chapter 8) tracked process information in the Working Record when she described Donna's in-session reactions, she did so in a relatively global way. As a consequence, she was left with an imprecise account of how Donna moved toward change—of how, for example, she arrived at the point of saying, "Vernon, I want my own money"—and what it was that she (the social worker) did to assist this shift. Although it is probably unrealistic to expect that we will ever know enough about all the interactive components and sequences of change to predict or even describe exactly how it occurs, systematically tracking processes of change should allow us to make finer discriminations about how a particular client is changing and, in turn, to provide the client with more precise intervention assistance.

Clinicians enter into a relationship with a client with some assumptions about how change occurs. These assumptions are more or less explicit, complex, flexible, and accurate, and they are more or less useful in suggesting how to intervene to help change processes along. We already know that preconceptions that are hidden, stereotypic, narrow, or rigid may lead us astray, yet having no preconceptions at all is not a desirable or possible alternative. Indeed, we all expend a great deal of effort learning about how problems develop and recede so that we will meet our clients with some idea about how to influence positive change.

CONTRIBUTIONS OF KNOWLEDGE STRUCTURES AND INFORMATIONAL CUES TO UNDERSTANDING CHANGE

Whatever they are, personal and formal preconceptions influence how we understand change and what we look for as we attempt to assess change processes. Unexamined, we follow our expectations mindlessly. We attend, code, store, and retrieve whatever is expected, familiar, vivid, personally salient, and intuitively correct. Alternatively, we can temper our spontaneous responding with mindful reflection, questioning, and searching for new information. We name and examine our assumptions; we question them, consider their strengths and limits, seek new ideas, stay open to intuitions and creative insights, and consider how else to think about, promote, and assess change.

Theoretical Knowledge About Change

Although our preconceptions about change are multiply informed, clinical theory is a major source of information about how people change. Different clinical theories provide us with different frameworks for thinking about change, different ways of trying to instigate it, and different configurations of cognitive, emotional, and behavioral shifts to look for when assessing processes of change. For example, cognitive theory suggests that people alter their dysfunctional appraisals and underlying assumptions when they are repeatedly confronted with information that contradicts their beliefs and when they are able to construct alternative interpretations (Evans & Hollon, 1988). Psychodynamically oriented short-term therapy emphasizes the primary role of the client-therapist interpersonal relationship in disconfirming the client's problematic patterns of relating (Strupp & Binder, 1984). Self-psychology proposes that the key process involves providing the proper empathic environment for developing the client's self-structures, that is, the capacity to regulate self-esteem, vitality, and cohesion (Baker & Baker, 1987). Behavior therapy emphasizes that changes are a function of the extent to which behaviors are cued and reinforced by environmental events (Bandura, 1986).

It seems likely that clinicians gravitate toward one or another of these perspectives for reasons other than the model's empirical track record. Evidence about the effectiveness of an intervention approach is often absent or ambiguous, but even if it is available, practitioners often choose theoretical models that "fit" with their preexisting schemas or classification categories about practice. For example, if the theory explains personally meaningful experiences, was employed in one's own therapy, or is favored by an impressive and respected teacher or supervisor, the model is likely to be adopted.

Current evidence suggests that any number of therapeutic models can be effectively employed in dealing with client problems (Orlinsky & Howard, 1986). One interpretation of this phenomenon is that theories are simply alternative languages for explaining the same underlying common processes of change (Mahoney, 1991; Goldfried, 1980). It is clearly important to have at least one well-developed, elaborate "language" for considering change. But given the differences in constructs, levels of abstraction, and problem foci among theoretical perspectives and the differences among the needs, capacities, and inclinations of clients, it seems important to also develop "multi-language" abilities, or as we say in Chapter 2, "theoretical pluralism."

Whatever theoretical model or models the clinician holds, he or she needs to remember that theories are useful for generating hypotheses, but they are not the best source of information for verifying them. To date, clinical scholars have provided an abundance of abstract notions about human problems and problem change but have generated little generalizable evidence about the actual mechanisms of such change. We know that people who participate in various forms of treatment sometimes improve, but we know very little about what actually changes and what drives the change.

For the most part, this state of knowledge extends to the situation of individual practitioners. Each of us has some general ideas about how change happens. For example:

> If I support my client, she will feel strong enough to take problem-solving steps. Once she has solved some of her life problems, she will be under less duress and she will feel more powerful as a person.

or,

> If I teach my client the skills he needs to resolve interpersonal problems, he will be able to reduce the conflicts he is having with significant others in his life.

However, how many of us would carefully track the extent to which support actually leads to empowerment and exactly how those powerful feelings are generated? How many of us would determine if and how our client was able to use skills training to his or her benefit? Our beliefs tend to be global; they do not incorporate the specific details of how change occurs. In their general terms, however, these beliefs leave us with the illusion that we already know how it all works.

The Role of Empathic Knowledge in Understanding and Assessing Change

Even though clinical intuitions are affected by our cognitive schemas and may be influenced by other information we store in memory, they sometimes provide us with novel ideas. Knowledge that is generated from empathy is necessarily colored by the clinician's basic ways of understanding; nonetheless, empathic knowledge probably carries the least "previous conceptualization" baggage. Empathy implies a special kind of closeness or overlap in feelings between the practitioner and client, but ideally the new information that empathy supplies is about the experiences of the client, not the projections of the practitioner. Jordan (1984) writes about this paradox in empathy. Her view is that by joining with the client, the clinician is able to retrieve a clearer sense of the client's uniqueness. The clinician "develops a more articulated and differentiated image of the other, and hence responds in a more accurate and specific way..." (p. 6).

Tuning into the client, developing a feel for what pulls him or her forward and draws him or her back, is one way of generating additional, particular information about how the client is changing or is likely to change. Through the processes of empathic attending—following the client along, experiencing his or her experiences, providing the words to express what he or she is feeling, maybe adding a few words that suggest a way out of the "cul-de-sac" of the moment—the clinician is able to both instigate change and generate ideas about how change happens. Moreover, when the clinician stores this information (explicit and tacit) in memory, it can also serve as raw material for subsequent intuitive insights.

> Jena, a social worker, is jogging around the track in back of the high school. It is about 9:30 on a damp, quiet October evening. Jena has stopped watching for muggers to appear from the shadows; she is gradually relaxing. Her ruminations about her day at the Women's Alcoholism Treatment Program have receded in her mind. For a while she attends to the sounds and feel of her running. Then a memory of a conversation she had with her brother earlier in the day comes to her mind. That memory some-how gives way to an awareness of the smell of the wet leaves that cover the ground next to the track, then her focus moves to an image of her client, Elizabeth, with her hand on her forehead, putting herself down for being too dependent. A series of thoughts unfold: "Elizabeth is making dependency bad because she thinks I think de-pendency is bad...she thinks I won't want to come through for her if she looks like she needs something from me...she is trying to manage her dependency...she can't take in what I am offering because she's afraid that wanting it is bad...."

These thoughts about Elizabeth, the clearest ones Jena has had about her in weeks, seemed to come from nowhere. In all probability they are the product of a mixture of information. In part, they may have come from the tacit (not explicitly conscious) information that Jena gained by attending closely and affectively to Elizabeth's struggles. Although this kind of empathic information is useful in its nonsymbolic, tacit form—to the extent that it guides the worker in staying connected to the client—once it becomes conscious and symbolized, it is potentially more useful, or at least useful in another way. In Jena's case, she can now turn this insight over in her mind, reflect on it, consider its validity, think what to do about it, and begin to explicitly track Elizabeth's struggles with dependency.

However, Jena's empathically generated ideas are not necessarily independent of the other kinds of knowledge—theoretical, empirical, personal, value-based—that Jena retains. For example, assume that Jena also has a strong general commitment to the primacy of the client's own sense of what she wants and needs and, thus, a commitment to listening closely to the client. These values play a part in influ-encing Jena's ideas about Elizabeth. Imagine also that Jena has a sense that her own personal struggles to become more independent have left her feeling slightly disconnected and isolated. This personal sense of the downside of independence probably adds a dimension, perhaps additional sensitivity. Further, over the last few years, perhaps Jena has read several contemporary pieces, some based on research, that emphasize the importance of close relationships in women's lives (e.g., Belle, 1982; Gilligan, 1982; Miller, 1984). Memories of these concepts and the fact that they are bolstered by data provide especially fertile ground for the empathic infor-mation that Jena retrieved and for the intuitive insight that she generated. Simply, knowledge from different sources became integrated and this integrated knowledge was enriched by the variety of sources that fed it.

A particularly important ingredient of this mix will be observations of change. Although evidence from observing change is also influenced by other kinds of knowl-edge, it adds relatively direct information about what it is that clients do (in this case, about what Elizabeth does) in order to achieve change. A discussion of the contributions of evidence follows.

To sum up, in attempting to understand change processes, clinicians are pulled toward the same kinds of habitual thinking patterns that characterize other aspects of clinical work (and thinking in general). These include overreliance on theory and underreliance on data; overreliance on automatic thinking and underreliance on mindful processing; allegiance to preconceived explanations about how change occurs and the kinds of change possible for certain kinds of clients; a readiness to focus exclusively on processes of individual change while ignoring processes of interpersonal or environmental change; and heuristic thinking that gives unwarranted weight to information that is readily available, suggests similarities to preexisting categories, or is vivid in detail. It bears repeating: Even though we would literally be lost without preconceptions and reduced to ponderous inefficiency without automatic and intuitive heuristic processing, it is important to occasionally check on the validity of these information sources and thinking processes and consider what else there is to know.

STRATEGIES FOR UNDERSTANDING AND ASSESSING CHANGE: THE ROLE OF PSYCHOTHERAPY PROCESS RESEARCH

Because psychotherapy process research is designed precisely to yield information about the processes that influence or add up to change, it seems reasonable to look to this body of knowledge for ideas about how to gain useful process information. The remainder of the chapter focuses on identifying potentially useful information-generating strategies from the domain of process research and adapting them to the special needs and constraints of clinical work.

Trends in Psychotherapy Process Research

The traditional strategy in psychotherapy process research has been to investigate the link between a potentially important process variable (e.g., therapist empathy, client compliance, therapist self-disclosure) and client outcomes. This kind of research is based on the assumption that out of all the events, characteristics, and conditions that interact to influence the client's end-of-treatment responses, single (or multiple) process variables will make a discernible difference in outcomes.[1] For the most part, this assumption is unfounded.

In their review of a decade of research on the relationship between psychotherapy process and outcome, Orlinsky and Howard (1986a) report inconsistent to weak relationships between therapy techniques (e.g., confrontation, interpretation, reflection, advice, support) and client outcome, but a significantly positive relationship between various dimensions of the therapeutic bond and outcome.[2] Similarly, their

---

[1]Typically, process factors were measured at a single point during the therapy or measured at multiple points and then averaged. Neither measurement strategy provides a close assessment of the flow of therapy processes.

[2]Orlinsky and Howard suggest that the therapeutic bond exerts influence through two pathways: 1) by mediating the client's ability to "absorb" the impact of other interventions; and 2) by directly strengthening the client's morale.

review of psychotherapy outcome research led Lambert and associates (Lambert, Shapiro, & Bergin, 1986) to conclude that the factors common to most therapies explain the largest share of client improvements. These common factors include respect, understanding, warmth, expectations for improvement, corrective experiences, exposure to feared situations, and encouragement to master situational problems. When theory-specific interventions are added to common factors, clients show increased gains, but no one particular intervention model (e.g., psychodynamic, client-centered, behavioral) seems to increase gains significantly over another. Exceptions are interventions that are tailored to address specific problems. For example, studies suggest that treatments designed especially for sexual dysfunctions, childhood behavior disorders, phobias and compulsions, and marital conflicts are superior to more general, albeit theoretically guided, treatment models in increasing client gains.

As a result of this body of findings, researchers have concluded that they stand to learn more about what is therapeutic by focusing less on techniques offered by the therapist and more on the activities undertaken by the client—the in-session and between-session steps he or she takes to accomplish change. Relatedly, instead of trying to find the one, definitive client variable that accounts for final outcome, the emerging process strategy is to investigate patterns of client behaviors within the context of smaller chunks, or episodes, of change (Greenberg & Pinsoff, 1986a). These changes in research strategy are based on the recognition that (1) the effect of one variable is likely to be obscured at a later measurement time, (2) averages of therapeutic conditions are too imprecise to afford useful information, (3) the critical change actions reside with the client, and (4) change is a complex, multiply influenced phenomenon that unfolds in a particular context (Greenberg & Pinsoff, 1986b; Reid, 1990; Jones, Cumming, & Horowitz, 1988).

Clinical Process Assessment

These shifts in methods and conceptions can be adapted to serve the purposes of clinical process assessment. Because these new approaches spring from the tradition of psychotherapy research, they give most emphasis to identifying the mechanisms of individual psychological change (Rice & Greenberg, 1984). Nonetheless, with additional effort and creativity, they can also be modified to accommodate a focus on the interactions among a variety of actors (e.g., family members, and representatives of organizations and social institutions). In all cases, however, the fundamental clinical process assessment task involves recognizing productive and unproductive processes of change.

Conceptualizing Change and Focusing Assessment

We assess process to identify the internal and interpersonal processes (steps, events, interactions, dynamics) that add up to progress (or regression) and, eventually, to meaningful change. Depending on our own conception of change, we watch for particular indications of movement—little shifts in affects, behaviors, understanding, ways of relating—toward accomplishment of some larger therapeutic task. Because these changes occur in various contexts, we also want to know what about these contexts supports or impedes client change. During and after each session, we note what we were doing as the client was pushing forward or sliding back. Did I shift the focus? Did I involve the client in rehearsing a problem-solving move? Did I give him an opportunity to fully express frustrations? Did I limit his complaining? In addition, we attempt to pull together information about the outside interactions and events that seemed to support or impede change.

With each case, the clinician and client begin by trying to determine what kind of change is most important, who needs to change, and what that change process is likely to entail.

CHANGES IN THERAPY AND IN LIFE   Due to convenience and conceptualization, most formal studies focus on change processes within the therapy hour. As social work clinicians, our interest includes but extends beyond these in-session shifts. Because the utility of the client's efforts depends in some large measure on whether he or she is supported, ignored, or assaulted in day-to-day interactions, we also have to be concerned with the evolution of change during the remaining 167 hours of the client's week (Orlinsky & Howard, 1986a; Kegan, 1982). We must understand how the client uses his or her new resolve in the outside world and how it is received.

Focusing on extra-therapy changes complicates the assessment task by requiring that we devise additional strategies for tracking the critical between-session moments. These strategies may necessitate spending time with the client in his or her natural environment in order to directly observe how things go or asking someone else (e.g., the teacher, parent, or family advocate) to watch for critical change moves. In many instances, however, a familiar and appropriate strategy for assessing between-session changes involves enlisting the client as an observer of his or her own change processes and then soliciting written self-reports or closely interviewing the client about what happened, for example, "when you spoke with the caseworker...," "when you got that paralyzed feeling...," "when you found out she'd been drinking again...." Although this kind of interviewing is a mainstay of clinical work, the difference here is that it is focused more precisely and systematically on locating the patterns of change or of hanging onto familiarity. The difference is that the social worker asks more precise questions, devises a systematic way of coding or organizing the client's responses, and carefully sorts through these responses in order to locate a pattern of change.

LOCUS OF THE CHANGE   Although the client is usually a key participant in the change process, he or she is not the only one who changes. As noted in Chapter 2, when the clinician thinks about what needs to happen to resolve a client's problem, her formulation may well take her beyond changes in the client's own attitudes, feelings, and actions.

> In order for Zelda to feel more hopeful, she needs to perceive real opportunities in her life, to have a safe place to live, a decent job, and some people who care about her. In order for her to perceive opportunities, they need to actually exist. In order for them to exist, I need to find, assess, and get Z. connected to them. In order for me to do that I need to....

> As one step in feeling less desolate and empty, Dennis needs to attend more to the feelings and needs of others in his life. As one step toward doing that, he needs

to reclaim his relationship with his mother. Instead of always relying on his wife to take care of interfamilial communications, occasionally he needs to be the one to call and write his mother, inquire about her health, etc. As one step in assisting him to do that, his wife needs to step back a little from some of these relational tasks and "quietly" support his efforts. In order for her to do that, D. needs to. . . .

To the extent that others play an important role in problem resolution, the clinician needs to know what it is that others do and how they come to do it. What is it about these interactions and negotiations (between the client and others and the worker and others) that add up to meaningful change?

MEANINGFUL CHUNKS OF CHANGE   In identifying what change episode(s) to assess, the worker is naming and drawing boundaries around opportunities for change for a particular client (cf. Rice & Greenberg, 1984; Greenberg & Pinsoff, 1986a; Schön, 1987). She is conceptualizing change. In effect, she is saying, "Given what this client is struggling with and what I know about how change occurs, these are the main things he will need to do or experience in order to achieve meaningful change." Rather than overwhelming herself by trying to capture every nuance of the therapy experience from beginning to end, the clinician focuses her assessment on the processes that occur in the context of episodes; she focuses on the opportunities to work on these main things.

Episodes are named according to the nature of the opportunity (e.g., an opportunity to forge or repair a therapeutic alliance, to resolve indecision and conflicting feelings, to exercise parental judgment and limit-setting, or, as in the example below, to initiate interpersonal action based on respect for one's own feelings and opinions). They can encompass change opportunities that occur during and outside of therapy, and they can involve the client or others or both as central actors. Change episodes are further delineated by specifying the circumstances that signal that the opportunity is at hand and that it is now resolved.

Indications of opportunities, called *markers*, are usually communications from the client that suggest that he or she is currently facing an issue that needs to be resolved. In work with Richard, the marker was defined as "Richard's communications about avoiding or struggling with expressing his own opinions." Consequently, when he explains, "and so my wife asked me what I wanted and I don't know why, but I said, 'it's up to you'", the social worker knew that a change opportunity was at hand. In fact, Richard was poised at the brink of an opportunity for change at the actual moment his wife asked him what he wanted and again as he recounted the interaction to the clinician. *Resolutions* are circumstances, usually communications, that indicate that the client has accomplished a therapeutic task (e.g., "and so I told her that I was worried about money and I wanted her to think about how she could help contribute to the family finances. . . .") Although resolutions are typically defined in positive terms, clinicians can also analyze and learn from nonresolution episodes in which opportunities present themselves but do not lead to completion of the task.

CHANGE WITHIN EPISODES   Having defined and identified key episodes, the next step is to define and then track the change processes within them. Exactly how a social worker understands and then defines these changes is influenced by the nature of the task to be resolved, her theoretical perspective, and her understanding of how a particular client is likely to change. In general terms, however, the clinician will be looking for changes in the client's relationship to himself or herself, to others, and to life circumstances.

> Last month, with my support, Terri made and kept an appointment for her baby at the clinic and followed through on advice about nutrition. This month, however, she has missed two appointments and her baby is not gaining weight. How did Terri's sense that "looking after my baby's health is important and I can do it" get diverted and how might it be reconstituted?

Taking the first part of the question, "how did Terri get diverted," some of the processes involved were clearly *interpersonal;* for example, Terri's mother yelled at her for spending too much money on a dress for the baby, her cousin stole her jacket, the baby caught a cold and was extra fussy, the social worker told Terri that she was becoming "a good little mother." Other processes, even though they may have occured in an interpersonal context, were more *circumstances or conditions;* for example, the bus was rerouted and Terri had to walk eight extra blocks to the bus stop, the outreach worker at the clinic resigned because of overwork. Still other processes were *personal or intrapersonal;* for example, Terri accidentally broke two baby bottles, she contracted a low-level flu, and over the course of the events noted above, she elaborated a view of herself as weak and ineffective—she felt that she would never have anything, that she could never do anything right, and that nothing really mattered anyway.

Although these changes in the client's relationships to self, others, and circumstances can be framed differently, at a general level, they can also be understood as changes in the client's intrapersonal and interpersonal communications. Overall, these shifts occur within the therapy, as the client is interacting with the clinician and usually communicating about other relationships, and they occur outside therapy, as the client is actually participating in the main relationships in her life. These communications—words, behaviors, emotions that convey meaning—can be analyzed according to function or the purpose of the communication (e.g., to control, elicit nurturing, encourage, withdraw, get distance, etc.), and in the case of verbal communications, they can also be analyzed according to content, or what is said (Greenberg, 1986; Benjamin, 1982).

To be more specific, analysis of interpersonal communications can convey movement toward the resolution of episodes in several ways. As noted above, the *content* of what the client is talking about may change. For example:

> Ellie began the session by talking about how mad she is at her landlord—he won't listen to her, he won't help her fix the cracks in the wall where the cold air comes in, he is patronizing, he ignores her, and no matter what she does, he won't come through for her. She ends the session by talking about what she's going to do next to influence him to take positive action.

Second, the *function* of the client's communication may change.

> As Ellie talked about the landlord and whether or not she has any power at all vis-á-vis him and the cold air blowing through her apartment, she shifted from freely disclosing, to withdrawing, to attempting to elicit caretaking, and then back to freely disclosing information. These changes in what she wants from me [the worker] or

how she places herself in relation to me may also signify something important about how she is inching toward the resolution of an episode.

Third, the clinician's communications provide part of the context for the client's change process (Rice & Greenberg, 1984). Although the content of the worker's communication is usually of lesser importance, the function of her communications is key and can be used as a way to untangle how the worker-client relationship influences change. Do the clinician's words serve to control, affirm, blame, encourage, nurture, teach, or what? For example, the social worker repeatedly wonders what Ellie wants from the landlord (prompts her to clarify her goals), empathizes with her frustration (affirms), gives her some ideas about what she might say (teaches), and listens closely to Ellie's ideas and recognizes their soundness (attends and encourages).

The main reason to understand the clinician's communication is to figure out whether certain kinds of communication are more likely to elicit client responses that show positive movement toward change. For example, when the worker accepts what the client says and adds an additional nuance of meaning, does the client go ahead to explore additional options or does she feel criticized or controlled?

As noted above, as Ellie talks to her social worker about her interactions with her landlord, she has an opportunity to alter her view of herself, of him, and of her relationship to him. Ellie may rely on these emerging possibilities and generate new ones in her next encounter with her landlord. This next face-to-face interaction with him provides another opportunity for change. The social worker can directly observe in-therapy change processes, but in most instances she relies on the client's verbal or written reports of the extra-therapy processes. She tracks Ellie's communication as Ellie talks about what happened in order to get some idea of how she moves toward change outside of the therapy and to get some idea of the environmental supports and barriers she experiences.

In addition to changes in interpersonal interactions, changes also unfold in intrapersonal dynamics, or in Benjamin's (1982) terms, the client's communications to herself. We can only infer what is happening inside the client by what she shows us on the outside: her words, emotions, body posture, and actions, which convey something about her relationship to herself. Ellie tells her social worker that she has about given up, she's just too tired to keep on trying to make things better (neglects self).

In summary, we have suggested that a productive strategy for assessing process is to focus on the processes of client change within specific "windows of opportunity" or episodes. At a general level, change can be conceptualized as difference in the client's relationship to himself or herself, others, or circumstances as observed in the client's interpersonal and intrapersonal communications. Although clinicians will need to conceptualize the exact nature of change they expect on a case-by-case basis, Table 9.1 summarizes the foregoing to illustrate that, in general, we are looking for multisystem and multilevel indications of the processes of change.

Tools for Assessing Processes of Change

Having a sense of the general territory of process assessment and understanding that the specific targets for assessment come from the clinician's general theory

TABLE 9.1
Focal Categories for Process Assessment

I. Change Episodes
  A. Within sessions/between sessions
  B. Change actions involving client and others
  C. Changes in the client's relationships to self, others, circumstances
    1. Communications (word, emotions, behaviors) signifying moment-to-moment shifts in the client's interpersonal and intrapersonal relationships
      a. content and function of communications
  D. Context for Change
    1. Communications from social worker, others, and circumstances that elicit (or block) change
      a. content and function of communications

---

of change and his or her understanding of what needs to happen in order for a particular client to accomplish meaningful change, the next step is to think about data-gathering strategies. The two main approaches for generating change process data include relying on observational coding systems (e.g., Sackett, 1978; Barlow, Hayes, & Nelson, 1984; Greenberg & Pinsoff, 1986b) and process measures (e.g., Rice & Saperia, 1984; Greenberg & Pinsoff, 1986b).

OBSERVATIONAL CODING SYSTEMS   Especially in past decades, social work clinicians perfected the art of free-form, retrospective coding, or, in more familiar terms, process recording (Kagle, 1991). As the name implies, social workers would undertake to recall and record the flow of events observed in the just-completed session.

> Mary Ellen slumped in her chair, sighed, and said: "It is really not worth talking about." I responded, "What would make it worth it." With a half-smile—almost taunting—Mary Ellen leaned forward and said, "All you want me to do is talk and you know it isn't going to do one damn bit of good." Overall, during the course of the session, Mary Ellen moved from a kind of stubborn and combative position to considering what she wanted for herself. When I paid too much notice to this shift, she reverted back to fighting me. I need to give her enough room to make some shifts without feeling that she is making concessions to me.

Along with the Working Record (see Chapter 8), most of the observational approaches described here can be understood as variants of process recording—variants that give additional focus and structure to the recording of process in order to generate information that is more specific and precise and, as a consequence, more readily translated into precise implications for intervention. Although free-form or narrative process recording gives the recorder more latitude in weaving together events in order to elaborate certain themes or to otherwise incorporate detail that might be missed or glossed over when relying on predetermined codes, having a system for recording that includes clear-cut rules about what gets called what may make the recording less arbitrary and more likely to detect and track a pattern. To reiterate a point made in earlier chapters, narrative and structured versions of process recording are not mutually exclusive options. Rather, each can be employed to fill out and complement the other.

Optimally, observational coding systems provide a set of reliable and valid categories that the clinician can use for describing the flow (sequence, pattern, and context) of change. Greenberg and Pinsoff (1986b) review several process research coding systems that can be adapted for use in clinical assessment. Brief descriptions of only a few coding systems are provided below.

Horowitz and his associates (Horowitz, 1979; Marmer, Wilner, & Horowitz, 1984) make the variable of recurring client states the target for process assessment. Conceptualized as configurations of subjective experience, feeling, tone, behavioral form, verbal content, and congruence between form and content, these momentary states can be operationalized for individual clients and observed over the course of an episode. The result is a record of change and hypotheses about the therapy interactions behind such changes. In a series of single case studies, Horowitz and associates found that raters could reliably identify states—in one case labeled as "artificial and engaging," "hurt, but working," "self-disgust," "competitive-angry," "hurt and not working"—and locate shifts from state to state from videotapes of therapy sessions. Although clinicians rarely have access to videotapes of sessions, once they have initially observed and defined the salient states for a particular client, they can track them using transcripts of audio-recorded sessions or their own retrospective process notes (see Session Process Summary, p. 176). Tracking client states can be useful to the extent that it prompts the clinician to specify the configurations of emotion, behavior, and thoughts that compose a client's functioning and to gain increased understanding about the conditions that prompt each pattern.

In recent years, several process researchers have relied on Benjamin's conceptual framework and coding categories to describe intrapersonal and interpersonal interactions, including worker-client interactions (e.g., Benjamin, 1979a,b; Greenberg, 1984; Henry, Schacht, & Strupp, 1986). Benjamin's Structural Analysis of Social Behavior (SASB; see Figure 9.1) is based on the assumption that human interactions can be distinguished on the basis of degrees of affiliation and interdependence (in the latter case, degrees of autonomy, submission, and control).

Moving counterclockwise around the figure, social behaviors or communications falling into the four quadrants would be warmly autonomous, warmly controlling or submissive, hostilely controlling or submissive, and hostilely autonomous.

By constructing a taxonomy of interpersonal and intrapersonal communications around the intersecting axes of affiliation and interdependence, SASB provides a way to describe and understand specific communications. As shown in Figure 9.2, the full SASB model is made up of three homologous circumplex surfaces, each representing a particular perspective or focus: A focus on what is happening to the other or to the self in interpersonal interactions or a focus on intrapersonal communications. Each surface contains 36 behaviors that reflect specific, stepwise proportions of affiliation and interdependence. In the simplified versions of the model, the 36 behaviors are collapsed into eight clusters or four quadrants (see Figure 9.3).

FIGURE 9.1
Basic dimensions of the SASB model. Source: S. B. Berlin and C. G. Johnson (1989). Dichotomous thinking vs. allowing differences. *Psychiatry: Interpersonal and Biological Processes, 52*, 79–95. Reprinted by permission.

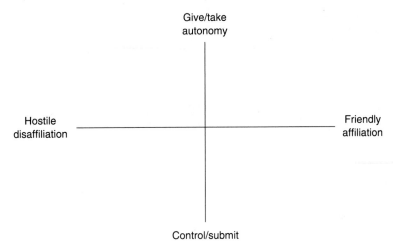

Using SASB to determine the meanings of interpersonal interactions requires making a series of decisions:

1. What is the communication to be coded?
2. Who are the referents in the interaction?
3. Is the current concern with the content or the function of the communication?
4. Is the communication focused on the other, on the self in response to the other, or reflective of internal directives to oneself?
5. How friendly is the communication?
6. How much interdependence does it contain?

Benjamin has provided a number of simple tools that a practitioner can use to aid in making these decisions. For example, the form presented in Figure 9.4 prompts the identification of the focus of a communication, the relative quantities (-9 to $+9$) of affiliation, and depending on the focus, the relative quantities of give autonomy–control, be separate–submit, or let self be–self-control.

For example, assume that the social worker wants to code some of her client's statements in the preceding session. The client said, "I have to do everything myself; Rob certainly isn't going to help out." In this case, the client is focusing on herself in relation to Rob. She and Rob are the referents, and the concern is on the content of the client's communication. As she talks about herself in relation to Rob, the worker hears little friendliness or affiliation. On the affiliation-hostility dimension, she codes the client as about -3. With respect to how autonomous-submissive the client sounds in this communication, the worker judges that she is fairly submissive, about a -6. When the clinician plots these points on the grid in the full model (starting at the midpoint of the second surface where the two main dimensions intersect, counting to the left 3 points (-3), and then counting down seven points (-7),

FIGURE 9.2

Results of Structural Analysis of Social Behavior (SASB). From L. S. Benjamin (1979). Structural analysis of differentiation failure. *Psychiatry, 42*, 1–23. Reprinted by permission.

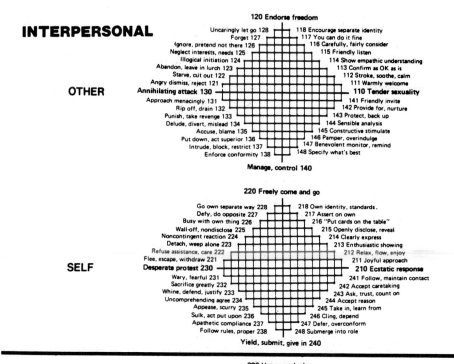

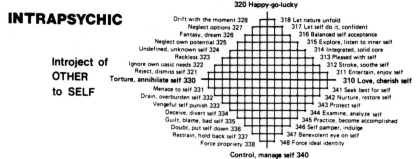

she arrives at the code, "apathetic compliance." If the practitioner does not need a precise code, she might follow the same general process using the cluster model. The cluster code most descriptive of the client's communication would be "sulking and scurrying."

Imagine that the worker responded to her client by saying, "You need to get a little more backbone, why are you doing all of the work?" In this case the focus of the communication is on the worker in relation to the client, and the clinician

FIGURE 9.3

Results of Cluster Version of Structural Analysis of Social Behavior (SASB). From L. S. Benjamin (1986). Use of the SASB dimensional model to develop treatment plans for personality disorders. I: Narcissism. *Journal of Personality Disorders, 1,* 43–70. Copyright 1986, The Guilford Press. Reprinted by permission.

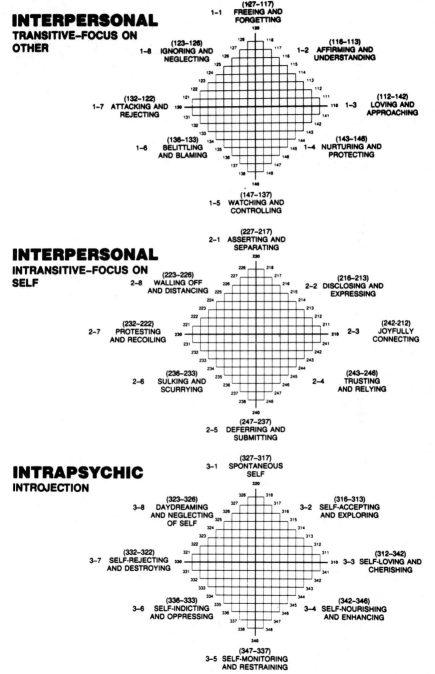

FIGURE 9.4

SASB Coding Guide. From L. S. Benjamin (1986). Adding social and intrapsychic descriptors to Axis I of DSM3. In T. Millon & G. L. Klerman (Eds.), *Contemporary Directions in Psychopatholgy.* New York: Guilford. Reprinted by permission.

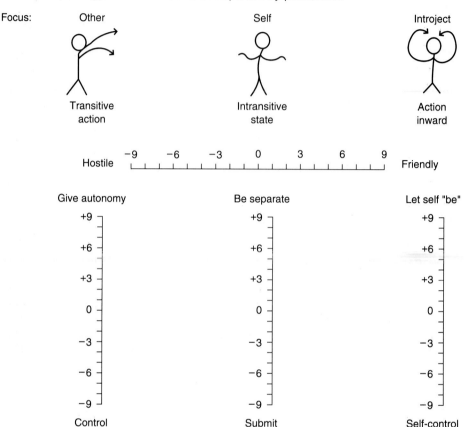

is primarily interested in coding the process or the function of the communication. The worker judges that her communication is mildly friendly, about +1, and moderately controlling, about −5. When she plots these points on the first surface of the full model (starting at the midpoint, counting right 1 point (+1) and then down 5 points (−5), drawing a line from the midpoint through the intersecting point) she arrives at the code "specify what's best." Using the cluster version (Figure 9.3), the cluster is "watching and controlling." Perhaps, in this instance, the worker will wonder if she needs to ease up on her own controlling communications, because the client seems to be struggling with resentful compliance.[3] Although learning to use the SASB coding system is arduous, its usefulness in increasing the precision of understanding more than compensates for the initial

---

[3]See Benjamin (1982, 1984, 1986) and Benjamin et al. (1986) for additional guidance in using SASB to code communication.

investment of effort. It is a complicated model that mirrors the complexity of human interchange. The main adaptation of SASB for clinical process assessment is to use it to code only selective segments of the therapy process. Moreover, once one has considerable practice in plotting degrees of interdependence and affiliation to locate the appropriate code, it becomes possible to complete this step mentally and still retain a fair amount of accuracy.

For example, Susan's social worker organized her process recordings to track Susan's efforts to resolve specific dysfunctional patterns of understanding and interacting. During the session, the worker listened closely for these repetitive themes, brought them to Susan's attention, and engaged her in understanding them and constructing more productive alternatives. After the session, the social worker recorded her recollections of how Susan moved to resolve these patterns. Within each occurrence or episode, she summarized chunks or segments of interactions and paraphrased the main messages conveyed in each segment; she (1) used SASB to code the paraphrases according to content and function of the client's communication and the function of the social worker's communication, (2) described the client's state (according to Horowitz's notion of client states), and (3) described the general tenor of the relationship.

☐   SESSION PROCESS SUMMARY

SEGMENT 1

Susan described her interaction with her boss as a way to explain her current sense of futility, frustration, etc. She explained that her boss is disorganized, keeps assigning her tasks but allows no opportunity for their completion, clutters her work space, interrupts her for conversation, misses a lot of work and then expects Susan to rush to make deadlines. In response, Susan mostly tries to comply with his requests, but she feels irritated and flustered, experiences little sense of accomplishment, and is preoccupied with how much she can't stand him.

Content

Boss interferes with S.'s efforts to do good work (SASB code: 137—Boss intrudes, blocks, restricts).
Susan tries to accommodate boss (SASB code: 237—apathetic compliance)

Function

Client: Susan discloses (215—openly disclose, reveal); accepts my prompts to elaborate and be more specific (245—take in, learn from); and searches for a fuller understanding of self in the situation (344—examine, analyze self).

Social Worker: Paraphrases (115—friendly listen) and asks for more specific descriptions (145—constructive stimulate) in order to sharpen Susan's understanding of the difficulty and leave some openings for her to think about how to handle it.

Overall Client State

Slightly anxious, organized, feelings and thoughts accessible.

Overall Relationship State

Cooperation, fairly even give-and-take.

SEGMENT 2

I asked Susan how this experience was like ones she'd had before, and she drew the parallel between this situation and the ones that occurred between her and her alcoholic father when she was a child. In his drunken state, no matter how late it was or what else she was doing, he would demand that S. come talk to him and keep him company for hours at a time. Even so, he did not genuinely try to elicit or pay attention to any of S's thoughts, but rather lectured at her or engaged in rambling monologues about his views on life. She tried to do what he wanted—sit and listen—in order to keep the peace, but she often felt scared, mad at him, sleepy, and confused. When he would demand that she say what she was thinking, her "mind was a blank."

Content

Father (and boss) interfere with her own activities (137—intrude, block, re-strict); have no regard for her opinions and desires (125—neglect interests and needs); and require that she attend to them (138—enforce conformity). Su-san complies but is upset and resentful (234—uncomprehending agree) and ultimately withdraws (225—wall-off, non-disclose).

Function

Client: Discloses (215—openly disclose, reveal); accepts input (245—take-in, learn from); analyzes and searches (344—examine, analyze self).

Social worker: Paraphrases and confirms reasonableness of feelings evoked by father (115, 116—friendly listen, show empathic understanding); sharpened definition of the pattern—feeling intruded upon and not recognized for her own ideas, etc; resentfully going along with the intrusion, and then withdrawing and giving up her own sense of things (144, 145—sensible analysis, constructive stimulate).

Overall Client State

Moderately anxious, disorganized, some thought blocking, struggling to find and express thoughts and feelings.

Overall Relationship State

Cooperative, friendly, more input and direction from me. I'm moving faster than S. and she's more fragmented and confused.

The main purpose for using this kind of coding system is the precision of description it can afford. If the codes fit the client's experience (if it has validity) and if it is used in a consistent (reliable) way, it assists the clinician in discerning a relatively precise and nuanced pattern of change over time. It should be evident that process coding, as in the example above, can be easily integrated into a format such as the Working Record to give a more complete and integrated picture of the client's process and progress.

Although Elliott's (1983, 1984, 1986) methods of Interpersonal Process Recall (IPR) are probably too time-consuming and complicated for routine clinic use, they also contain germs of ideas about how to get useful process information. First introduced by Kagan (1975), IPR places the client or the therapist or both in the role of "expert witness" and asks them to identify the significant moments of change in the therapy (Elliott, 1984, p. 249). It is based on several of the assumptions that we have already articulated: (1) Therapists and particularly clients are in a unique position to comment on the processes of psychosocial change; (2) their phenomenological views are made more useful by anchoring them to specific behavioral events; (3) psychotherapy research can gain most from focusing on critical change events or "turning points"; and (4) these critical moments need to be studied "closely and comprehensively" (Elliott, 1986, p. 251).

More specifically, IPR is an interview-based method in which an interviewer and a client (or therapist) reviews an audiotape or videotape of a just-completed therapy session and the informant is prompted to remember and disclose his or her views of particularly meaningful moments — the "fleeting impressions and reactions that would ordinarily be forgotten or merged into more global perceptions" (Elliott, 1986, p. 503). Although the informant's recollections can be focused on a range of therapy occurrences (e.g., perceived empathy, affective states, therapist intentions), for the purposes of tracking client change, they are most usefully aimed toward significant change events — events or interactions that helped or hindered change. The procedure can be conducted in standard or abbreviated ways (Elliott, Shapiro, & McGlenn, 1986); it can be used with rating-scale, free-response, or combined formats;[4] and, as noted, it can focus on either the client or the therapist as the recall informant. The strength of IPR is that it primes the informant to reconstruct vivid memories of specific therapy experiences. For example, in reviewing a replay of the session, the client is in a position to stop the tape at significant moments and say, "this helped because..." or "when you said..., I felt hopeless again because...."

Elliott provides specific guidelines for using IPR when the purpose is to retrieve qualitative information about how a significant event evolved:

1. The informant describes in as much detail as possible what was going on before the event. For clients, the focus is on intentions and covert experiences; for therapists, the focus is on cues provided by the client to which the therapist responded and the covert decision process that led to the subsequent significant intervention.
2. The informant is asked, first, to explain in more detail what made the event significantly helpful or hindering; second, to describe the speaker's intention; and third, to describe the immediate overt or covert impact of the event on the client.
3. The informant describes what happened following the event, in particular, the further covert or overt impact of the event on the client. Finally, the informant summarizes by describing the nature of the change involved in the event. (1984, p. 253)

Elliott goes on to explain how measurement validity can be understood in this context. He suggests that informants' responses are valid to the extent that a network of underlying assumptions are met: that the informant (1) is aware of what she or he was experiencing at the time, (2) remembers those experiences during

---

[4]For example, informants may use a simple Likert scale of therapist helpfulness to rate therapist responses or locate and provide qualitative description of the significant therapy moments (Elliott, 1984).

recall, (3) has the language capability to describe the experience, (4) is willing to reveal the experience, (5) avoids fabrication, and (6) focuses on responses to specific events rather than summarizing reactions to report more global or general responses (Elliott, 1986, pp. 518–520).[5] Elliot's practice of asking informants to take a "there-and-then" perspective and to distinguish "then" from "now" perceptions may help informants to focus more closely on their original reactions. In all cases, however, their responses are inevitably reconstructed. This fact does not detract from the usefulness of reports. Even though their recollections are probably some synthesis of original reactions to the therapy, current reactions to those reactions, and explanations of both, clients (and therapists) are still providing a relatively close account of how they viewed specific therapy events. Elliott suggests that one of the most worrisome threats to the validity of IPR data is the possibility that the client will report what he or she thinks the interviewer wants to hear, and relatedly, that the interviewer will ask leading questions or put words in the client's mouth. In the same way that clinicians discipline themselves to create a context in which clients feel able to find and express their own views, the interviewer (who in clinical adaptations of the procedure may be the clinician) works to create the same conditions. He or she asks for the client's frank reactions, accepts them, and gives the client uninterrupted time to construct them.

As is often the case with researchers who are also clinicians, Elliott does not apply his full research armamentarium to every clinical case he sees. Rather, he adapts his research tools to serve the assessment needs of the clinical encounter, and he understands that his experiences as a researcher contribute to his expertise as a clinician:

> My research with IPR has changed how I do therapy: In using IPR over the past few
> years I have seen that clients are much more aware of what is going on in the therapy
> process than most therapists are willing to give them credit for. For example, many
> are quite aware of their own defensive processes, even though they might never spon-
> taneously admit this to the therapist. This understanding has helped me to discover
> the usefulness of carrying out IPR-like procedures during therapy sessions and has led
> me to be much freer in discussing the process of therapy with clients. (1986, p. 524)

In a similar vein, clinicians might adapt IPR for clinical use by routinely asking clients to give their impressions about what was most meaningful, difficult, useful, hindering—either in the preceding moment or over the course of the session. Further, interactions that are viewed as significant by the client may be designated for special coding, as in the example above.

In assessing the process of change, practitioners need a systematic way to understand and describe it—one that fits the way the client is working and illuminates his or her unique struggles, constraints, small shifts, and surges forward and backward. Such a system might be an adaptation of any or all the examples provided above, or it might stem from the client's and worker's own concepts and words.

---

[5]In most respects, these considerations apply to all retrospective reports. However, because remembering is ordinarily understood as retrieval that is affected by the current context (e.g., Fiske & Taylor, 1984), the assumption that the client calls up the original experience in an unrevised form is impossible to maintain.

The main point is to have a systematic, accurate, feasible, and useful way to see and note how change is occurring so that practitioners can understand it and help it along.

PROCESS MEASURES AND REPORT FORMS.   In addition to finding, adapting, or creating a systematic way to observe and describe the flow of change, clinicians can also rely on process instruments to supplement their understanding of change. Berlin has adapted a brief report form to be completed by clients immediately following a session (see Figure 5.1). Orlinsky and Howard (1986b) have developed both therapist and client versions of the Therapy Session Report designed to be completed in about 15 minutes after each therapy session. Each version of their fixed-choice questionnaire consists of 152 questions that focus on several aspects of the client's (or practitioner's) experiences and perceptions during the session. Some of these include topics discussed and the concerns they expressed; aims and intents; feelings about the session; therapist's interventions; client's behavior, affect, and self-adaptation; and overall evaluation of the session. Abbreviated versions of the Therapy Session Report appear in Appendix 9A at the end of this chapter. Although these questionnaires may be too lengthy and elaborate for weekly use as a part of ongoing clinical assessment, selected sections may be used.

Stiles (1980) offers a Session Evaluation Questionnaire (SEQ), which practitioners and clients can fill out after each session (see Table 9.2). The SEQ consists of 22 bipolar adjective scales. Items composing the first half of the SEQ form two distinct factors named depth/value and smoothness/ease. The second half of the SEQ provides a single "postsession feelings" factor. The advantages of this instrument for clinical use are its relative brevity and focus on both client's and therapist's reactions to the just-completed session.

Despite the fact that much of the work toward change occurs outside of therapy, few instruments for reporting on intersession activities are noted in the literature (see Pinsoff, 1982, for an exception). At the same time, however, many clinicians routinely ask clients to keep track of salient events that occur between sessions and design self-monitoring formats to aid clients in that task. For example, Lisa and her social worker developed the following self-monitoring format for her to use in keeping track of her efforts to develop a more distinct sense of self. The idea was that Lisa would stay cognizant of these efforts and record them according to the following scheme at least twice a day:

Goal: *Self-defining (finding, expressing, valuing my own opinions, ideas, and desires).*

What was the opportunity?

- *Jack said he would help with the yard work, but then backed out.*

How did I respond?

- *At first I fumed, slammed a few doors, and felt like my day was ruined. Then, I went to him and said that I planned to work in the yard. I said I would like his company and his help. But if he had other plans, that was fine. I said that one thing I needed him to do*

*was turn over the soil in the front flower bed. I asked if I could count
on him to start on it within the next hour.*

How did it go?

- *It went great. He said yes. I didn't quite know what to do. I am so
used to being mad at him. Of course, he procrastinated and was late
starting the job. But he did it.*

What can I do next?

- *Tell him thanks. And pat myself on the back, too.*

David kept a journal in which he recorded his thoughts about those situations that prompted him to operate out of competing dysfunctional assumptions (I am weak and defective; I have the potential to be superior) and those that helped him access

TABLE 9.2
Session Evaluation Questionnaire (SEQ)

Completed by:

Cl. Code:

Date and Session No.:

Directions:　Please place an X on each line to show how you feel about this session.

This session was:

1. BAD	—	—	—	—	—	—	—	— GOOD
2. SAFE	—	—	—	—	—	—	—	— DANGEROUS
3. DIFFICULT	—	—	—	—	—	—	—	— EASY
4. VALUABLE	—	—	—	—	—	—	—	— WORTHLESS
5. SHALLOW	—	—	—	—	—	—	—	— DEEP
6. EXCITING	—	—	—	—	—	—	—	— CALM
7. UNPLEASANT	—	—	—	—	—	—	—	— PLEASANT
8. FULL	—	—	—	—	—	—	—	— EMPTY
9. SLOW	—	—	—	—	—	—	—	— FAST
10. SPECIAL	—	—	—	—	—	—	—	— ORDINARY
11. ROUGH	—	—	—	—	—	—	—	— SMOOTH

Right now I feel:

1. HAPPY	—	—	—	—	—	—	—	— SAD
2. ANGRY	—	—	—	—	—	—	—	— PLEASED
3. CONFIDENT	—	—	—	—	—	—	—	— AFRAID
4. UNCERTAIN	—	—	—	—	—	—	—	— DEFINITE
5. INVOLVED	—	—	—	—	—	—	—	— DETACHED
6. UGLY	—	—	—	—	—	—	—	— BEAUTIFUL
7. POWERFUL	—	—	—	—	—	—	—	— POWERLESS
8. TENSE	—	—	—	—	—	—	—	— RELAXED
9. FRIENDLY	—	—	—	—	—	—	—	— UNFRIENDLY
10. WEAK	—	—	—	—	—	—	—	— STRONG
11. SHARP	—	—	—	—	—	—	—	— DULL

and elaborate a newer set of ideas that focused him on the optimistic and competent pursuit of more "human scale" goals:

1-29-89

Weak Self	Superior Self	"I-Can-Do-It Self"
▪ *Can't finish this paper. Feel stupid. Don't belong in this class.*	▪ *It is going to be great. Prof. will be impressed. I'll show those other jerks.*	▪ *My goal is clarity & cohesiveness. I can do that. One step at a time.*

Blanca used her journal to help her think through what it is that pulls her back into a relationship with her boyfriend despite his abusive behavior toward her and her children.

> Rick came by this afternoon with some flowers for me and ice-cream for the kids. He said he was sorry about two days ago and wanted me to take him back. With his hair all slicked back, he looked like a lost little boy. I felt myself starting to feel sorry for him. He said that he needed me and that he is confused and frustrated. He said he thinks that I need him too, that we belong together. More and more I felt myself wanting to reach to him and put my arms around him. But I held back. I hesitated. But he knows how to get to me. And he knows that he does.

Of course, all clients are not equally able to discern their own extra-therapy change processes or put them into words. It is often the case that the main benefit of self-monitoring is to increase these abilities in people who are not very aware of the choice points in their day-to-day experiences. In order for that to happen, the clinician needs to take pains to design a self-monitoring system that matches the client's abilities, time, style, and major motives. Of course, there are also instances when self-monitoring is not feasible or useful, for example, when the client is in the midst of an overwhelming crisis.

SUMMARY

Implicit in all clinical work is the obligation to keep track of how the work is unfolding (how clients are changing) and to analyze the factors (therapy related, environmental, client-related) that support or hinder that process. Because it often occurs at an intuitive level, tracking change processes is especially vulnerable to all the common biases of thinking outlined in earlier chapters of the book. Although there may be utility in following an intuitive track to understanding, intuitions can be improved by articulating them, reflecting on them, and modifying them. In this chapter, we have proposed some ways to supplement casual observation of client change by borrowing, putting together, and adapting ideas and tools from psychotherapy process research. In the next chapter, we provide an extended example of how a particular model of process assessment, task analysis, can be used to generate information about the process of change. This example shows how many of the concepts and tools discussed in this chapter can be used together in an integrated research/assessment methodology.

APPENDIX 9A: THERAPY SESSION REPORT FORMS

Patient's Form

A. How do you feel about the session that you have just completed? (Circle the one answer that best applies.)

_____ 1. Perfect	_____ 5. Fair
_____ 2. Excellent	_____ 6. Pretty poor
_____ 3. Very good	_____ 7. Very poor
_____ 4. Pretty good	

B. What did you want or hope to get out of this session? (For each item, circle the answer that best applies.)

This session I hoped or wanted to:	No	Some	A Lot
1. Get a chance to let go and get things off my chest	0	1	2
2. Learn more about what to do in therapy, and what to expect from it	0	1	2
3. Get help in talking about what is troubling me	0	1	2
4. Get relief from tension or unpleasant feelings	0	1	2
5. Understand the reasons behind my feelings and behavior	0	1	2
6. Get some reassurance about how I'm doing	0	1	2
7. Get confidence to try new things, to be a different kind of person	0	1	2
8. Find out what my feelings really are, and what I really want	0	1	2
9. Get advice on how to deal with my life and with other people	0	1	2
10. Have my therapist respond to me on a person-to-person basis	0	1	2
11. Get better self-control	0	1	2
12. Get straight on which things I think and feel are real and which are mostly in my mind	0	1	2
13. Work out a particular problem that's been bothering me	0	1	2

C. What do you feel that you got out of this Session? (For each item, circle the answer that best applies.)

I feel that I got:	No	Some	A Lot
1. A chance to let go and get things off my chest	0	1	2
2. Hope: a feeling that things can work out for me	0	1	2
3. Help in talking about what was really troubling me	0	1	2
4. Relief from tensions or unpleasant feelings	0	1	2
5. More understanding of the reasons behind my behavior and feelings	0	1	2
6. Reassurance and encouragement about how I'm doing	0	1	2
7. Confidence to try to do things differently	0	1	2
8. More ability to feel my feelings, to know what I really want	0	1	2
9. Ideas for better ways of dealing with people and problems	0	1	2
10. More of a person-to-person relationship with my therapist	0	1	2
11. Better self-control over my moods and actions	0	1	2
12. A more realistic evaluation of my thoughts and feelings	0	1	2
13. Nothing in particular: I feel the same as I did before the session	0	1	2
14. Other:_____	0	1	2

D. 15. How did you feel about coming to therapy this session?
    1. Eager; could hardly wait to get here
    2. Very much looking forward to coming
    3. Somewhat looking forward to coming
    4. Neutral about coming
    5. Somewhat reluctant to come
    6. Unwilling; felt I didn't want to come at all

E. 16. How much progress do you feel you made in dealing with your problems this session?
    1. A great deal of progress
    2. Considerable progress
    3. Moderate progress
    4. Some progress
    5. Didn't get anywhere this session
    6. In some ways my problems seem to have gotten worse this session

F. 17. How well do you feel that you are getting along, emotionally and psychologically, at this time?

I am getting along:
1. Very well; much the way I would like to
2. Quite well; no important complaints
3. Fairly well; have my ups and downs
4. So-so; manage to keep going with some effort
5. Fairly poorly; life gets pretty tough for me at times
6. Quite poorly; can barely manage to deal with things

G. 18. To what extent are you looking forward to your next session?
1. Intensely; wish it were much sooner
2. Very much; wish it were sooner
3. Pretty much; will be pleased when the time comes
4. Moderately; it is scheduled and I guess I'll be there
5. Very little; I'm not too sure I will want to come

H. 19. How well did your therapist seem to understand what you were feeling and thinking this session?

My therapist:
1. Understood exactly how I thought and felt
2. Understood very well how I thought and felt
3. Understood pretty well, but there were some things he (she) didn't seem to grasp
4. Didn't understand too well how I thought and felt
5. Misunderstood how I thought and felt

I. 20. How helpful do you feel your therapist was to you this session?
1. Completely helpful
2. Very helpful
3. Pretty helpful
4. Somewhat helpful
5. Slightly helpful
6. Not at all helpful

J. During this session, how much:

	Slightly or Not At All	Some	Pretty Much	Very Much
21. Did your therapist talk?	0	1	2	3
22. Was your therapist attentive to what you were trying to get across?	0	1	2	3
23. Did your therapist tend to accept or agree with your ideas and point of view?	0	1	2	3
24. Was your therapist negative or critical towards you?	0	1	2	3
25. Did your therapist take initiative in bringing up things to talk about?	0	1	2	3
26. Did your therapist try to get you to change your point of view or way of doing things?	0	1	2	3
27. Was your therapist friendly and warm toward you?	0	1	2	3
28. Did your therapist show feeling?	0	1	2	3

K. How did your therapist seem to feel during this session? (For each item, circle the answer that best applies).

My therapist seemed:

	No	Some	A lot		No	Some	A lot
29. Pleased	0	1	2	43. Attracted	0	1	2
30. Thoughtful	0	1	2	44. Confident	0	1	2
31. Annoyed	0	1	2	45. Relaxed	0	1	2
32. Bored	0	1	2	46. Interested	0	1	2
33. Sympathetic	0	1	2	47. Unsure	0	1	2
34. Cheerful	0	1	2	48. Optimistic	0	1	2
35. Frustrated	0	1	2	49. Distracted	0	1	2
36. Involved	0	1	2	50. Affectionate	0	1	2
37. Playful	0	1	2	51. Alert	0	1	2
38. Demanding	0	1	2	52. Close	0	1	2
39. Apprehensive	0	1	2	53. Tired	0	1	2
40. Effective	0	1	2	54. Other: _____	0	1	2
41. Perplexed	0	1	2	55. Other: _____	0	1	2
42. Detached	0	1	2	56. Other: _____	0	1	2

BE SURE THAT YOU HAVE CHECKED EVERY ITEM

L. If you wish, give a brief formulation of the significant events or dynamics of this session:

Additional Comments:

Therapist's Form

A. How do you feel about the session that you have just completed? This session was: (Circle the one answer which best applies.)

1. Perfect
2. Excellent
3. Very Good
4. Pretty Good
5. Fair
6. Pretty Poor
7. Very Poor

B. What did your patient seem to want this session? (For each item, circle the answer that best applies.)

This session my patient seemed to want:	Not at all	Some	A lot
1. A chance to let go and express feelings	0	1	2
2. To learn more about what to do in therapy and what to expect from it	0	1	2
3. To avoid dealing with anxiety-arousing concerns	0	1	2
4. Relief from tension or unhappy feelings	0	1	2
5. To understand the reasons behind problematic feelings or behavior	0	1	2
6. Reassurance, sympathy, or approval from me	0	1	2
7. To evade or withdraw from effective contact with me	0	1	2
8. To explore emerging feelings and experiences	0	1	2
9. Advice on how to deal more effectively with self or others	0	1	2
10. To get a personal response from me	0	1	2
11. Help in controlling feelings or impulses	0	1	2
12. Help in evaluating feelings and reactions	0	1	2
13. To work through a particular problem	0	1	2
14. My frank opinion or evaluation	0	1	2
15. Other: _____	0	1	2

C. In what direction were you working with your patient this session? (For each item, circle the answer that best applies.)

I was working toward:	Not at all	Some	A lot
1. Helping my patient feel accepted in our relationship	0	1	2
2. Getting a better understanding of my patient, of what was really going on	0	1	2

I was working toward:	Not at all	Some	A lot
3. Helping my patient talk about his or her feelings and concerns	0	1	2
4. Helping my patient get relief from tensions or unhappy feelings	0	1	2
5. Helping my patient understand the reasons behind his or her reactions	0	1	2
6. Supporting my patient's self-esteem and confidence	0	1	2
7. Encouraging attempts to change and try new ways of behaving	0	1	2
8. Moving my patient closer to experiencing emergent feelings	0	1	2
9. Helping my patient learn new ways for dealing with self and others	0	1	2
10. Establishing a genuine person-to-person relationship with my patient	0	1	2
11. Helping my patient get better self-control over feelings and impulses	0	1	2
12. Helping my patient realistically evaluate reactions and feelings	0	1	2
13. Sharing empathically in what my patient was experiencing	0	1	2
14. Getting my patient to take a more active role and responsibility for progress in therapy	0	1	2

D. 15. How much were you looking forward to seeing your patient this session?
1. I definitely anticipated a meaningful or pleasant session.
2. I had some pleasant anticipation.
3. I had no particular anticipations but found myself pleased to see my patient when the time came.
4. I felt neutral about seeing my patient this session.
5. I anticipated a trying or somewhat unpleasant session.

E. 16. To what extent did your own state of mind or personal reactions tend to interfere with your therapeutic efforts during this session?
1. Considerably
2. Moderately
3. Somewhat
4. Slightly
5. Not at all

F. 17. To what extent did you reveal your spontaneous impressions or reactions to your patient this session?
1. Considerably
2. Moderately
3. Somewhat
4. Slightly
5. Not at all

G. 18. To what extent were you in touch with your patient's feelings?
    1. Completely
    2. Almost completely
    3. A great deal
    4. A fair amount
    5. Some
    6. Little

H. 19. How much of what your patient said and did do you feel you understood?
    1. Everything
    2. Almost all
    3. A great deal
    4. A fair amount
    5. Some
    6. Little

I. 20. How helpful do you feel that you were to your patient this session?
    1. Completely helpful
    2. Very helpful
    3. Pretty helpful
    4. Somewhat helpful
    5. Slightly helpful
    6. Not at all helpful

J. During this session, how much:	Slightly or not at all	Some	Pretty much	Very much
21. Did you talk?	0	1	2	3
22. Were you attentive to what your patient was trying to get across?	0	1	2	3
23. Did you tend to agree with or accept your patient's ideas or suggestions?	0	1	2	3
24. Were you critical or disapproving towards your patient?	0	1	2	3
25. Did you take initiative in defining the issues that were talked about?	0	1	2	3
26. Did you try to change your patient's point of view or way of doing things?	0	1	2	3
27. Were you warm and friendly towards your patient?	0	1	2	3
28. Did you express feeling?	0	1	2	3

K. How did you feel during this session? (For each item, circle the answer that best applies).

During this session I felt:

	No	Some	A lot		No	Some	A lot
29. Pleased	0	1	2	43. Attracted	0	1	2
30. Thoughtful	0	1	2	44. Confident	0	1	2
31. Annoyed	0	1	2	45. Relaxed	0	1	2
32. Bored	0	1	2	46. Interested	0	1	2
33. Sympathetic	0	1	2	47. Unsure	0	1	2
34. Cheerful	0	1	2	48. Optimistic	0	1	2
35. Frustrated	0	1	2	49. Distracted	0	1	2
36. Involved	0	1	2	50. Affectionate	0	1	2
37. Playful	0	1	2	51. Alert	0	1	2
38. Demanding	0	1	2	52. Close	0	1	2
39. Apprehensive	0	1	2	53. Tired	0	1	2
40. Effective	0	1	2	54. Sexually stimulating	0	1	2
41. Perplexed	0	1	2	55. Headachey or ill	0	1	2
42. Detached	0	1	2	56. Other: _____	0	1	2

BE SURE THAT YOU HAVE CHECKED EVERY ITEM

L. If you wish, give a brief formulation of the significant events or dynamics of this session:

Additional Comments:

10 | Using Task Analysis to Assess Processes of Change

T he purpose of this chapter is to describe the task-analysis approach for assessing client change processes and then provide an extended example of how task analysis is used to illuminate clinical questions. In particular, task-analytic methods are useful in trying to discern how clients work to change their problematic circumstances and, by extension, how social workers might be most helpful in assisting this change.

The processes of client change must be observed and understood in order to mobilize and support those change processes more effectively. The purpose of this chapter is to provide an explanation and example of a comprehensive approach for keeping track of how clients change. This approach, called task analysis, is a change-process research strategy (cf. Reid, 1990) that pulls together into one assessment method many of the assumptions and procedures introduced in Chapter 9. Task analysis consists of a set of intensive, inductive, and discovery-oriented procedures for generating theoretically guided and empirically based hypotheses about how clients change.

In developing task analysis, psychotherapy researchers Laura Rice and Leslie Greenberg (1984) drew on Newell and Simon's (1972) approach to locating the steps or tasks that make up successful problem solving. Rice and Greenberg's adaptation similarly outlines a method to uncover the steps clients undertake in accomplishing therapeutic work. Although conducting a complete task analysis of client change can be an awesome undertaking (cf. Berlin, Mann, & Grossman, 1991; Reid, 1990), the basic components of this method are potentially very useful for clinical work and can be modified to meet (or almost meet) the feasibility requirements of practitioner assessments (Berlin, 1990). In conducting a task analysis, the clinician does the following:

1. Articulates his or her general theoretical assumptions (general theory) about the processes of change
2. Identifies a key aspect of change (a critical change event or episode) for study and specifies the client communications that indicate that the change opportunity

is at hand (marker) and those that signify positive resolution of the episode (resolution)

3. Specifies a theory-based model (rational model) of how change occurs for the event
4. Specifies the clinical interventions and environmental supports (task environment) that provide the therapeutic context for client changes[1]
5. Reviews session transcripts and intersession reports to observe how the client effects change
6. Uses these observations to revise the rational model and construct a first empirical model (performance model)
7. Observes more events and revises the first performance model to devise a theoretically guided and data-based model of change; makes additional observations and revisions so long as they yield new information[2]

In the following section, we use a case example to explore how task-analysis guidelines can be flexibly followed to provide a feasible (though still time-consuming) procedure for collecting information that is immediately useful for ongoing clinical work.[3]

Phoebe sits down in her social worker's office and says that she is depressed and upset over her break-up with her boyfriend. Phoebe and her social worker, Laura, have been working together for almost a year battling Phoebe's sense of defeat, diffuseness, and ineffectiveness primarily by focusing on improving the conditions of her life. With a great deal of active support, advice, and guided practice, Phoebe moved into a new apartment in a safer neighborhood, got a more responsible job, and started taking better care of herself and her things—cooking for herself, paying closer attention to her appearance, exercising, paying her bills, keeping her apartment cleaned up and organized, and inviting friends over. All these achievements not only improved the quality of her life in concrete ways, but they also added to her still vulnerable sense that she can make good things happen, that she is "somebody." Now she feels like she is back to square one—an empty nonentity. As usual, the question is what needs to happen over the next weeks and months to make Phoebe feel different and better. How do people dig themselves out of these kinds of dilemmas? How might Phoebe do it?

Laura puzzled over these questions after she first saw Phoebe but, in the press of other demands, put them aside. Before seeing Phoebe for the second time, she gave them some serious thought. She tried to figure out how Phoebe might move from being stuck in this depressed experience to feeling competent, substantial,

---

[1]Although Rice and Greenberg do not emphasize the extra-therapy context of change, it seems important to pay attention to what happens outside of therapy in order to move beyond a narrow conception of psychosocial interventions and change.

[2]In the case of research applications, studies to verify the benefits of following the steps of the model compose the final stage of the task-analysis approach.

[3]This example is based on one case drawn from a small sample task-analysis study conducted by Berlin, Mann, & Grossman (1991). For the purposes of illustration, aspects of the task analysis of this case have been modified to take into account the time and resource constraints of clinical practice and show how to carry out the steps in a relatively simple and feasible, but still meaningful, way.

distinct, and loveable. In other words, Laura asked herself to articulate her own theory of change.[4]

Following Rice and Greenberg's directions for conducting a task analysis, Laura first specified her overall assumptions or general theory about psychosocial change and, particularly, change out of depression. As noted, when she first started seeing Phoebe over a year ago, Laura assumed that, to a great extent, Phoebe's problem was a function of her not taking good care of herself and acting as if she could never have anything or do anything worthwhile. During the work that ensued, Laura's strategy was to influence Phoebe to change her mind and feelings by changing her behavior and the concrete conditions of her life. The tasks they worked on involved self-enhancing actions that led to a redefinition of herself as a competent "somebody" who had "gotten herself a life."

Today, Laura still saw Phoebe's problem as primarily one of self-conceptualization. However, because many of the concrete attributes of Phoebe's life were still intact (excepting the relationship), Laura's inclination was to focus more directly on cognitive-emotional change. Her sense of what needed to change and ideas about how change would happen were both heavily influenced by a version of cognitive theory she had learned in school. These preconceptions were intertwined with ideas from other theoretical allegiances as well as her own personal and professional experiences.

Laura listed several assumptions about how cognitive-emotional problems develop and change. By translating her ideas into words she was able to examine her assumptions and alter them when she found gaps or views that did not withstand her own critical scrutiny. The assumptions that Laura specified are listed below.

☐ GENERAL THEORY OF HOW COGNITIVE-EMOTIONAL PROBLEMS DEVELOP AND CHANGE

1. How a person functions is influenced by how he or she interprets information about himself or herself, the world, and interactions with the world (e.g., Bandura, 1986; Mahoney, 1980, 1991).
2. The information consists of environmental and interpersonal "messages," as well as the person's own thoughts, behaviors, and emotions (Bandura, 1986; Mahoney, 1980, 1991).
3. Attempts to improve functioning should differentially focus on altering environmental constraints and demands, what the person can do, what he or she feels, and his or her expectations, appraisals, and understanding of what all this means personally and for his or her prospects in the world (Nurius & Berlin, 1993).
4. Even though environmental events may allow a variety of interpretations and responses, habitual ways of understanding can trap one in a narrow

[4]Laura was not able to finish this initial task before seeing Phoebe again. Indeed, her initial outlay of time was only a small portion of the several hours she eventually devoted to trying to understand how Phoebe changed. Practitioners are usually not in a position to make such heavy investments of time with more than one case during any one period. However, the experience that is gained by conducting a thorough process assessment gives one a basis for discerning the unique change characteristics of subsequent clients without having to repeat all the steps in the painstaking way that is described here.

range of actions and reactions (Arnkoff, 1980; Evans & Hollon, 1988; Jack, 1991; Nurius & Berlin, 1993).

5. Over the course of development and as a result of experience, individuals develop relatively stable habits of understanding or interpreting. These habits of attending, encoding, remembering, and inferring are guided by cognitive-emotional schemas (networks of classification categories and associated emotions that are stored in memory) (Fiske & Taylor, 1984; Bower, 1981; Evans & Hollon, 1988; Meichenbaum & Gilmore, 1984).

6. Depressive schemas encompass classification categories related to deprivation, loss, relentless demands, and personal weakness (Kovacs & Beck, 1978; Jack, 1991).

7. When environmental events are perceived as similar to features of depressive self-schemas, these cognitive-emotional networks of meaning are activated and function to direct attention to the depressing features of situations, prime memories of depressing events, and give depressing interpretations to events. As thoughts and feelings of personal weakness, hopelessness, and despair predominate, the individual becomes less active, productive, and socially engaged. His or her preoccupation and withdrawal may contribute to a worsening of interpersonal relationships and other life problems, and, in turn, recognition of these continuing failures serve to reactivate and elaborate the depressing self-schemas (Evans & Hollon, 1988; Kovacs & Beck, 1978; Ingram, 1984).

8. Individuals can move out of depressed states by developing and using alternative schemas to read personal and situational information. This can mean (1) creating or finding situations that do not have as many depressing features; (2) priming (or consciously directing one's attention to) alternative schemas; or (3) focusing on and accommodating facets of information that lead to positive self-schemas (Evans & Hollon, 1988; Nurius & Berlin, 1993; Fiske & Taylor, 1984; Beck & Young, 1985; Kovacs & Beck, 1978).

Although these general theoretical assumptions reflect a cognitive perspective on change, it should be clear that a similar list could be made for any theoretical perspective or mix of perspectives (e.g., family systems, psychodynamic, ecological, behavioral). Articulating guiding assumptions in this way prompts clinicians to think through, further develop, and wonder about the implications of their change-related beliefs. On the other hand, as discussed in Chapter 1, the more we specify and elaborate our own theories of change and become experts on them, the less likely we are to alter these beliefs in the face of contradictory information. There is no real protection against this confirmatory bias except to watch for it and remind ourselves that evolution of knowledge depends on discovery, not confirmation of what we have always thought. Accordingly, Laura might take a moment to feel proud of herself for pulling together her list of theoretical assumptions, but then go on to find the evidence that will alter it and make it more accurate and useful.

Guided by these assumptions about change, Laura went on to pinpoint critical change episodes or opportunities for important therapeutic work. Specifying episodes allowed her to focus her assessment efforts on the aspects of Pheobe's change work that seemed most critical. She designated episodes as the opportunities that came up (both in and outside of therapy) for Phoebe to alter her negative appraisals of specific events in her life, and to alter the more general, cross-situational beliefs that supported the depressing appraisals. As a part of thinking through how Phoebe might go about resolving these two kinds of episodes, Laura specified markers (beginnings) and resolutions (ends) for each episode and conceptualized intervening steps. These activities constitute what Rice and Greenberg call developing a rational model of change. It is a "rational" model because it is generated by rational thinking—by thinking about what theory, research results, practice experience, and the experience of "stepping into the client's shoes" say about how the client is likely to resolve episodes.

Laura's rational model for resolving one of the types of episodes, altering basic beliefs, included the following steps:

☐   RATIONAL MODEL FOR CHANGING BASIC BELIEFS

Marker: Phoebe expresses a dysfunctional appraisal that has been identified (or can be identified) as reflecting a core belief.

1. She clarifies the general theme of the appraisal and its cross-situational nature (e.g., touches on what happened, the personal meaning of what happened, how this is the usual direction that her interpretations of meaning seem to take her).
2. She places the basic assumption(s) or core belief(s) in a historical context (in effect,"these are some early situations in which I developed or used this belief and this is the way it was adaptive, or was meant to be adaptive, in those earlier times").
3. She focuses on the limiting consequences of the belief in the current situation (e.g., on how her attempts to protect herself from hurt by withdrawing keep her feeling cut off, ignored, and lonely).
4. She identifies her personal values, desires, and attributes and then identifies possibilities within the situation that might allow her to act according to these values, desires, and attributes and at the same time dispute her dysfunctional belief (e.g., what I really want is . . . ; sure, sometimes I have been able to . . . ; well, maybe I could . . .).
5. She articulates alternative beliefs or assumptions and experiments with them; that is, she uses them to direct actions and thoughts outside therapy (e.g., she consciously tries some different ways of responding to situations that are in line with a more hopeful, connected, initiating view of herself).
6. *Resolution*: She reports the ability to consciously access and enact more adaptive responses to life situations.

Similarly, Laura mapped a rational model for altering dysfunctional appraisals. Although this model was similar to the model for changing basic beliefs, it focused less on establishing the historical context and cross-situational pattern of appraisals and focused more on problem solving as a way to generate alternative solutions to the here-and-now problems that Phoebe felt were bringing her down.[5] Although many clients seem to require several experiences of working to move beyond dysfunctional appraisals in order to recognize the general themes that run through them, based on their previous work together, Laura assumed that Phoebe would more readily recognize her basic beliefs and be able to work immediately on modifying them.

Having considered what Phoebe would have to do to move out of her recent lapse into depressive functioning, Laura's next step was to try to define the conditions or context that would support Phoebe in making these moves. In the language of Rice and Greenberg, her next "thought-experiment" was to specify the task environment. As we have already noted in Chapter 9, there were really two environments she needed to think about: the one she created within the sessions and Phoebe's extra-therapy environment.

In specifying the in- and extra-session task environment, Laura thought about how she would promote and support Phoebe's accomplishment of each of the steps outlined in the Rational Model; the qualities of the therapy relationship that might give Phoebe a different and better sense of herself; the basic structure of the therapy; and the extra-therapy conditions that would support change. Although Laura's ideas remained relatively general, writing them down gave her a chance to review what she did and did not want to do and to set guidelines to follow as she moved through the therapy.

One can not and should not try to preplan all the therapeutic moves. As Schön (1987) implies, therapeutic work involves moment-to-moment experimentation and spontaneous improvisation: The clinician responds to the client, notices what happens, tries something different, and sees what happens next. Nevertheless, bringing some ideas to the session about how to help the client take steps towards change is a critical feature of professional helping. But how does the worker figure out what to do—what does he or she put into her plans? Most importantly, the plan needs to fit the problem. There needs to be a logical and, where possible, an empirical connection between a certain kind of "task environment" and completing a specific task. We take up this issue in more detail in Chapter 11.[6]

☐ **TASK ENVIRONMENT**

1. Use questions, prompts, and paraphrases to focus Phoebe on (a) recognizing the "themes" in her reactions, (b) further clarifying them as basic beliefs, and (c) tracing their influence in her life. Recognize the "internal validity"

---

[5]In the interests of space, the rational model for resolving dysfunctional appraisals is not included here. The remainder of the example will continue to focus only on "the resolving dysfunctional beliefs" episodes.

[6]Throughout the project, Laura allowed herself to come back to her "task-environment list" to refine it and add to it. Unlike a psychotherapy researcher conducting a controlled experiment, she did not need to have her intervention strategy completely worked out ahead of time.

of these beliefs, but gradually introduce some "emotionally tinged" language to begin to clarify their negative consequences. Join Phoebe in the search but do not take it over; let the discoveries be hers.

2. Consider the circumstances that led Phoebe to adopt this network of beliefs as the framework for her view of reality. Focus Phoebe on remembering the details of these formative situations so that she can get a full sense of how she was trying to somehow make things okay in adopting the beliefs. Use questions, prompts, and paraphrases—same as above.

3. Use paraphrases that highlight the punitive side of the beliefs; focus on feelings; use prompts and questions to help her recognize and underscore the outmoded nature of the dysfunctional assumptions and the discrepancy between the original (or current) adaptive intent of the assumptions and their actual consequences. Don't move too fast.

4. Focus Phoebe on her other goals, hopes, aspirations, and abilities that do not fit with the beliefs. Use questions and prompts along the lines of: "If . . . isn't working or doesn't quite fit any more, then what would?" "If you were really to take account of the things that are most important to you now as an adult woman, or the new hopes that you have for yourself, or the possibilities that this situation might allow, what would you believe about yourself . . . ?"

5. Focus Phoebe on further defining and elaborating alternative beliefs and help her plan how to develop and enact them between sessions.

Corrective interactions. I want to interact with Phoebe so that (1) she will formulate and express her thoughts and feelings, (2) she will experience me as attending to and valuing what she offers, (3) she will gain a stronger sense of her own identity through what I reflect back to her, and (4) she will experience me as extending myself for her—giving her some ideas, possibilities, ways of trying, and so forth. That means I need to listen carefully, move at her pace and not rush her, give her accurate reflections and paraphrases, extend myself—be disclosive, present, and willing to give some advice and opinions (the latter with a light touch). I also need to look for signs that P. sees me as neglectful or judgmental and be ready to engage her in analyzing those perceptions.

Structure. Flexibly follow guidelines for cognitive therapy for depression (Beck, Rush, Shaw, & Emery, 1979). For example, set agenda at beginning of session, ask P. to summarize main points at end of session, give homework assignments.

Outside therapy. On a day-to-day basis, Phoebe needs opportunities to (1) notice her dysfunctional ways of viewing herself and consider their accuracy or utility; (2) eventually try alternative ways of thinking, acting, and interacting; (3) get positive responses to her efforts, and (4) notice and accurately interpret those responses. With respect to her interactions, Phoebe needs a social context in which her friends, family, and coworkers listen to her, acknowledge what she has to say, and show that they respect her ideas and opinions even if they are not perfectly formulated. In addition, Phoebe needs a context— time, reminders, absence of hassles, frame of mind—to do some intrapersonal work between sessions, for example, to differentiate her grief over the loss of her relationship from a loss of self, and to differentiate the loss of this relation-ship from hopelessness about ever participating in a sustaining and mutually respectful relationship.

In working with Phoebe, Laura focused on helping her to create and make use of a constructive external task environment, that is, to ask for and recognize the kind of positive social attention she required and establish an appropriate time and place to engage in reflective exercises.[7] In many cases, however, the practitioner is called on to structure the external environment herself: meet with the family, pave the way with the welfare department, go along for the first visit to the day-care center, and so forth.

By the time Laura had completed the steps listed above (specified the general theory, rational model, and task environment), a month had elapsed. Although she had been seeing Phoebe all along, she was now ready to revise her theoretical or rational model of how Phoebe resolved episodes. This involved recording episodes, observing and describing what happened within them, pulling together common patterns in the descriptions, and revising the theoretical model of change according to the patterns that emerged.

As a lone practitioner, without the benefit of transcribers, coders, sophisticated recording equipment, or very much time, Laura relied on her own recall, brief therapy notes, and audio recordings of the sessions to reconstruct what Phoebe did from the episode's marker to its resolution. During sessions, she noted the beginnings and ends of episodes and the time (how far into the audiotape) they occurred. Immediately after the session, she made some rough notes about her perceptions of Phoebe's process and then listened to the appropriate section of the audiotape to bring in more detail and prime her own recall.

As Laura was making notes about how Phoebe seemed to move through the episode, she realized that she needed some systematic way to describe what was happening if she wanted to locate patterns. For example, she knew it would be confusing to describe the same process as "describing feelings" in one place and "searching for explanations" in another. She reviewed her rational model and her own notes several times to locate and define the most precise labels for Phoebe's change processes.

CODING CATEGORIES

1. Describes—recounts without searching for new understanding
2. Explores—brings in additional information, searches for new understanding (e.g., explores situation, historical context, conflicting responses, etc.)
3. Slides back to operating according to dysfunctional assumptions

---

[7]Laura had already surmised that several people in Phoebe's life were supportive or potentially supportive and that if Phoebe was sufficiently direct and specific, she could evoke recognition, respect, and affirmation from at least some of them.

4. Synthesizes a new realization—pulls explorations together to reach a new level of understanding (e.g., about the meaning of her dysfunctional views or about more adaptive ways to respond)
5. Problem-solves or plans—generates ideas about how to carry out additional explorations or actions between sessions
6. Reports on (successful or unsuccessful) efforts to accommodate alternative assumptions between sessions

Over the course of actually using these codes, Laura recognized their inadequacy and worked to refine and add to them.[8] Even so, her coding system remained rudimentary—better than no coding system at all and not as good as a system containing reliable, valid, mutually exclusive, and exhaustive codes.

When Laura had used these codes to describe how Phoebe worked to resolve several episodes, she looked for similarities in how Phoebe moved through them. Her idea was to look not only for patterns that would confirm the rational model, but for patterns that differed from it. The illustration below shows how Laura coded her recollections (assisted by the audiotape) of one episode that occurred toward the end of the therapy.

☐ SESSION 24: MAY 2, 1989

P: At work in these meetings, I feel like I don't want to open my mouth. It is like whatever I have to say just isn't worth it.... So, I say things in kind of a retreating way...like, don't mind me, but.... [Marker: Describes dys. assumption]
L: Right, like "what I have to say is probably useless, but.... "
P: And then I feel blank.... I can't find anything to say. [Elaborates]
L: So you kind of undermine yourself and then feel empty or blank.
P: Yeah, but the other day I just reminded myself that this was the kind of situation where I would feel insecure and blank and all of that was just old stuff. I did have things to say, so I screwed up my courage and did it. It didn't come out the way I wanted it to, but people still listened to me. [Pulls together realization of alternative—first pass].
L: They didn't need for it to be perfect.
P: It is kind of humbling to be taken seriously even if I'm not expressing things the way I want to...to realize that the substance is there and others have room for my weaknesses, even if I don't. So I just focused on that and said, well, why can't I do that for myself. [Explores alternative]
L: You'd like to do that for yourself.
P: Yeah, I want to. [Expresses commitment to alternative]
L: It sounds like you already took a big step toward that...you caught yourself putting yourself down and didn't like it. You said, "do I really want to be undermining myself in this way?" And then you came up with an

---

[8]She added the categories of "Elaborates," "Counterposes," "Distances or Recognizes Dissonance," and "Expresses Commitment or Ownership" to accommodate actions that fell outside the scope of the original coding categories.

answer—decided to muster your courage and take the plunge. You were a little rough and frayed around the edges, but it came out fine—people paid attention to you. They weren't critical of you or judging you for not being completely smooth and poised.

P: Yeah, even though I still don't want to be that rough and frayed person.... One of the things I've invested in is not having anybody see me making mistakes. I would rather be invisible and not think about how they're seeing me. I'd rather have them write me off and have my standards than to let go of my standards. It was even worse before. [Associates back to dys. assumption, distances from it]

L: You're past the worst part, but it still grabs you sometimes, this feeling that it is truly bad and awful to make mistakes and to have people see you make mistakes.... So, what is this scathing intolerance?

P: I guess my fear of being disrespected, like my mom was ... and just believing that the only way to be respected is to not ever make mistakes. The only way to get my dad to respect me, anyway.... And, you know, just feeling paralyzed because of that and not having parents that were jumping in there doing anything because they were too afraid of their own mistakes.... And there is this basic feeling that I just don't belong, don't deserve, don't deserve to be here. And that's one thing that I've been struggling with. [Explores historical antecedents; pulls together clearer sense of dys. assumption]

L: How?

P: Well, I blank out when I think about it (laughs). I just don't know how to really believe that I have a right to exist and be recognized and visible ... flaws or no flaws. That's a pretty hard one to address because it's just so deeply rooted in that basic "I'm sorry" stance to the world.... But I guess I haven't answered your question. [Recognizes dissonance; explores difficulty of letting go]

L: So, how do people get the feeling that they do have a right to exist?

P: In the beginning, by being responded to that way by their parents. Just to be recognized as a person in their own right. And whatever they are thinking or feeling or being at the time, that's good, that's them, who they are. And we've talked a lot about that.... ways of nurturing the little interests and things that make a person who they are.... You know, and I'm still trying to enjoy and think about the ways that other people do that for me—ways I get that from certain friends. I'm trying to enjoy that and think about it ... [Explores alternative]

L: So, you pay attention to the ways that other people recognize you and are trying to make that a part of your experience and history, too.

P: Yeah, so that's a change. That's something in the past I wasn't able to accept. I was too embarrassed or too vulnerable or something. [Explores alternative and dysfunctional assumption; owns alternative]

L: And now?

P: Now I like it. [Claims ownership of alternative]

L: So, some things have changed? Maybe you?

P: Yeah, and I need to work to fill that in—keep acting like I deserve to be here, like in the meeting, and keeping myself open to people who respect and look out for me. At least that is something new—being able to see it when it happens. [Plans about how to act on basis of alternative]

L: Right. (Brief discussion of progress vis-à-vis homework)...You know I'm curious about how your father would react if he heard you talking about feeling blank and paralyzed and that it is better to be invisible than to make mistakes. Is this how he wanted it to turn out?

P: No. He'd probably cry. [Explores interpersonal situation that supports alternative; elaborates alternative]

L: He'd cry because...the sacrifice is too much? You've given up too much?

P: Yeah. I think he'd just be confused because he thought he loved me so much...and, you know, in many ways he did, even more now, but... (gives more detail on experience with father). [Explores interpersonal situation]

L: But is this kind of selflessness and invisibility what your father wanted?

P: It isn't. [Explores interpersonal situation; elaborates alternative]

L: And in terms of your deserving to be noticed, heard, paid attention to?

P: He'd want that for me. [Explores interpersonal situation; elaborates alternative]

L: (Pause) And if you were to have a thoughtful discussion with your mother about the struggles you're having in your life now, what would she say?

P: She'd say she has the same ones. (Gives more detail about her mother's and grandmother's struggles to feel whole, deserving, and acceptable). [Explores interpersonal situations that support alternative; Explores historical antecedents for dys. assumption and alternative assumption]

L: If you had a chance to answer one of those self-effacing letters your grandma wrote to her family when she was a young woman, what would you want to say to her?

P: All I'd want to say is, "You are somebody." [Explores interpersonal situation that support alternative; elaborates alternative]

L: You'd want to give your grandma encouragement and appreciate her...and same for your mother? And maybe the same for the little girl who needed some specific recognition?

P: Same for her. (Pause) I think it helps for me to spend more time thinking about my mom and my grandma and to have compassion for them. It's like...it sort of lets me have more compassion for myself. [Resolution: Pulls together a fuller sense of the alternative]

P: [following week] I called my mom and talked with her about grandma—thanked her for sending me her letters—and said how proud I was of grandma for being so tough. I said that it was sad that grandma never really felt it...never felt tough or strong within herself. And I told my mom that I thought she was kind of tough, too. [Reports back on extra-therapy efforts to operate according to alternative]

Laura reviewed her coded descriptions of four episodes over and over, comparing two episodes at a time, then adding a third, and finally, a fourth. With each addition, Laura revised her framework of Phoebe's pattern of change. She synthesized the codes from the episodes to summarize the essential steps and variations on them (Schefler, 1983) that Phoebe used in moving from dysfunctional assumptions to more adaptive responding. When Laura had a revised model of change worked out, she went back to her original case notes to tally up how many of the four episodes actually contained the steps in her model. She retained steps if they occurred in three out of four of the episodes.

The result of this considerable body of work was a first performance model of change. As we have indicated, this model stems from practice wisdom, theory, and empirical observation. It represents a set of warranted hypotheses about how Phoebe performs as she goes about changing a specific dilemma within a specific context or task environment.

☐   HOW PHOEBE RESOLVES DYSFUNCTIONAL ASSUMPTIONS:
FIRST PERFORMANCE MODEL

1. Describes dysfunctional assumption
2. Explores and expands meaning in contexts of current, interpersonal situation and historical antecedents
3. Pulls together a clearer realization of the meaning of the assumption
4. Finds the core meaning dissonant
5. Brings in additional information to form the basis of an alternative assumption
6. Counterposes interpersonal behaviors, cognitions, and emotions that support or flow from the alternative perspective with a stronger emotional experiences of the dysfunctional assumption
7. Differentiates situations that pull for the alternative vs. the assumption and finds experiences with the alternative on which to build
8. Pulls together a more vivid, complex realization of alternative
9. Plans to carry out further explorations of alternative assumption between sessions
10. Reports back on between-session feelings, actions, and insights that reinforced the alternative

This performance model of how Phoebe goes about moving beyond dysfunctional views of herself and her world is a summary of the variety of patterns of task accomplishment that she used. It is the clearest, most common, and basic pattern that Laura was able to pick out from all the back and forth, repetition, and varying sequences. Although it represents what Laura saw and heard Phoebe doing, it also represents Laura's own thinking about those processes—the ways her thoughts about Phoebe's change processes changed.

In general terms, her observation-based ideas about how Phoebe goes about changing are now much more precise, complex, and clear. At least some of that new precision is reflected in the performance model. It may be that even more of it is also available to Laura in an intuitive, unarticulated form. On both explicit and intuitive levels, Laura has a clearer sense of how Phoebe gets work done and how she herself can help Phoebe.

The performance model resembles the original rational, or theory-based, model of change, but it also contains some differences. For example, the observations suggested that when Phoebe explored her dysfunctional assumption and brought together a fuller sense of its cognitive, emotional, relational aspects, the force of that realization seemed to prompt a recoiling, a strong sense that "this is really not a good guideline for my life" (see #2 and #3 in the Performance Model). That undermining of the dysfunctional assumption seemed much more solid when Phoebe came to it on her own than when Laura led her to it through a directive process of logical analysis.

It also became apparent to Laura that when Phoebe turned from thinking and talking about how she might understand herself in an alternative way to talking about all the compelling reasons the dysfunctional assumption was true, it was not necessarily a negative move (see #6). It seemed to Laura that counterposing evidence in favor of the alternative assumption with evidence in favor of the original assumption was a constructive part of how Phoebe worked things out for herself. Reexperiencing the strong pull of the dysfunctional assumption—the security inherent in certainty and the concomitant constriction—and doing so in the context that offered other possibilities eventually seemed to allow Phoebe to move toward those new possibilities. Finally, the process of identifying and reflecting on the aspects of Phoebe's situation that pulled for the dysfunctional assumption and those that pulled for the alternative (see #7) gave Phoebe the opportunity to exert more control over her prevailing perspective. She could both prepare herself to respond to the dysfunctional cues in another way and seek out more supportive environments. As a part of this step, Phoebe also dwelled on memories of having already relied on the alternative perspective in previous situations.

As noted above, these discoveries and the careful thinking and attention that made them possible allow Laura to be more precise and on target in assisting Phoebe. For example, she learned not to block Phoebe from moving back to explore dysfunctional assumptions; she began to recognize and use the subtle cues that would prompt Phoebe to fully explore the pros and cons of her dysfunctional assumptions rather than lead her through a more structured analysis of their maladaptive nature; she encouraged Phoebe to explore the situational cues for dysfunctional and more adaptive assumptions; and she primed Phoebe to develop an alternative perspective that was grounded in real experience—that had vivid detail and emotional meaning. Most importantly, the practice of thinking through her own change-related assumptions, staying open to divergences from those assumptions, and engaging in careful observation improved the quality of Laura's empathy and became part of her usual clinical mode.

SUMMARY

The main message of the last two chapters is that it is important to attend to the processes of change in order to become more sensitive and effective in assisting those processes. As we have suggested, this assessment work can be done on a comprehensive scale, as in the case of task analysis, or on a more modest scale by incorporating specific assessment procedures and tools into one's usual process assessment. In all cases, the point is to identify one's own assumptions about how change occurs and to modify those views based on careful attention to new information.

As already noted, in practice it is artificial and counterproductive to separate assessments of progress and process. In an earlier era, when the research emphasis was squarely focused on documenting therapy outcomes, it was easier to delineate research approaches that detected processes leading to outcomes and those that focused on the outcomes per se. In light of more recent understanding that outcome is often arbitrary designation (Is it what you measure during the final therapy session? Six weeks later? Or when the person faces his or her first big crisis?) and that it is extremely difficult to trace a line of influence from therapy processes to an exact, single-point measure of outcome, the trend has been to look also for intermediate outcomes, that is, signs of progress. As we noted, when the increments of progress being scrutinized become small enough, they begin to resemble steps toward change; the building blocks of change.

Despite these blurred distinctions, it still seems possible to implement a two-pronged assessment strategy: assessing increments of problem change (e.g., lessening depression, marital stress, neglectful parenting, inadequate resources) and assessing the processes (explorations, expressions of feelings, enactive tasks, relationship dynamics, interpersonal supports, etc.) that add up to progress. In the mode of the clinical researcher, one might also go on to conduct controlled tests to verify the relationship between change processes and intermediate outcomes.

The fundamental questions that drive all these investigative efforts are, "How do clients resolve their problems and reach their goals?" and "How can practitioners help them in that process?" We continue our discussion of how practitioners decide what to do in the following chapter.

4 INTERVENTION DECISION MAKING

11 | Deciding What To Do

T his chapter focuses on the process of deciding how to intervene. It revisits earlier discussions about assessment to focus more explicitly on the link between understanding the client and his or her problems and generating actions to minimize those problems. The chapter addresses several issues that arise as a result of working to specify the intervention implications of various assessment conclusions. It also provides examples of decision-making models.

I. How Social Workers Figure Out What to Do
   A. Comparison and classification
   B. Theory
   C. Creative innovation

II. How Assessments Inform Decisions About Intervention

III. Intervention Guidlines
   A. Changing behaviors
   B. Changing cognitions
   C. Changing emotions
   D. Changing interpersonal interactions
   E. Changing situations
      1. The influence of problem severity
      2. The influence of client strengths and social resources
      3. The influences of motivations, resistances, and coping styles
      4. The influence of incoming information about progress and process

IV. A Treatment Selection Model

V. Linking Treatments to Clients and/or Problems
   A. Prescription or problem solving
   B. Predicting change
      1. Pretreatment predictors
      2. Common factors
      3. Is predictability an illusion?

    C. What do clinicians really do? (Approaches vs. responses)

    D. Knowing more than you can say

VI. Summary

Social workers seek to understand their clients in order to have a basis for figuring out what to do to be most helpful. Central to this approach is the notion that *somehow* information about the client's problems, resources, progress, and change process will reveal how to mobilize and support positive change. Although we have addressed this idea throughout the book, we want to take it up in a more explicit manner here. Specifically, the issue that we want to pursue is, what is involved in this "somehow"? How does this revelation transpire? How do social workers move from understanding to action? How do practitioners decide what to do? How do they translate decisions into proficient and effective action? How can this decision-action process be improved?

Take a moment and think about how *you* figure out what to do. Are your intervention communications and actions the result of carefully crafted plans or do they stem from spontaneous improvisation? What is the balance? Are they influenced more by your repertoire of skills than the needs of the client? Are they focused on accomplishing specific goals or do you just "go with the flow"?

> Chizuko Bell is a 50-year-old Japanese American woman who complains of depression. She has been married for 25 years to Wilford Bell, an airline pilot. Chizuko and her husband have raised two daughters; the oldest is working in an East Coast city and the youngest is now in college in a neighboring state. Chizuko says she is close to her daughters but does not hear much from them. She misses them but is also thankful that they are out of the house because they both became very rebellious during their high school years. Wilford is away for blocks of several days on international flights and is then home again for extended periods. When at home, he plays golf avidly and, according to Chizuko, is distant and remote. Chizuko has worked off and on during her adult life as a medical technologist. She finds the work boring. Her parents, first-generation Japanese immigrants, have died within the past 3 years. Chizuko weeps openly when she talks of them. Chizuko spent her young childhood in an internment camp in Wyoming. She says that experience drew her family closer together. Now Chizuko talks of feeling useless and insignificant. Her life, she says, is empty and has no purpose.

What else do you want to know about Chizuko in order to help her? Why is the available or additional information important? What will it tell you about how to start and what to do?

> Mavis Jeppson is a 29-year-old Caucasian woman who currently resides at the St. Alphonsis Shelter for Homeless Women. Two days ago, she attempted suicide by cutting her wrists with a paring knife. She was released to the shelter from the emergency room where it was determined that her cuts were relatively superficial and that she was not at serious risk of harming herself. Mavis has worked as a fruit picker and cannery worker. When the canning factory closed, she came to the city to try to find work. She and her two children, 3-year-old Karla and 5-year-old Kevin, ended up living in her car for two months until Mavis was reported to the Child Protection Agency for leaving her children unattended. The children have been placed in temporary foster care. Mavis is not married to the children's father, has not had contact with him

for a couple of years, and reports that he has no resources to contribute to t
says that her life is about as low-down as a life can get and she sees no way c

How can you help Mavis? What kind of information are you looking for in figuring
this out? Will your approach be different for her than for Chizuko? What are the
cues that guide you in these choices?

HOW SOCIAL WORKERS FIGURE OUT WHAT TO DO

In one of the few investigations of how social workers actually generate helping
actions, Harrison (1991) conducted in-depth interviews with 25 community-oriented
British social workers. His findings suggest that social workers use three interrelated
cognitive approaches or guides to practice: comparison and classification, applying
portions of generic theories, and searching for creative alternatives. Although some
of the workers in Harrison's study tended to rely on one approach over the others,
the approaches are not mutually exclusive. Often workers employed all three—either
in a sequential pattern or practically simultaneously.

Comparison and Classification

Comparison and classification makes up the basic problem-solving paradigm. This
method of formulating solutions is a fundamental and pervasive form of Western
thinking. Briefly, comparison and classification involves specifying a problem situation in detail, comparing the situation to others so that it can be classified, and
linking the class to resources for change. When one can accurately portray the
salient elements of the problem situation, the desired state, and the operations
that are necessary in moving from the current to desired state, comparison and
classification works. Of course, this is no small order in the unruly, complicated
world of social problems. As we know , in the midst of overwhelming detail and
uncertainty about which detail is most important, practitioners tend to rely on
heuristics or information-processing shortcuts; that is, they tend to use information that is readily available, fits familiar patterns, or confirms favored beliefs and
hunches.

Theory

Harrison (1991) suggests that when classifying the unique attributes of individuals
and matching them to intervention options did not work out, social workers in
his sample often turned to guidelines from generic theories. Harrison uses the
term "generic theory" to represent formulations stemming from what is commonly
referred to in Britain as "unitary approaches" or what we might call "systems theory."
In unitary approaches,

> the same processes are applied with different "systems" or sets of people and social
> institutions that interact with one another dynamically. Sometimes individuals are
> looked at as systems in and of themselves, but usually the term is reserved for people

in relationships with other close individuals, families, neighbourhoods, communities, and larger social groups. (p. 110)[1]

The implications of turning to generic theories often included moving away from case-by-case definitions of problems to more generic, community ones. Taking a kind of "we are all connected and suffer this problem together" approach, workers were prompted to bring all of affected individuals into the process of defining a common problem and working toward solutions that would "maintain what was desirable in communities and . . . change what was not" (p. 117).

Creative Innovation

Finally, Harrison found that workers sometimes tried to locate solutions outside the bounds of classification systems and general theories. In the absense of a good rule about what to do, they made something up. They created new responses. "This [creative] mode is one of seeking potentially helpful ideas from any source, and combining them in new ways, or in ways new to the situation at hand" (p. 126). The innovation social workers described often involved discovering analogies from seemingly different situations and testing their applicability via thought experiments: "I wonder what would happen if. . . ."

To sum up, at the most fundamental level, decisions about how to intervene tend to be the result of classification and comparison; matching features of knowledge about the problem, the client, and the change process with knowledge about how to assist change. In effect, we say to ourselves, "given the way the client and I understand the problem, given the kind of outcome the client and I are working toward, given the personal and social resources with which we have to work, and given what we know about how change seems to occur or is occuring, what do we need to do to get from point A to point B? What does logic suggest? What does theory suggest? What does research suggest? What does my intuition or creativity tell me?" Because the issues with which we are dealing are often much more complicated than our classification schemes, we also need to be able to step back and reconsider what we are missing that might be important and what is irrelevant. We need the flexibility to be able to reclassify on the basis of alternative theories; for example, "this is not an individual problem, it is a housing project or a neighborhood problem," or "I should stop focusing on what the client cannot do and focus more on what she can do and what she wants for herself." We also must be able to quiet the problem-solving mind so that ideas that escape intentional, "brain-racking," efforts might coalesce and come into awareness.

[1]Harrison quotes a definition of the unitary approach from Timms and Timms: "This is a term of recent origin in social work, describing a move away from the conceptualisation of social work as a grouping of distinct, separable methods (for instance, *casework*, *groupwork*, and *community work*) aimed at correcting problems in either the client, or his immediate environment, or 'society' in general. The unitary approach, usually based on a version of systems theory, assumes that social work is one thing, differentially manifested, and that its targets and those for whom social work is undertaken can all be encompassed in one over-arching framework" (Timms & Timms, 1982, p. 202, as cited in Harrison, 1991, p. 110).

HOW ASSESSMENTS INFORM DECISIONS
ABOUT INTERVENTION

Faced with wanting to be helpful, the issue of assessment becomes more focused and critical. The focus is on selecting and understanding the things that will allow the worker and the client to create difference. This assessment process is continuous throughout the worker-client encounter. As we noted in previous chapters, practitioners begin with an initial assessment task and continue to rework their understanding of the client and his or her problems so that they can locate, create, or refine ways to effect change. In Table 11.1, we summarize points made in earlier chapters about the potential contributions of assessment to intervention efforts. We will elaborate on these points in an attempt to sketch out a preliminary model of the assessment-intervention connection. This framework is an example of how social work practitioners can explicate (and then examine) their own decision guides. It is an "idealized" or "rational" model (see Chapter 10) in the sense that it provides directions that are largely the result of logic (our logic as it is informed by various theoretical preferences and empirical findings) and ought to work under ideal conditions. Under real conditions, suggested interventive actions would need to be adjusted, adapted, and even abandoned.

In Table 11.1, we simply articulate the broad intervention implications of various kinds of assessment data. The scope and locus of problem, the conditions that maintain it, and client goals inform the selection of targets for change. Information about personal and social resources and about the patterns and results of early efforts to accomplish change give cues about how the change can be encouraged. But clearly, these broad suggestions about what to do need to be further refined; they need to stimulate additional searching for ideas about how certain kinds of changes occur. The following questions illustrate that kind of searching. How do people change their behaviors? How do they change the ways they think and feel about things? How do homeless people find housing and jobs? How does a mentally ill person find a supportive niche outside the hospital? How does a neighborhood become a haven for its residents instead of a battleground? How do these changes occur and what is my role in this change process? How will I focus the effort? What are the steps that the client and I need to take? Who else will we involve in this plan?

In order to accomodate a variety of situations and states that might be targeted for change, the worker needs a variety of ways for conceptualizing change and helping it along. The client is a primary source of information in developing a perspective about how change might happen. For example, factors such as (1) how he or she described the problem, (2) how he or she struggles with issues, (3) how other people figure in, (4) the things that really matter to him or her, (5) the kind of change the client seeks, (6) why the client thinks it will or will not happen, and (7) the ways he or she tries to change and to hang on to stability tell the clinician much about how the change process will unfold. Practitioners listen to these accounts and understand them according to their own personal and formal theories about problems and change. These frameworks are an additional resource

TABLE 11.1
Contributions of Assessment to Intervention

INITIAL ASSESSMENT	INTERVENTION
People-Problems	What will be the scope of the intervention effort? Will it focus on specific symptoms, reactions, or dilemmas or more complicated patterns of personal identity and social structure?
Goals	What outcome are we seeking?
Situations and Dispositions	How can the intervention strategy (task environment) address the main factors blocking accomplishment of goals? What or who will be the locus of the change action?
Strengths and Deficits	How can personal strengths and social resources be mobilized to generate and implement solutions? How will this change process occur? What are the main in- and extra-session opportunities?
	How serious are the deficits? How can the intervention be adjusted to account for degree of impairment, risk, dangerousness, the range of negatively affected individuals?
ASSESSING PROGRESS	
Is the situation improving?	How does the intervention strategy need to be modified?
Has the goal been achieved or redefined?	How does the intervention strategy need to be modified?
ASSESSING PROCESS	
How is change occurring?	What do the client and I need to do to capitalize on these change processes?

in forging a useful perspective about change. Whether clinicians simply borrow theories to fit the problem or find a way to integrate different perspectives into one overarching theoretical perspective, they need access to a relatively large repertoire of explanatory frameworks and intervention skills in order to draw on those that most directly address the targets and goals for change. Common targets and goals include (1) personal characteristics (behaviors, cognitions, emotions), (2) interpersonal interactions, (3) social situations, or (4) various combinations of the above. Practitioners also need to stay in touch with empirical evidence and their own experiences about which approaches seem to work best with which problems and goals. When we push ourselves to articulate how we match treatments to problems, we come up with the following guidelines.

INTERVENTION GUIDELINES

Changing Behaviors

If the change target primarily involves *behavioral* excesses and deficits, borrow from behavioral frameworks (e.g., Bandura, 1977, 1986; Wachtel, 1987; Wheelis, 1973) and behavioral techniques (e.g., Barlow, 1985; Linehan, 1987a, b; Steketee & Foa, 1985; Wachtel & Wachtel, 1986b).

Essentially, competent action requires appropriate subskills, incentives, environmental supports, and reasonably accurate judgments about capabilities in a given situation (Bandura, 1986). In helping clients to acquire these components, use prompts, questions, suggestions, modeling, coaching, and feedback:

1. Specify what the client wants to accomplish.
2. Differentiate realistic expectations for early efforts.
3. Identify and review incentives and supports for new action.
4. Identify and practice necessary steps and subskills.
5. Anticipate and plan for personal and social resistances that may be aroused.
6. Take action, observe, refine plan, and recycle through steps again.
7. Consider how these new actions alter self-concepts, feelings, and relationships.

Depending on the client's problems and goals, consider specific, empirically tested intervention approaches, for example, coping skills training (Goldfried & Davison, 1976), exposure therapy (Marks, 1987), relaxation training, relapse prevention training (Marlatt & Gorden, 1985), stress innoculation (Meichenbaum, 1977), parent training (Pinkston, Friedman, & Polster, 1981; Reid, Taplin, & Loeber, 1981), assertiveness training (Linehan, 1979), and anger control (Novaco, 1975).

Changing Cognitions

If the change target primarily involves *dysfunctional* beliefs, borrow from cognitive frameworks, for example, cognitive behavioral (Beck, Rush, Shaw, & Emery, 1979; Meichenbaum, 1977), cognitive developmental (Mahoney, 1991), cognitive interpersonal frameworks (Safran & Segal, 1990), and cognitive techniques (e.g., Freeman, Simon, Beutler, & Arkowitz, 1989).

At the simplest level, in order for people to change their core beliefs, they need to understand the subjective nature of these beliefs, repeatedly encounter and perceive evidence that contradicts them, and develop an alternative set of beliefs that account for many of the "facts" explained by the original perspective (Evans & Hollon, 1988).

Use questions, pharaphrases, prompts, probes, and specific data-gathering homework exercises to support the client to do the following:

1. Clarify her current dysfunctional perspective
2. Catch herself in the act of using that perspective to make sense of particular situations

3. Understand what it is about current situations that pulls for this dysfunctional viewpoint
4. Understand the historical origins of the beliefs and how they were adaptive or served an adaptive intent in that earlier context
5. Gain a tangible, experiential awareness that, at least currently, this viewpoint is partial, constructed, and generating negative consequences
6. Attend to previously ignored or new cues that suggest other ways of assigning meaning
7. Generate and practice alternative frameworks for understanding and action
8. Catch herself interpreting according to old perspective and consciously substitute more productive ways of understanding
9. Explore relative advantages and disadvantages, pulls and resistances associated with the two systems for understanding
10. Realize that dysfunctional perspectives remain accessible and prepare to tolerate and move beyond them when they recur

Depending on the specific nature of the client's cognitive problems and goals, consider empirically tested, cognitive intervention approaches (e.g., Abramson, Alloy, & Metalsky, 1988; Berlin, Mann, & Grossman, 1991; Horowitz, 1991) and techniques, for example, mastery and pleasure exercises (Beck et al., 1979), self talk (Mahoney, 1991; Meichenbaum, 1977), life review (Mahoney, 1991), change history exercises (Bandler & Grinder, 1979; Kelly, 1955), and mirror time (Mahoney, 1991).

Changing Emotions

If the change target primarily involves constricted, conflicted, or upsetting *feelings*, the goal usually involves helping the client experience and make constructive use of the adaptive information contained in the emotion. This work should be guided by theoretical frameworks focusing on emotions (e.g., Gendlin, 1981; Greenberg & Safran, 1987; Lazarus, 1991; Rice & Saperia, 1984), and expressive or experiential therapeutic techniques (Daldrup, Beutler, Engle, & Greenberg, 1988; Greenberg, Safran, & Rice, 1989; Rice & Saperia, 1984; Safran & Greenberg, 1991).

Use paraphrases, evocative language, silence, reflection, focusing, and enactive exercises to assist the client in doing the following:

1. Experiencing his or her primary (spontaneous, unlearned) emotions; attending to sensations, images, felt needs
2. Symbolizing feelings; saying what they mean
3. Gaining awareness of additional information while the emotion is still felt: for example, experiencing the action implications of the emotion (e.g., defend self, seek comfort, find safety), noting other cues in the situation that might have been overlooked or misinterpreted, and exploring depths and intensity of feeling to the point of generating reactivity (a feeling of dissonance with the extremity of the feeling) and then moving to focus on moderating aspects of the situation, memories, or opposing feelings
4. Enacting adaptive implications of emotions

5. Repeatedly practicing experiencing emotions, reading their adaptive cues, taking constructive action
6. Considering the meaning of these emotions and actions for "self-concepts" and relationships

Depending on the specific nature of the client's emotion-related dilemmas, consider empirically tested, expressive intervention approaches, for example, focusing (Gendlin, 1981), two-chair work (Daldrup, Beutler, Greenberg, & Engle, 1988; Greenberg, 1984), evocative unfolding (Rice, 1974; Rice & Saperia, 1984), completing unfinished business (Greenberg & Safran, 1987), and guided imagery (Anderson, 1980; Edwards, 1989).

Changing Interpersonal Interactions

If the change target primarily involves conflicted or restrictive *interpersonal interactions*, borrow from interpersonal theoretical frameworks and techniques (e.g., Boyd-Franklin, 1989; Fortune, 1985; Gurman, Kniskern, & Pinsoff, 1986; Hartman & Laird, 1983; Imber-Black, 1988; Lerner, 1985, 1989; McGoldrick, Anderson, & Walsh, 1989; McGoldrick, Pearce, & Giordano, 1982; Minuchin & Fishman, 1981; Wachtel & Wachtel, 1986).

With affected individuals, use questions, prompts, paraphrases, and directions to focus clients on doing the following:

1. Specifying conflicting and common desires
2. Delineating problematic interpersonal patterns and the motivations, communications, and perceptions that maintain them
3. Sorting among individual and common desires to choose goals for change
4. Identifying and practicing alternative communications

Consider empirically tested, interpersonal intervention approaches: for example, family support (Seitz, Rosenbaum, & Aptel, 1985; Weissbourd & Kagan, 1989), psycho-education (Anderson, Reiss, & Hogarty, 1986), communication exercises (Gottman, Notarius, Gonso, & Markman, 1976; Guerney, 1977; Stuart, 1980; Tolson, 1977), family problem solving (Reid, 1985), family reunification (Rooney, 1981), and family preservation (Whittaker, Kinney, Tracy, & Booth, 1990).

Changing Situations

If the change target primarily involves untenable *social situations*, borrow from theoretical frameworks and techniques that focus on mobilizing resources and changing neighborhoods, communities, and organizations (e.g., Erlich & Rivera, 1992; Grief & Lynch, 1983; Rappaport, Swift, & Hess, 1984; Smale, Tuson, Cooper, Wardle, & Crosbie, 1988).

1. Specify what needs to change.
2. Delineate the people, groups, or organizations who can influence change and the access route to these influential people.

3. Assess the motivations and resistances of the people and groups who need to be involved in the change effort.
4. Engage their cooperation.
5. Work with people and group(s) to develop short-term and long-term goals and strategies.

Depending on the nature of the situational issues to be addressed, consider empirically tested social mobilization, support, and change approaches: for example, self-help support and action groups (Almeleh, Soifer, Gottlieb, & Gutierrez, in press; Lieberman & Videka-Sherman, 1986; Powell, 1990; Rappaport, Reischi, & Zimmerman, 1992; Zimmerman & Rappaport, 1988), community support models (Kisthard, 1992; Rapp, 1992; Test et al., 1991), advocacy (Nulman, 1983; Rose, 1990), finding resources (Gambrill, 1983), community organizing (Gutierrez & Lewis, 1992), and political action (Murdach, 1982).

Moreover, the social worker also needs to consider what theories and research evidence say about other variations in the targets for change. For example:

- If the change targets are more complicated personal identity configurations, as opposed to more narrowly delineated problems, then consider a lengthier intervention process that focuses on understanding the early context and adaptive intent of basic self-views and worldviews (Berlin, Mann, & Grossman, 1991).
- If the change targets are more complicated social structures and multilevel patterns, consider a longer intervention process focusing on a range of interacting problem dynamics; specify short- and long-term goals.
- If the change targets consist of a combination of the above, consider longer treatments, list change targets by priority, work out timing, and specify short- and long-term goals.

THE INFLUENCE OF PROBLEM SEVERITY   The practitioner also needs to adjust interventions to account for degrees of impairment, risk for worsening, dangerousness, and number of people who are adversely affected. For example:

- If the individual is seriously impaired with respect to judgment, self-care, safety, and so forth, consider the following:

hospitalization

community supervision

mobilizing family/friendship support

psychiatric consultation

long-term community support (e.g., housing, work, supportive relationships with family and friends, coping and stress management, medication management, and health care)

- If the individual is at risk for harming himself or others, consider the following:

immediate crisis intervention to determine the client's and others' need for protection

- If the negative effects of the problem situation extend to others, consider the following:

  group problem solving

  psycho-education

  support groups

  respite care

- If the negative effects on the client and others are escalating, consider the following:

  crisis intervention

  group problem solving

  respite care

  interventions listed under serious impairment

THE INFLUENCE OF CLIENT STRENGTHS AND SOCIAL RESOURCES.   The practitioner also needs to build intervention efforts on a client's strengths and available social resources. In all the instances noted earlier, consider how available or potential assets can be supported and employed as a major force in the change process:

- Does the client have a network of friends or family who have the potential to be supportive?
- Does the client have aspirations and hopes?
- Does he or she function well in one or more domains of his or her life? Does he or she have particular skills?
- Does the client have a good sense of humor?
- Does the client look to others for guidance and help?
- Is the client able to function independently?
- Does the client live in a resource-rich community or a community in which appropriate resources might be patched together?

Find a way to harness these strengths—notice them, play to them, build a plan around them, and instigate change with them. Here and in all the other steps, emphasis needs to be given to understanding how this particular client—who comes from a given culture, economic situation, family background, and network of relationships, and who carries his or her own views of problems and goals and solutions—is likely to effect positive change.

THE INFLUENCE OF MOTIVATIONS, RESISTANCES, AND COPING STYLES.   In building interventions to fit what clients want, need, and can use, the worker needs to fine-tune intervention efforts according to the client's and other actors' motivations, resistance, and coping styles. For example:

- Where is the push for change, who has it, and how can it be protected and enhanced?
- What are the interfering personal fears, interpersonal patterns, and social structures?
- How can they be minimized?

- How does the client go about reducing stress and fearfulness (e.g., denial, with-drawal, self-blame, support-seeking, problem-solving action, self-management, blaming others)?
- Can these coping patterns be used or managed?
- Do they need to be altered?

THE INFLUENCE OF INCOMING INFORMATION ABOUT PROGRESS AND PROCESS

Finally, the practitioner needs to continually adjust or alter interventions according to incoming information about the progress and process of change. For example:

> If the client is not making the expected progress, the worker must question why. "Are the client and I waiting for each other to provide the focus and direction? Is the big issue between the client and her partner? Is the client's life so chaotic that what I of-fer in the outpatient clinic is wiped away the minute he leaves? How can I readjust my approach to check out some of these hunches? Now that we are working together, do I see patterns that tell me something about how this client accomplishes change? How can I adjust my approach to provide more opportunities for these patterns to emerge and to support them when they do?"

A significant amount of theoretical knowledge, empirical findings, and prac-tice wisdom is encapsulated in the practice guidelines provided in this chapter. Nonetheless, they are not exhaustive or exact; nor are they meant to be prescrip-tive. They leave a great deal of a room for creativity and experimentation. The work of Beutler and Clarkin (1990) represents an alternative and more systematic effort to match interventions to problems. Their approach is heroic in its complexity and is characterized by its personal psychological perspective, strong empirical base, and prescriptive classification and comparison approach. We recommend a thor-ough reading of Beutler and Clarkin's book, but we briefly highlight aspects of their model here.

A TREATMENT SELECTION MODEL

Drawing from several theory-based approaches to change (e.g., cognitive, behavioral, psychodynamic, expressive, family systems) as well as the work of other researchers seeking robust techniques across theories (e.g., Lazarus, 1981; Norcross, 1986a, b), Beutler and Clarkin started out by developing a list of variables that might be expected to interact with interventions to influence outcome. They went on locate the most promising predictors "by tabulating the relationship of these variables to differential outcome rates reported in the empirical literature (Beutler, 1979, 1983, 1991; Frances, Clarkin, & Perry, 1984). The resulting treatment selection model is theoretically grounded and builds on the accumulation of previous empirical work. As noted, it is based on a classification and comparison approach to intervention decision making, and it looks primarily to pretreatment assessment data to find the client and problem characteristics that need to be considered in selecting treatments. To date, results of attempts to test parts of the model tend to support its predictions (Beutler, Engle, et al., 1991; Beutler, Mohr, et al., 1991). It is likely, however, that further tests will suggest modifications.

The Beutler and Clarkin model lays out a sequence of increasingly fine-grained decisions that lead to the selection and modulation of therapeutic strategies and techniques. As noted, the nature of the decision points in the model are based on the authors' synthesis of empirical and theoretical literature about the dimensions or variables most likely to predict clients' intervention. The variables they view as most important are contained within four major categories: patient predisposing variables, treatment context, relationship variables, and strategies and techniques (see Figure 11.1). Decisions made within each of these categories are directly or indirectly influenced by all the previous decisions. Moreover, the variables within each category often influence each other.

Starting with "patient predisposing variables," Beutler and Clarkin pull together a number of client-related characteristics that are frequently highlighted as related to therapy outcome. They include the following:

Problem area

Symptoms or syndrome

Expectations about therapy

Expectations about social roles

Problem severity

Current problem-solving efforts

Motivation and compliance

Problem complexity

Interpersonal reactance

Coping style

Environmental stressors

Environmental resources

Having developed a perspective on which client characteristics are likely to be predictive of outcomes, Beutler and Clarkin go on to link these characteristics with their views of available treatment options, including treatment context, relationship possibilities, and strategies and techniques.

Beutler and Clarkin recommend distinguishing among interventive procedures according to their distinctive goals, tasks, and procedural requirements. This is a critical step that is often overlooked in discussions of matching clients to intervention. It is also overlooked in actual practice. Theorists, teachers, supervisors, and line practitioners all seem to agree that assessing clients is important because certain person and problem constellations tend to call for certain interventions. So far, so good. But unless we also clarify intervention options and understand their objectives and requirements, we are left with complicated details about the client, on the one hand, and very little to match that understanding with, on the other.

Beutler and Clarkin classify therapeutic procedures according to several hierarchically arranged dimensions: the breadth of their primary outcome goals, the level or depth of experience the procedure addresses, mediating tasks, and therapy structure. By matching intervention characteristics to client characteristics,

FIGURE 11.1
Beulter and Clarkin's Model of treatment selection decisions. *From: Beulter and Clarkin, 1990; reprinted by permission.*

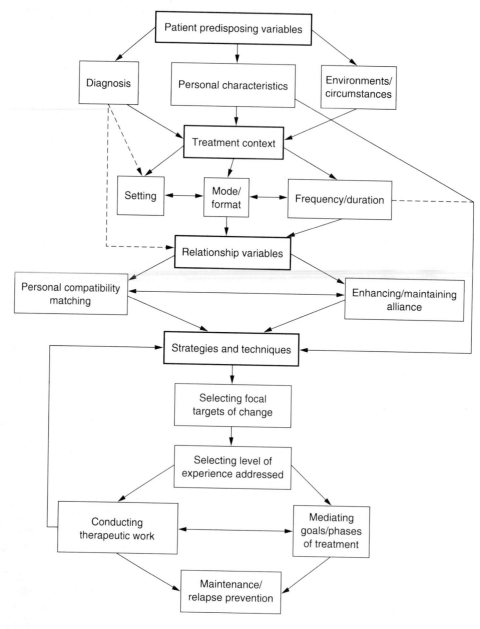

the model sequentially generates an overall focus (matches the breadth of focus of the intervention to the complexity of the client's problem), a potential menu of intervention options (matches the level of experience targeted by the intervention with client's coping style), and fine-tuned activities (matches overall focus and phase-specific goals with the client's current level of stress, reactance, and problem-solving progress).

LINKING TREATMENTS TO CLIENTS AND/OR PROBLEMS

Going through the exercise of trying to closely link dimensions of the client's experience to intervention actions is useful because it reminds us of things to think about and try with specific clients; it alerts us to categories of interventions we need to learn more about; and it allows us to critically review our linking strategies (for example, "does this really make sense?"). But engaging in this process also raises other important questions and issues about clinical decisions. For example: Does linking treatments to client experiences mean that the clinician prescribes interventions? What is the client's role? What dimensions of the client experience are the best clues to how interventions should be chosen and altered? What intervention possibilities actually exist? What happens to all these guidelines and plans in the actual client and worker interaction? Are these few guidelines really all we know how to do?

Prescription or Problem Solving

In the same way that assessing the problem is a shared effort involving both the clinician and the client, figuring out what to do about the problem optimally involves both people over the entire course of the therapy. Although the clinician is expected to bring to the process ideas about different ways to approach change, this does not mean that he or she can reliably prescribe effective means for achieving change. "Take these two little pills (or follow this interpersonal skills training exercises) and your battering husband will become gentle; your acting-out children will become cooperative; a no-cost, high-quality nursing home will spring up to take care of your aging, ill mother; and you will find the sense of purpose and competence and security that has eluded you for the past 40 years." Although we should have some good ideas about how to start working on these problems and some warranted options to try, we do not know how to prescribe precisely the treatment that will reliably make problems go away. We cannot know in advance if the theory or evidence or personal bias that we are drawing on will help or if it will need to be adjusted for this particular client at this moment in time. We can increase the probabilities of being helpful by relying on theories that have the most direct bearing on the client's problems and by considering interventions that have been tried before with similar clients. But in the final analysis, our good ideas are only good if they make sense to this client. If he or she can grab onto them, rework them, and link them up with some of his or her own ideas, then they are good. We err when our zeal to accurately classify rides roughshod over the client's own sensibilities.

For reasons that are both pragmatic and value based, we need to work *with* the client, not *on* the client. It is important to focus more on enhancing active engagement than on compliance, and to think of the change process more in terms of collaborative problem solving and empowerment than prescription.

Predicting Change

Practitioners, in search of good ideas to bring to the problem-solving process, usually seek ideas that involve predicting change. Essentially, practitioners try to figure out which factors are most important predictors of how clients or problems will change. There are several approaches to this predicting task. Traditionally, most emphasis has been placed on finding the client or problem characteristics that will predict responses to particular kinds of interventions. Because psychotherapy studies have failed to find many robust treatment-by-client interactions, theorists have been pressed to think about predicting change in different ways. One alternative suggests that various kinds of interventions exert positive influence through a set of common factors that provide a supportive boost to almost everyone (Frank, 1982; Goldfried, 1980). A similar perspective suggests that the real power behind therapeutic change resides in the relationship between the client and practitioner (e.g., Orlinsky & Howard, 1986a; Strupp & Binder, 1984). Another position is that the most direct way to predict how people will respond to various therapeutic approaches is to observe them in the process of change (Greenberg & Pinsoff, 1986a; Rice & Greenberg, 1984). Finally, there is a point of view that suspects predictability is an illusion (Goldstein, 1992; Harrison, 1991; Saleebey, 1992).

PRETREATMENT PREDICTORS   The assumption that pretreatment variables— client and problem characteristics—will predict responses to different kinds of interventions has strong intuitive appeal. The importance of tailoring interventions to fit clients' particular needs is repeatedly addressed in social work direct practice literature (cf. Rosen, Proctor, & Livne, 1985). As noted in Chapter 9, there is evidence to suggest that some treatments that have been specifically designed to interfere with particular problems, for example, sexual dysfunctions, phobias and compulsions, childhood behavior disorders, and marital conflicts, show superior outcomes. Even so, the preponderance of psychotherapy studies have failed to reveal consistent differences in the effects of different therapies (e.g., Lambert, Shapiro, & Bergin, 1986; Luborsky, Singer, & Luborsky, 1975; Smith, Glass, & Miller, 1980). At the same time, the considerable within-condition variance that psychotherapy studies have found indicates that clients do respond differently to similar treatments. We know that, given the same interventions, some clients do better than others, but we do not know very much about why (Beutler, 1991). Only a few investigations have been specifically designed to focus on untangling the ways in which client characteristics join up with treatment techniques to facilitate positive change (e.g., Beutler Mohr, Graw, Engle, & MacDonald, 1991).

In part, this must be because the untangling task is not an easy one. In his review of summaries of research reported in the *Handbook of Psychotherapy and Behavior Change* (Garfield & Bergin, 1986), Beutler (1991) counted 175 categories of patient characteristics and 40 categories of therapist characteristics that have been advanced as potential influences in treatment. Combining these client and therapist characteristics with the 50 or more categories that emerge from the 300-plus brand-name treatments presents an overwhelming number of client-therapy-therapist interactions that could be studied in order to locate the optimal combinations (p. 226–227). Beutler (1991) notes that many of the client and therapist variables that have been explored as potential predictors have only weak connections to theories of psychotherapy, were not measured in reliable and valid ways, and were often "selected on the basis of convenience and, perhaps spurious, earlier empirical findings" (p. 227). This observation suggests that the enormity of the research task to locate meaningful interactions can be decreased and the potential for its success increased by ensuring that there is good reason (e.g., theoretical backing or converging empirical findings) that a given variable will make a difference. As noted above, Beutler and Clarkin (1990) have taken this approach in their work to construct a treatment selection model.

COMMON FACTORS   In the face of "no difference" findings, some theorists (e.g., Frank, 1982; Garfield, 1980; Goldfried, 1980; Parloff, 1986) have focused their attention on the common features of different therapies. They suggest that despite technical variations between different therapies, change occurs because of the so-called nonspecific variables that are common across therapies (e.g., empathy, respect, positive expectations, encouragement, exposure to what is feared, corrective experiences, and emotional arousal). Based on their review of studies examining the relationship between psychotherapy processes and outcome, Orlinsky and Howard (1986) report inconsistent to weak relationships between therapy techniques (e.g., confrontation, interpretation, reflection, advice, support) and client outcome, but a significantly positive relationship between various dimensions of the therapeutic bond. These findings support the perspective of many theorists who believe that the power of change does not reside in specific techniques, but rather in the dynamics of the client and therapist relationship. As Strupp and Binder (1984) see it, "One changes as one lives through affectively painful but engrained interpersonal scenarios, and as the therapeutic relationship gives them outcomes different from those expected, anticipated, feared, and sometimes hoped for" (p. 35). Similarly, Kempler (1980) explains that

> all of us—therapists, patients, people—change according to what happens or doesn't happen between ourselves and certain powerful or influential significant others regardless of how those others are empowered—through one's love, one's respect, or the others' force. The how, of course, contributes to the character of the changing. The ingredient essential in the changing process from my perspective is the presence of a worthy other: someone to be reckoned with, someone who can empower, to measure oneself by or to lay oneself in the hands of, the worthy witness who knows when and how to give a hand or point a finger. (p. 289)

At the same time, others suggest that different approaches do influence different effects, but to date researchers have not been able to detect which approaches affect which outcomes. For example, Stiles (1983) reports data that indicate that different psychotherapies utilize strikingly divergent techniques (Brunink & Schroeder, 1979; Hill, Thames, & Rardin, 1979; Stiles, 1979; Strupp, 1955). Even though these different techniques do not seem to generate different degrees of improvement, Stiles suggests that they open up "different ranges of options for their clients," that is, different pathways to improvement and different models of health (pp. 186–187). In these terms, the hypothesis to be tested is "that different therapies turn out systematically different kinds of healthy people" (p. 187).

As we noted in Chapter 9, an increasingly influential perspective argues that the absence of differential effects results from inadequate understanding of the mechanisms of change within each approach. Rice and Greenberg (1984) elaborate: "It seems to be assumed that the specified treatment variable, when administered to a group of clients homogeneous on some individual difference variable, will 'take' in a similar fashion with most of the clients, resulting in a relatively homogeneous client response to treatment" (p. 12). They go on to suggest that this perspective is a variant of the uniformity myth, in this case, a myth that there is uniformity in the change process: Clients who have some similar characteristics or traits will respond to the same therapy in the same fashion and thereby achieve similar results. Furthermore, they claim that this myth has led to both statistical and conceptual problems in psychotherapy research. In a sense, the major statistical problem occurs because the myth is not true; clients are not uniform. In many studies, the differences between clients is so great that it is impossible to determine whether there are differences between treatments. The conceptual problem arises when clients are considered to be "fixed variables."

As Mischel (1973) has pointed out, in the domain of personality, human beings are just too good at making discriminations to be treated as fixed variables in person-situation interactions, and thus the research focus must shift from "attempting to compare and generalize about what different individuals are like to an assessment of what they do behaviorally and cognitively in relation to the psychological conditions in which they do it" (p. 265).

Rice and Greenberg's conclusion is that, instead of grouping people together in some static trait category, the criterion for forming samples should be that clients are in a similar "problem-space." Instead of studying kinds of people, they suggest studying kinds of therapy episodes. Their notion is that intense scrutiny of how clients go about changing within episodes will help to illuminate the differential effects question by specifying what client performance strategies are set in motion by what therapist interventions at what particular points in therapy (p. 13).

As you will recall, this rationale is the basis for the task analysis approach to process assessment discussed in Chapters 9 and 10. In the "assessment to intervention" example mentioned earlier we have, however, relied on static trait and process approaches to matching interventions with clients. In the initial stages of intervention, we think that one needs to at least consider how particular kinds of clients are likely to go about the change process. As soon as possible, however, the practitioner is well advised to observe how each individual client reacts to specific change opportunities, because these process data provide the most direct cues about how to support client change. Moreover, we continue to believe that both common and diverse factors can influence therapy outcomes. Although change occurs in the context of important interpersonal relationships, we assume that the operation and focus of the relationships do matter.

IS PREDICTABILITY AN ILLUSION?   Is prediction even possible? It takes little argument to persuade social workers that life is not very static, uniform, stable, consistent, or predictable. As Goldstein (1992) suggests, "given the contingencies, quirks, and sometimes risks of daily life, it is safe to say that mind and body are altogether restless, in motion, and at least slightly out of balance, and watchful to monitor and cope with whatever may come along next" (p. 34).

We believe that even if our physical, social, economic, and personal worlds are not entirely predictable, neither are they totally random. We think that life is characterized by a tension between stability and plasticity, predictability and surprise, regularities and chaos. The fact that humans are able to cope with what comes along next suggests that we all have discerned some regularities in the way life works. We agree that life is uncertain and that predictability is often illusive. This means that tidy cause-and-effect relationships will be hard to find and, if found, may not be very meaningful. However we should not give up trying to discern patterns and regularities that give us at least a partial picture of how people manage themselves and their lives. As we have noted earlier, the fluidity of human life and experience inclines us to look more closely to process characteristics (how people are changing) than to static pretreatment variables for the most direct ideas about how to help that change.

What Do Clinicians Really Do?
(Approaches vs. Responses)

It is worth considering what possibilities exist with respect to intervention choices. The number of therapy approaches seems to be steadily on the rise. By some accounts there are currently about 330 different ways to achieve psychological relief, but when it comes down to the kinds of things that clinicians actually say to clients in therapy, there are significantly fewer categories of responses. For example, Hill's (1989) categorization includes nine therapist response groups: approval, providing information, direct guidance, closed question, open question, paraphrase, interpretation, confrontation, and self-disclosure. Elliott and his associates (Elliott, Hill, Stiles, Friedlander, Mahrer, & Margison, 1987) found six categories of therapy responses: questions, providing information, advising, reflecting, interpretation, and self-disclosure.

There is evidence to suggest that practitioners make different use of these response categories depending on their theoretical orientations (cf. Stiles, 1983). Although we usually think of therapy as including much more than response categories (e.g., content, relational context, affect, purpose, theoretical and value assumptions), it may sometimes be helpful to consider the paired-down choices (e.g., should I confront, question, paraphrase, etc.?) and include them in our skill repertoire. In her intensive study of eight short-term psychotherapy cases, Hill (1989) found that self-disclosure, intrepretation, and approval were rated by all the clients as helpful. Seven of eight clients found paraphrasing helpful. Direct guidance, open questions, and confrontation were seen as helpful by some clients. Although closed questions and providing information were frequently used, they were rarely viewed as helpful, and closed questions were sometimes seen as hindering. With respect to therapeutic communications, we also know from Benjamin's (1984) SASB model (see Chapter 9) that different therapist communications tend to evoke different interpersonal responses on the dimensions of autonomy-submission and hostility-affiliation.

Knowing More Than You Can Say

Performing the assessment-to-intervention (see p. 211) exercise convinced us that we do not know enough about how to help people solve problems but that we do know more than we can say. Simon (1969) observes, "The capacity of the human mind for formulating and solving complex problems is very small compared with the size of the problem whose solution is required for objectively rational behavior in the real world" (pp. 198,199). Nonetheless, in spite of hugely complex problems and limited information-processessing capacities, humans solve problems. We figure things out, adapt, adjust, and, so far, survive. Our models of reality (including models of helping) are clearly imperfect and always will be, but they bear sufficient correspondence to the way things operate to have allowed us some arenas of progress.

At the same time, a lot of what we know as humans and practitioners is not easily verbalized. It is one thing to interact with a client—to adjust, modulate, intensify, try-and-err, and try something a little different—and quite another to explain to oneself or others what all those variations are about and why one chooses to use them. We do not know and cannot say everything we did. Our ability to discern and respond is greatly extended because we do not have to consciously "think through" every little perception that registers and every little response we make. We conduct much of our problem solving and decision making at an automatic, unconscious level.

It is important to remember, however, that this unconscious feature does not necessarily make the knowledge any more perfect. In fact, much of this book argues for reflecting back on some of these automatic decisions to ensure that they take us in useful directions. At the same time, Schön (1983) reminds us of the importance of knowledge that is revealed and gained through action.

> Common sense admits the category of "know-how," and it does not stretch common sense to say that the know-how is in the action—that a tightrope walker's know-how, for example, lies in and is revealed by the way he takes his trip across the wire, or that a big-league pitcher's know-how is in his way of pitching to a batter's weakness,

changing his pace, or distributing his energies over the course of a game. There is nothing to suggest that know-how consists of rules or plans that our minds entertain prior to action. Although we sometimes think before acting, it is also true that in much of the spontaneous behavior of skillful practice we reveal a kind of know-how that does not stem from a prior intellectual operation. (Schön, 1983, pp. 50–51)

In his work, Schön (1983, 1987) draws distinctions between knowing that is synonymous with action (knowing-in-action); planning or thinking through actions to be taken (reflection-on-action), and on-line improvisation and problem solving (reflection-in-action). He goes on to argue that educational programs for practitioners are usually inadequate in the sense that trainees tend to be exposed to massive doses of theory and research that provide guidance about what to do under static, ideal conditions, but that offer very little opportunity to learn how to meet the demands of uncertainty, uniqueness, and ambiguity that are the hallmarks of real-world practice. They have few opportunities for practice ("knowing-in-action") or for reflecting on practice before, after, or during practice ("reflection-on-action" and "reflection-in-action").

Schön notes the importance of applied science *and* research-based techniques in professional practice but argues that science and technical knowledge are most useful when artfully applied. The artistry of problem framing, implementation, and improvisations are "all necessary to mediate the use in practice of applied science and technique" (Schön, 1987, p. 13). To illustrate:

☐   Inez is an intake social worker. She is a real "pro." After having conducted over 8,000 intake interviews, Inez carries them out smoothly, with great skill and poise. Without a great deal of conscious deliberation, she executes smooth sequences of activity, recognition, decisions, and judgment. Inez's knowledge is mostly "know-how" or knowledge that is revealed in action. She is not very good at describing what she does, but she is very good at doing it.

Inez's automatic routines work very well. Clients like her; she collects a lot of information in a short time; and she seems to have great instincts for knowing who should work with which clients. But given the irregularities of clinical practice, she often encounters situations that do not quite fit her procedural categories. Luckily, she has the acuity to recognize those instances, reassess the situation, try something different, see how that works out, and move ahead. Inez has mastered the arts of problem framing, implementation, and improvisation.

Inez's artistry is continually nourished by her experiences, by her ongoing actions and interactions. It is also renewed by her mindfulness about her work. She reflects back on her own actions and wonders if she did the best thing, if she really understood what the client was saying, what would have happened if she had taken another course. Sometimes she wonders if she is getting too callous or if she too readily diagnoses individual problems and overlooks the community and neighborhood contributions to the problems. These reflections have an effect on her subsequent work. Moreover, she is still open to incorporating new ideas. She is willing to learn from the young social work interns and psychiatry residents who rotate through her operation every year. She reads, consults with others, and attends conferences and workshops. And she thinks about how to implement these new ideas.

It might be tempting to say that Inez is "a natural." She certainly seems like she was born to do this work. But her knowledge is not a function of genetics. Like the tightrope walker and the baseball player, she has worked hard—with deliberateness—to develop her artistry. As a part of her education, she studied a set of general rules from applied social science theories and research-based techniques. From all the talk at school about "individualizing," "use of self," "empathy," "common sense," she developed some general ideas about how to generate responses to unique situations, and she began the painstaking process of translating all the "book learning," this rational and technical knowledge, into effective actions via practice.

At first her efforts were self-conscious and sometimes awkward. Nonetheless, she could describe, quite fluently, what she was doing. "I am trying to start where the client is." "I am trying to get agreement on a target problem." "I am trying to make the client feel respected." Gradually, she became more practiced, more proficient; her actions became more routinized. She also got better at transposing plans into action, reframing, and improvising. Over the years, she has learned new theories and techniques and how to execute innumerable variations (more than she can say) on all her theoretical and empirical knowledge. She has not become less articulate, just more proficient.

SUMMARY

In this chapter, we have discussed intervention action, moving from assessment or understanding to action. We believe that effective action is based on an evolving understanding and the premeditated plans and creative innovations that can emanate from it. Part of this understanding is informed by what Schön might call technical rationality, by theoretical and empirical knowledge about people, social situations, problems, and change. We recommend using this kind of understanding to plan ahead—to think through the options that are likely to be most helpful to the client given how you understand him or her and how both of you look at the goals of your work together.

Another part of the understanding and planning occurs in process. It occurs as the practitioner tries to change the problem. To paraphrase Schön (1983), in the same move, the practitioner tests his or her hypothesis of what the problem is about, tries to effect a change, and explores the problem further (p. 151). We think it is important to use the concept of reflection-in-action. At the same time, the artistry of implementation, reframing, and improvisation comes about via practice, reflection, and more practice (reflection-in-action, reflection-on-action, and more reflection-in-action).

12 | Summary

S ocial workers are asked to assist clients in undoing or minimizing the consequences of serious social, physical, and psychological deprivations and intrusions. As direct-service practitioners, we perform our work by securing close relationships with clients, enabling us to generate solutions that fit with their sensibilities and capacities and that offer the experience of human connection and support. We look to theories and research to supplement our personal knowledge about how people progress through difficult circumstances, and we rely heavily on the results of our moment-to-moment direct experiences of working with the client and our observations of what happens when we try to help.

As we abstract knowledge from all these sources and expand our schemas about practice—expand the categories we have for understanding client situations and for generating interventive actions—we become more complex thinkers, more sophisticated clinicians. We become more able to discern subtle distinctions and to construct differential responses. As we expand our ability to generate ideas about a large range of phenomena, we become more secure in what we know and less likely to encounter situations that cause us to question or revise our entire framework. Similarly, as we take actions that seem to prompt positive responses, we tend to rely on those actions. In Bandura's (1986) words, "hitting upon a sufficient alternative is likely to dissuade the search for an even better one" (p. 131).

Despite this conservative aspect of expertise, being expert is a good thing. Within the domain of his or her own expertise, the expert clinician is able to generate more options and show greater flexibility in understanding and responding than the novice. But expert and novice alike need to be concerned about the extent to which their clinical decisions are diminished (or improved) by the way they are thinking about the case.

Because judgments are generally dominated by knowledge structures (schemata) and heuristic information-processessing shortcuts, clinical judgments can be more influenced by tangential considerations—for example, the practitioner's personal life, the predilections of a favorite professor, the vividness of certain client responses, or the practitioner's habits of diagnosing—than by the client's needs, interests, and capabilities. We need to be aware of these habits of mind and continually step back to consider whether the knowledge we are generating serves the client.

Do the ideas that I am generating serve the client?

Am I relying on the most relevant theories (experts' theories)—the ones that bear directly on the client's dilemma and are, in some version, comprehensible to and usable by him?

Am I taking into account empirically generated knowledge and considering relevant findings from good studies?

Am I sufficiently aware of my own personal beliefs and values to know, within a given circumstance, whether they are helpful, inadequate, or destructive?

Do I learn from my own practice experience? Do I have a system for tracking and organizing the critical aspects of that experience? Is the client getting better? How is that happening? What is getting in the way?

Do I maximize opportunities for discovery and new learning by continuously looking beyond "what works" for what might work better, by consciously looking for the unexpected, and by reconsidering conclusions arrived at on the basis of automatic thinking and the biases inherent therein?

Throughout the book, we have offered guidelines like the ones listed above, but nowhere have we spelled out the exact way to make constructive clinical decisions. If there is such a way, frankly, we do not know it. We continue to believe that there is more than one useful way to think about and respond to a client situation. At the same time, we also believe that all ways of understanding and responding are not equally useful. Our advice is to think about this, reconsider that, look at things from another way, put your "toe in the water," try something, and learn from your experience.

We advise you to be aware of preconceptions you have about your client, yet we also know that without them, clinicians would literally be lost. Moreover, if one has had a rich personal and professional life, including a good professional education, the resultant schemas for understanding are likely to be quite helpful. From this "on the one hand" and "on the other hand" equivocation, the clearest thing we can say is to be mindful of your preconceptions: Question them, seek to alter them through exploration and an intent to discover, and finally, subject them to the critical, "client-serving" test: Do your preconceptions provide you with increased understanding and generate actions that help the client get better?

Be wary of behavioral confirmation, the kind of self-fulfilling prophesying that leads clients to respond in a way that supports the clinician's preconceptions. Prompting someone to respond in exactly the way you expect limits the flow of new information and thereby limits the possibilities for creative and on-target interventive responses. On the other hand, therapy is often characterized as a social influence process. It is routine for clinicians to try explicitly to influence their clients to adopt new perspectives. For example, clinicians commonly model a "this problem is understandable and potentially solvable" attitude to their clients. The hope is that clients will incorporate this sense of optimism and use it to fuel work on what had originally seemed like overwhelming and intractable situations.

Although the most successful and ethical therapeutic work is focused toward the client's goals and fits with how he or she operates, when the client improves, these improvements are almost inevitably colored by the therapist's views. Shaping the client's responses is part of the process, but it can go too far. Once again, there is no exact guideline. We can only ask ourselves if the ways we are influencing seem to be helping the client realize what he or she wants.

We note that information-processing heuristics are necessary, efficient, and often accurate. They allow us to respond quickly without getting bogged down in overwhelming detail. Indeed, life without heuristics would plunge us into a deep abyss of obsessiveness: "Should I tie my shoes this way or this way?" "Should I say hello and then offer her a seat or should it be the reverse?"

On the other hand, thinking shortcuts can sometimes blur the really critical distinctions that might otherwise influence decisions in another, more useful direction. We do not have sufficient on-line memory to hold all the potentially important variables in our minds at one time or to weigh how much we want each to influence our judgments. Nonetheless, we can review the judgments and wonder if and how our biases interfere with generating more useful conclusions.

Certainly, gathering quantitative and qualitative evidence about how the client is or is not progressing introduces an important stream of information to deliberations about how to understand and assist the client. The rules of science are designed to protect findings from the theoretical, personal, and thinking process biases that we have been discussing. But the protection is never complete. The nature of the questions that are asked, the kinds of information that are taken as data, and the ways findings are interpreted are all necessarily influenced by preconceptions. Moreover, "a little evidence can be a dangerous thing" if it becomes a barrier to further discovery.

As Kirk and Miller (1986) suggest, the unique contribution of empiricism is not that findings are entirely free of the "footprints" of the researcher, but rather that empiricism produces demonstrable knowledge. In contrast to logical argument and personal opinion, empiricism generates reproducible (reliable), publicly observable demonstration. This publicly observable quality gives empirical knowledge a measure of objectivity in the sense of agreement among observers. Even so, the "facts" of experience are still mutable—open to question, changeable, and relative. They allow us warrantable conjectures, not absolute truth (Mahoney, 1976). Kirk and Miller (1986) explain this as follows:

> A commitment to objectivity does not imply a desire to "objectify" the subject matter by "overmeasurement" (Etzioni, 1964), or to facilitate authoritarian social relation- ships by treating human beings as though they were certain features they may happen to have. It does not presuppose any radically positivist view of the world; it emphati- cally eschews the search for final, absolute "truth".... (p. 11)
>
>   Relaxing certain of the narrow definitions of the hypothetico-deductive mode... facilitates discovery of the new and unexpected. It would be an error, however, to drop the scientific concern for objectivity. The scientific credo is one good way to permit

the resolution of a conflict of opinion. It is not the only way; the scholastic solution, still prevalent in many disciplines... relies on argument and rhetoric rather than on argument and demonstrations. (p. 18)

Despite the importance of empirical knowledge, it is insufficient for guiding practice. Clear theoretical conceptualization, commitments and values, spontaneous improvisation, intuitive hunches, empathic understanding, and empirically derived data are interdependent components of a dynamic knowledge that is relevant to practice (Reid, 1990). Each component carries a particular strength that is best suited for addressing particular questions. For example, intuition plays an important role in the process of discovery; knowledge generated from empathy contributes to an affective understanding of the client's dilemma; observational knowledge is particularly useful for testing conclusions; and theories give us clues about what to look for and how to organize and understand what we observe. Together, these sources of knowledge provide a filled-out picture; each offers a context for and a check on the others. If parts of the picture do not fit, we are alerted to what we might have missed or misinterpreted.

> Janine Elliot, MSW, is sitting in on the staff meeting of the family counseling agency where she has been employed for 2 years. She is dutifully trying to pull herself out of a personal reverie in order to concentrate on the words of her colleague, Stewart Halstom. He appears, thankfully, to be bringing his case presentation to a close. "Actually, I'm not sure why I think that the main dynamic behind James's stealing is a 'family secret,'" he offers, "somehow, it just feels right." Ah yes, Janine thinks, the feel-right criteria... never mind that at James's school, stealing is the norm, or that he is stealing pencils and candy while the other kids are taking bicycles and jackets. Never mind that the only secret in his family is that his Mom is so overwhelmed with having to deal with little Rupert, Lee Ann, and Benjie—and the welfare worker—and Mr. Halstrom that she hasn't even talked to James about his stealing.... No longer able to contain herself, Janine shifts in her chair and says, "You know, Stewart, it doesn't feel right to me."

If you were at the meeting, would you take a side in the ensuing discussion? Would you agree with Stewart or think Janine made a good point? How would you figure it out? Maybe Janine is overreacting and Stewart is on to something. Perhaps he has picked up cues from the client family that he has subsequently forgotten but that have nonetheless influenced his impressions about a family secret and emerge now as intuition. It is also possible that, for reasons having little to do with his clients, he is so enamored with certain family treatment concepts that he tends to rely on them whether they fit or not.

Perhaps, then, Janine Elliot's more data-driven assessment approach yields superior explanations and blueprints for treatment. She is, after all, admirably careful in the way she ties her conclusions to observable evidence. Such practices could give her the advantage—but not necessarily. It may be that, aside from the data in hand, she has such a limited fund of knowledge about this and similar situations (e.g., limited theoretical understanding of the dynamics of poor families, a poor empathic grasp of the client's particular dilemma) that she fails to fully grasp the incompleteness or narrowness of her conclusions.

Without data, intuitive breakthroughs and even more explicit theories are ephemeral. They constitute the stories we make up about what is happening with our clients and what would help them. Similarly, without pertinent prior knowledge about what to look for and how to understand what we find, the data-driven explanations that we generate may give us a lot of evidence about nothing.

If you were participating in the meeting, you might want to pursue the following line of questioning:

> Stewart, what is the evidence for the family secret explanation? In the absence of evidence, what is the source of this hunch? Are you operating from a set of beliefs about what generates stealing in kids? What are they? Where do they come from? Does this explanation make sense to James and his family? Are they able to use it to increase their understanding of the problem and what to do about it? What kinds of intervention strategies does this explanation suggest? How have you acted on them in working with James and his family? What has been the result? Is the situation improving? Is there anything else about the situation or anything that James, his mother, or the teacher has said or done that would suggest an alternative way to understand and intervene?

How would you want to follow-up with Janine? Although she seems to be on a reasonable track, you might ask her what she makes of her observations:

> What does this all add up to? How should we put these facts together to understand James' stealing? Does this kind of explanation make sense to James and his family? Are they able to use it to increase their understanding and options? Does it suggest intervention strategies to you? How would you proceed? Is there an alternative way to understand this same evidence? Is there other evidence that you are not focusing on that might suggest different ways of understanding and intervening?

We hope that these are the kinds of questions you will ask yourself as you gather, weigh, and make judgments about information that ultimately bears on clients' well-being.

From its infancy to the present, social work has struggled with a dualism that defines direct practice as an art and a science (Weick, 1987). In part, the art-science tension endures because the profession finds itself unable to accept an either-or resolution. The clinician is artful—she or he relies on intuition, creativity, and empathy—yet social work is more than art. The clinician grounds her or his inferences in recognizable patterns of personal-social interplay, yet the practitioner is not just a scientific thinker. She or he constructs plausible explanations of human functioning and yet is more than a theorist.

"Human sociocultural conduct is not reducible to any simple formula but may be discovered and explored through a variety of philosophical, theoretical, and methodological passageways. The more diversity of approach, conception, and strategy there is within the discipline, the better—we then have more chances for surprises, success, and learning from error" (Estroff, 1981, p. 17).

References

Abelson, R. P. (1976). Script processing in attitude formation and decision making. In J. S. Carroll & J. W. Payne (Eds.), *Cognition and social behavior* (pp. 33-46). Hillsdale, NJ: Erlbaum.

Abramson, L. Y., Alloy, L. B., & Metalsky, G. I. (1988). The cognitive diathesis stress theories of depression: Toward an adequate evaluation of the theories' validities. In L.B. Alloy (Ed.), *Cognitive processes in depression* (pp. 3–30). New York: Guilford.

Alloy, L. B., & Abramson, L. Y. (1988). Depressive realism: Four theoretical perspectives. In L. B. Alloy (Ed.), *Cognitive processes in depression* (pp. 223–265). New York: Guilford.

Almeleh, N., Soifer, S., Gottlieb, N., & Gutierrez, L. (in press). Women achieving personal and political empowerment through workplace activism. *Affilia: Journal of Women and Social Work.*

American Psychiatric Association. (1987). DSM-III-R: Diagnostic and statistical manual of mental disorders (3rd ed.). Washington, DC: Author.

Anderson, C. M., Reiss, D. J., & Hogarty, G. E. (1986). *Schizophrenia and the family: A practitioner's guide to psychoeducation and management.* New York: Guilford.

Anderson, J. R. (1990) *Cognitive Psychology and its Implications* (3rd ed.). New York: W. H. Freeman & Co.

Anderson, M. P. (1980). Imaginal processes: Therapeutic applications and theoretical models. In M. J. Mahoney (Ed.), *Psychotherapy process* (pp. 211–248). New York: Guilford.

Arnkoff, D. B. (1980). Psychotherapy from the perspective of cognitive theory. In M. J. Mahoney (Ed.), *Psychotherapy process* (pp. 339–361). New York: Plenum.

Ash, P. (1949). The reliability of psychiatric diagnoses. *Journal of Abnormal and Social Psychology, 44,* 272–277.

Baker, H. S., & Baker, M. N. (1987). Heinz Kohuts self-psychology: An overview. *American Journal of Psychiatry, 144,* 1–9.

Bales, R. F. (1950). Interaction process analysis: A method for the study of small groups. Cambridge, MA: Addison-Wesley.

Bandler, R., & Grinder, J. (1979). *Frogs into princes: Neurolinguistic programming.* Moab, UT: Real People Press.

Bandura, A. (1977). *Social learning theory.* Englewood Cliffs, NJ: Prentice Hall.

Bandura, A. (1986). *Social foundations of thought and action: A social cognitive theory.* New Jersey: Prentice Hall.

Barlow, D. H. (Ed.). (1985). *Clinical handbook of psychological disorders*. New York: Guilford.

Barlow, D. H., Hayes, S. C., & Nelson, R. O. (1984). *The scientist practitioner*. New York: Pergamon Press.

Bartlett, M. S. (1946). On the theoretical specification of sampling properties of autocorrelated time-series. *Journal of Royal Statistical Society (Series B), 8,* 27–47.

Batson, C. D. (1975). Attribution as a mediator of bias in helping. *Journal of Personality and Social Psychology, 72,* 455–466.

Batson, C. D., Jones, C. H., & Cochran, P. J. (1979). Attributional bias in counselors' diagnoses: The effect of resources on perception of need. *Journal of Applied Social Psychology, 9,* 377–393.

Batson, C. D. & Marz, B. (1979). Dispositional bias in trained therapists' diagnoses: Does it exist? *Journal of Applied Social Psychology, 5,* 476–489.

Batson, C. D., O'Quin, K., & Pych, V. (1982). An attribution theory analysis of trained helpers' inferences about clients' needs. In T. A. Wills (Ed.), *Basic Processes in Helping Relationships* (pp. 59–80). New York: Academic Press.

Battle, C., Imber, S. D., Hoehn-Saric, R., Stone, A. R., Nash, E. H., & Frank, J. D. (1966). Target complaints as criteria of improvement. *American Journal of Psychotherapy, 20,* 184–192.

Beach, S. R. H., Abramson, L. Y., & Levine, F. M. (1981). Attributional reformulation of learned helplessness and depression: Therapeutic implications. In J. F. Clarkin & H. I. Glazer (Eds.), *Depression: Behavioral and directive intervention strategies* (pp. 131–165). New York: Garland Press.

Beck, A. T., Rush, A. J., Shaw, B. F. & Emery, G. (1979). *Cognitive therapy for depression*. New York: Guilford.

Beck, A. T. Ward, C. H., Mendelson, M., Mock, J., & Erbaugh, T. (1961). An inventory for measuring depression. *Archives of General Psychiatry, 4,* 561–571.

Beck, A. T., & Young, J. E. (1985). Depression. In D. H. Barlow (Ed.), *Clinical handbook of psychological disorders* pp. 204–244. New York: Guilford.

Beere, C. A. (1979). *Women and women's issues: A handbook of tests and measures.* San Francisco, CA: Jossey-Bass.

Bellack, A. S., Hersen, M., & Himmelhoch, J. M. (1980). Social skills training for depression: A treatment manual. *JSAS Catalog of Selected Documents in Psychology, 10,* 92.

Belle, D. (1982). *Lives in stress: Women and depression.* San Diego: Sage Publication.

Benbenishty, R., & Ben Zahem, A. (1988). Computer-aided process of monitoring task-centered family interventions. *Social Work Research and Abstracts, 24*(1), 7–9.

Benjamin, L. S. (1979a). Structural analysis of differentiation failure. *Psychiatry: Journal for the Study of Interpersonal Processes, 42,* 1–23.

Benjamin, L. S. (1979b). Use of structural analysis of social behavior (SASB) and Markov chains to study dyadic interactions. *Journal of Abnormal Psychology, 88,* 303–319.

Benjamin, L. S. (1982). Use of structural analysis of social behavior (SASB) to guide interventions in psychotherapy. In J. Anchin & D. Kiesler (Eds.), *Handbook of interpersonal psychotherapy* (pp. 190–212). Oxford, England: Pergamon.

Benjamin, L. S. (1984). Principles of prediction using structural analysis of social behavior (SASB). In R. A. Zucker, J. Aronoff, & A. J. Radin (Eds.), *Personality and the prediction of behavior*. New York: Academic Press.

Benjamin, L. S. (1986). Adding social and intrapsychic descriptions to axis 1 of DSM3. In T. Millon & G. L. Klerman (Eds.), *Contemporary directions in psychopathology* (pp. 599–638). New York: Guilford.

Benjamin, L. S. (1987). Use of the SASB dimensional model to develop treatment plans for personality disorders. I: Narcissism. *Journal of Personality Disorders, 1,* 43–70.

Benjamin, L. S., Foster, S. W., Giat-Roberto, L., & Estroff, S. E. (1986). Breaking the family code: Analyzing videotapes of family interactions by structural analysis of social behavior. In L. S. Greenberg & W. M. Pinsoff (Eds.) (pp. 391–438). *The psychotherapeutic process: A research handbook.* New York: Guilford.

Benson, H. (1975). *The Relaxation response.* New York: Morrow.

Berlin, S. B. (1983). Single case evaluation: Another version. *Social Work Research and Abstracts, 19,* 3–19.

Berlin, S. B. (1990). The utility of change-process research for the education of practitioners and single-case evaluation. In L. Videka-Sherman & W. J. Reid (Eds.), *Advances in clinical social work research* (pp. 159–162). Silver Springs, MD: NASW Press.

Berlin, S. B. (1992). Therapy Events Forms. Unpublished instrument.

Berlin, S. B., & Johnson, C. G. (1989). Women and autonomy: Using structural analysis of social behavior to find autonomy within connections. *Psychiatry: Interpersonal and biological processes, 52,* 79–95.

Berlin, S. B., & Jones, L. E. (1983). Life after welfare: AFDC termination among long-term recipients. *Social Service Review, 57,* 378–402.

Berlin, S. B., Mann, K. B., & Grossman, S. F. (1991). Task-analysis of cognitive therapy for depression. *Social Work Research and Abstracts, 27,* 3–11.

Beutler, L. E. (1979). Toward specific psychological therapies for specific conditions. *Journal of Consulting and Clinical Psychology, 47,* 882–897.

Beutler, L. E. (1983). *Eclectic psychotherapy: A systematic approach.* New York: Pergamon.

Beutler, L. E. (1991). Have all won and must all have prizes? Revisiting Luborsky et al.'s verdict. *Journal of Consulting and Clinical Psychology, 59,* 226–232.

Beutler, L. E., & Clarkin, J. F. (1990). *Systematic treatment selection.* New York: Brunner/Mazel.

Beutler, L. E., Engle, D., Mohr, D., Daldrup, R. J., Bergan, J., Meredith, K., & Merry, W. (1991). Predictors of differential response to cognitive, experiential, and self-directed psychotherapeutic procedures. *Journal of Consulting and Clinical Psychology, 59,* 333–340.

Beutler, L. E., Mohr, D. C., Graw, K., Engle, D., & MacDonald, R. (1991). Looking for differential treatment effects: Cross-cultural predictors of differential psychotherapy efficacy. *Journal of Psychotherapy Integration, 1,* 121–141.

Bishop, J. B., & Richards, T. F. (1984). Counselor theoretical orientation as related to intake judgments. *Journal of Counseling Psychology, 31,* 398–401.

Bloom, M. (1975). *The paradox of helping: Introduction to the philosophy of scientific practice.* New York: John Wiley & Sons.

Bloom, M., & Fischer, J. (1982). *Evaluating practice: Guidelines for the accountable professional.* Englewood Cliffs, NJ: Prentice Hall.

Bordin, E. (1979). The generalizability of the psychoanalytic concept of the working alliance. *Psychotherapy: Theory Research and Practice, 16,* 252–260.

Borreson, A. M. (1965). Counselor influence on diagnostic classification of client problems. *Journal of Counseling Psychology, 12,* 252–258.

Boverman, I. K., Boverman, D. M., Clarkson, F. E., Rosenkranz, P. S., & Vogel, S. R. (1970). Sex-role stereotypes and clinical judgments of mental health. *Journal of Consulting and Clinical Psychology, 34,* 1–7.

Bower, G. H. (1981). Mood and memory. *American Psychologist, 36,* 129–148.

Bowers, K. S. (1981). Knowing more than we say leads to saying more than we know: On being implicitly informed. In D. Manasson (Ed.), *Toward a psychology of situations: An interactional perspective.* Hillsdale, NJ: Erlbaum.

Bowers, K. S. (1984). On being unconsciously influenced and informed. In K. S. Bowers

& D. Meichenbaum (Eds.), *The unconscious reconsidered* (pp. 227–272). New York: John Wiley & Sons.

Bowlby, J. (1977). The making and breaking of affectional bonds. *British Journal of Psychiatry, 130,* 201–210, 421–431.

Box, G. E., & Jenkins, G. (1970). *Time series analysis: Forecasting and control.* San Francisco: Holden-Day.

Box, G. E., & Tiao, G. C. (1975). Intervention analysis with applications to economic and environmental problems. *Journal of the American Statistical Association, 70,* 70–92.

Boyd-Franklin, N. (1989). *Black families in therapy: A multisystems approach.* New York: Guilford.

Briar, S., & Miller, H. (1971). *Problems and issues in social casework.* New York: Columbia University Press.

Brodsky, A. M. (1989). Sex, race and class issues in psychotherapy research. In A. M. Brodsky, J. D. Frank, A. E. Kazdin, M. J. Mahoney, & H. H. Strupp (Eds.) *Psychotherapy Research and Behavior Change* (pp. 123–150). Washington, D.C.: American Psychological Association.

Broverman, I. K., Broverman, D. M., Clarkson, F. E., Rosenkranz, P. S. & Vogel, S. R. (1970). Sex, race, stereotypes and clinical judgments of mental health. *Journal of Consulting and Clinical Psychology, 34,* 1–7.

Brower, A. M. (1988). Can the ecological model guide social work practice? *Social Service Review, 62,* 411–429.

Brunink, S. A., & Schroeder, H. E. (1979). Verbal therapeutic behavior of expert psychoanalytically-oriented, Gestalt, and Behavior therapists. *Journal of Consulting and Clinical Psychology, 47,* 567–574.

Bryman, A. (1984). The debate about quantitative and qualitative research: A question of method or epistemology? *British Journal of Sociology 35,* 75–92.

Budd, K., Rogers, A., & Schilmoeller, K. (1972). *Observation Training Manual.* University of Kansas: Department of Human Development.

Caldwell, Betty, M. HOME. Center for Child Development and Education, University of Arkansas at Little Rock, 33rd and University Avenue, Little Rock, Arkansas 72204.

Campbell, D. T. (1960). Blind variation and selective retention in creative thought as in other knowledge processes. *Psychological Review, 67,* 380–400.

Campbell, D. T., & Stanley, J. C. (1963). *Experimental and quasi- experimental designs for research.* Chicago: Rand-McNally & Co.

Cantor, N., & Kihlstrom, J. F. (1987). *Personality and social intelligence.* Englewood Cliffs, NJ: Prentice Hall.

Cantril, H. (1965). *The pattern of human concerns.* New Brunswick, NJ: Rutgers University Press.

Caplan, N., & Nelson, S. (1973). On being useful: The nature and consequence of psychological research on social problems. *American Psychologist, 28,* 199–211.

Chapman, L. J., and Chapman, J. P. (1969). Illusory correlation as an obstacle to the use of valid psychodiagnostic signs. *Journal of Abnormal Psychology, 74,* 271–280.

Chi, M. T. H., Fillovich, P. J., & Glaser, R. (1981). Categorization and representation of physics problems by experts and novices. *Cognitive Science, 5,* 121–152.

Chun, K., Cobb, S., & French, J. (1975). *Measures for psychological assessment.* Ann Arbor, MI: Institute for Social Research.

Ciarlo, J. A., Brown, T. R., Edwards, D. W., Kiresuk, T. J., & Newman, F. L. (1986). Chapter 2: A taxonomy of client outcome measures. In NIMH, Series FN No. 9, *Assessing mental health treatment outcome measurement techniques* (pp. 4–31). (DDHS Publication No. ADM 86-1301). Washington, DC: Superintendent of Documents, U.S. Government Printing Office.

Clark, C. F. (1988). Computer application in social work. *Social Work Research and Abstracts, 24*(1), 15–19.

Cohen, J. (1962). The statistical power of abnormal-social psychological research. *Journal of Abnormal and Social Psychology, 65*, 145–153.

Cohen, J. (1969). *Statistical power analysis in the behavioral sciences.* New York: Academic Press.

Cook, T. D., & Campbell, D. T. (1979). *Quasi-experimentation: Design and analysis for field settings.* Chicago: Rand-McNally & Co.

Crane, J. A. (1976). The power of social intervention experiments to discriminate between experimental and control groups. *Social Service Review.* 224–242.

Daldrup, R. J., Beutler, L. E., Engle, D., & Greenberg, L. S. (1988). *Focused expressive psychotherapy: Freeing the overcontrolled patient.* New York: Guilford.

Dangel, R. F., & Polster, R. A. (1988). *Teaching child management skills.* New York: Pergamon/Allyn & Bacon.

Davis, L. E., and Proctor, E. K. (1989). *Race, gender and class: Guidelines for practice with individuals, families and groups.* Englewood Cliffs, NJ: Prentice-Hall.

Dewey, J. (1971). *How we Think.* Chicago: Regency. (Originally published 1933.)

Edelson, J. (1985). Rapid-assessment instruments for evaluating practice with children and youth. *Journal of Social Service Research, 8*(38), 17–31.

Edwards, D. J. (1989). Cognitive restructuring through guided imagery: Lessons from Gestalt Therapy. In A. Freeman, K. M. Simon, L. E. Beutler, & H. Arkowitz (Eds.), *Comprehensive handbook of cognitive therapy* (pp. 283–298). New York: Plenum.

Eells, K., & Guppy, W. (1963). Counselors' valuations of and preferences for different types of counseling problems. *Journal of Counseling Psychology, 10*, 146–155.

Elliott, R. (1983). "That in your hands...": A comprehensive process analysis of a significant event in psychotherapy. *Psychiatry, 46*, 113–129.

Elliott, R. (1984). A discovery-oriented approach to significant events in psychotherapy: Interpersonal process recall and comprehensive process analysis. In L. Rice & L. S. Greenberg (Eds.), *Patterns of change* (pp. 249–286). New York: Guilford.

Elliott, R. (1986). Interpersonal process recall (IPR) as a psychotherapy process research method. In L. S. Greenberg & W. M. Pinsoff (Eds.), *The psychotherapeutic process: A research handbook* (pp. 503–527). New York: Guilford.

Elliott, R., Hill, C. E., Stiles, W. B., Friedlander, M. L., Mahrer, A. R., & Margison, F. R. (1987). Primary therapist response modes: Comparison of six rating systems. *Journal of Consulting and Clinical Psychology, 55*, 218–223.

Elliott, R., Shapiro, D. A., & McGlenn, M. (1986, June). *Brief structured recall: A more efficient method for identifying and describing significant therapy events.* Paper presented at meeting of Society for Psychotherapy Research, Wellesley, MA.

Ellis, A. (1973). *Humanistic psychotherapy.* New York: McGraw-Hill.

Elson, M. (1986). *Self-psychology in clinical social work.* New York: W. W. Norton.

Erlich, J., & Rivera, F. (Eds.). (1992). *Community organizing in a diverse society.* Boston: Allyn & Bacon.

Estroff, S. E. (1981). *Making It Crazy.* Berkeley: University of California Press, p. 17.

Etzioni, A. (1964). *Modern organizations.* Englewood Cliffs, NJ: Prentice Hall.

Evans, M. D., & Hollon, S. D. (1988). Patterns of personal and causal inference: Implications for the cognitive therapy of depression. In L. B. Alloy (Ed.), *Cognitive processes in depression* (pp. 344–377). New York: Guilford.

Feld, S., & Radin, N. (1982). *Social psychology for social work and the mental health professions.* New York: Columbia University Press.

Filsinger, E. E. (Ed.). (1983). *Marriage and family assessment: A sourcebook for family therapy.* Beverly Hills, Sage.

Finn, J. (1988). Microcomputers in private, nonprofit agencies: A survey of trends and training requirements. *Social Work Research and Abstracts, 24*(1), 10–14.

Fischer, J. & Corcoran, K. (1987) *Measures for Clinical Practice: A Sourcebook.* New York: The Free Press.

Fischoff, B. (1975). Hindsight and Foresight: The effect of outcome knowledge on judgment under uncertainty. *Journal of Experimental Psychology: Human Perception and Performance, 1,* 288–99.

Fiske, S. T., & Taylor, S. E. (1984). *Social cognition.* Reading, MA: Addison-Wesley.

Fortune, A. E. (Ed) (1985). *Task-centered practice with families and groups.* New York: Springer, pp. 173–174.

Frances, A., Clarkin, J., & Perry, S. (1984). *Differential therapeutics in psychiatry.* New York: Brunner/Mazel.

Frank, J. D. (1982). Therapeutic components shared by all psychotherapies. In J. H. Harvey & M. M. Parks (Eds.), *The master lecture series, Vol. 1: Psychotherapy research and behavior change* (pp. 73–122). Washington, D.C.: American Psychological Association.

Franklin, D. (1985). Differential assessments: The influence of class and race. *Social Service Review, 59,* 44–61.

Fredman, N., & Sherman, R. (1987). *Handbook of measurements for marriage and family therapy.* New York: Brunner/Mazel.

Freeman, A., Simon, K. M., Beutler, L. E. & Arkowitz, H. (1989). *Comprehensive handbook of cognitive therapy.* New York: Plenum Press.

Freud, S. (1963). *Introductory lectures on psychoanalysis.* In J. Strachey (Ed. and Trans.), *The standard edition of the complete psychological works of Sigmund Freud* (Vols. 15 and 16). London: Hogarth. (First German edition published 1917).

Freud, S. (1964). *New introductory lectures on psychoanalysis.* In J. Strachey (Ed. and Trans.), The standard edition of the complete psychological works of Sigmund Freud (Vol. 22). London: Hogarth. (First German edition published 1933).

Gambrill, E. (1983). *Casework: A competency-based approach* (pp. 205–222). Englewood Cliffs, NJ: Prentice Hall.

Gambrill, E., & Barth, R. P. (1980). Single-case study designs revisited. *Social Work Research and Abstracts, 16*(3), 15–20.

Gambrill, E., & Butterfield, W. (1988). Computers as practice and research tools. *Social Work Research and Abstracts, 24*(1), 4–6.

Garfield, S. L. (1980). *Psychotherapy: An eclectic approach.* New York: John Wiley & Sons.

Garfield, S. L., & Bergin, A.E. (Eds.). (1986). *Handbook of psychotherapy and behavior change.* New York: John Wiley.

Gauron, E. F., & Dickenson, J. K. (1969). The influence of seeing the patient first on diagnostic decision-making in psychiatry. *American Journal of Psychiatry, 126,* 199–205.

Gendlin, E. T. (1970). *Experiencing and the creation of meaning.* New York: MacMillan.

Gendlin, E. T. (1981). *Focusing.* New York: Bantam.

Germain, C., & Gitterman, A. (1980). *The life model of social work practice.* New York: Columbia University Press.

Getzels, J. W. & Csikszentmihalyi, M. (1976). *The creative vision: A longitudinal study of problem finding in art.* New York: Wiley.

Ghiselin, B. (1955). *The creative process.* New York: The New American Library.

Gilligan, C. (1982). *In a different voice.* Cambridge, MA: Harvard University Press.

Glass, G. V., McGaw, B., & Smith, M. L. (1981). *Meta-analysis in social research.* Beverly Hills, CA: Sage Publications.

Glass, G. V., Willson, V. L., & Gottman, J.M. (1975). *Design and analysis of time-series experiments.* Boulder, CO: Colorado Association of University Presses.

Goffman, E. (1961). *Asylums: Essays on the social situation of mental patients and other inmates.* Garden City: Anchor Books.

Goldfried, M. A. (1980). Toward the delineation of therapeutic change principles. *American Psychologist, 35,* (11), 991–999.

Goldfried, M. R., & Davison, G. C. (1976). *Clinical behavior therapy.* New York: Holt, Rinehart, & Winston.

Goldstein, A. P. (1962). *Therapist-patient expectations in psychotherapy.* New York: Pergamon Press.

Goldstein, E. G. (1980). Knowledge base of clinical social work. *Social Work,* 173–78.

Goldstein, H. (1992). Victors or victims: Contrasting views of clients in social work practice. In D. Saleebeg (Ed.), *The strengths perspective on social work practice* (pp. 27–38). New York: Longman.

Gottman, J. M. (1981). *Time-series analysis.* Cambridge, England: Cambridge University Press.

Gottman, J. M., & Leiblum, S. R. (1974). *How to do psychotherapy and how to evaluate it.* New York: Holt, Rinehart and Winston.

Gottman, J. M., Notarius, C., Gonso, J., & Markman, H. (1976). *A couple's guide to communication.* Champaign, IL: Research Press.

Gould, K. (1984, March). A feminist perspective on the person-in-situation complex or practice with women. Paper presented at the meeting of the Council on Social Work Education, Detroit, MI.

Greenberg, L. S. (1984). A task analysis of intrapersonal conflict resolution. In L. N. Rice & L. S. Greenberg (Eds.), *Patterns of change: Intensive analysis of psychotherapy process* (pp. 67–123). New York: Guilford.

Greenberg, L. S. (1986). Change process research. *Journal of Consulting and Clinical Psychology, 54,* 4–9.

Greenberg, L. S., & Pinsoff, W. M. (1986a). Process research: Current trends and future perspectives. In L. S. Greenberg & W. M. Pinsoff (Eds.), *The psychotherapeutic process: A research handbook* (pp. 3–20). New York: Guilford.

Greenberg, L. S., & Pinsoff, W. M. (Eds.). (1986b). *The psychotherapeutic process: A research handbook.* New York: Guilford.

Greenberg, L. S., & Safran, J. D. (1987). *Emotion in psychotherapy.* New York: Guilford.

Greenberg, L. S., Safran, J. D., & Rice, L. N. (1989). Experiential therapy. In A. Freeman, K. M. Simon, L. E. Beutler, & H. Arkowitz (Eds.), *Comprehensive handbook of cognitive therapy* (pp. 169–187). New York: Plenum.

Greif, G. L., & Lynch, A. A. (1983). The eco-systems perspective. In C. H. Meyer (Ed.), *Clinical social work in the eco-systems perspective.* New York: Columbia University press.

Greist, J. H. et al. (1983). Clinical computer applications in mental health. *Journal of Medical Systems, 7,* 175–185.

Gruber, H. (1981). *Darwin on man* (2nd ed.). Chicago: University of Chicago Press.

Guerney, B. G., Jr. (1977). *Relationship enhancement.* San Francisco: Jossey-Bass.

Guidano, V. F., & Liotti, G. (1983). *Cognitive processes and emotional disorders.* New York: Guilford.

Gurman, A. S., Kniskern, D. P., & Pinsoff, W. M. (1986). Research on marital and family therapies. In S. F. Garfield & A. E. Bergin (Eds.), *Handbook of psychotherapy and behavior change* (pp. 565–624). New York: John Wiley & Sons.

Gutierrez, L., & Lewis, E. (1992). A feminist perspective on organizing with women of color. In J. Erlich & F. Rivera (Eds.), *Community organizing in a diverse society* (pp. 113–132). Boston: Allyn & Bacon.

Hammond, K. W., & Gottfredson, D. K. (1984). The VA mental health information system package, *Computer Use in Social Services Network Newsletter, 4,* 6.

Harrison, W. D. (1991). *Seeking common ground: A theory of social work in social care.* Aldershot, England: Avebury.

Hartman, A., & Laird, J. (1983). *Family centered social work practice.* New York: The Free Press.

Hayes, S. N., & Wilson, C. C. (1979). *Behavioral assessment: Recent advances in methods, concepts and applications.* San Francisco: Jossey-Bass Publishers.

Henry, W. P., Schact, T. E., & Strupp, H. H. (1986). Structural analysis of social behavior: Application to a study of interpersonal process in differential psychotherapeutic outcome. *Journal of Consulting and Clinical Psychology, 54,* 27–31.

Heppner, P. P., & Peterson, C. H. (1982). The development and implications of a personal problem-solving inventory. *Journal of Counseling Psychology, 29,* 66–75.

Hersen, M., & Barlow, D. H. (Eds.) (1976). *Single-case experimental designs: Strategies for studying behavior.* New York: Pergamon.

Hill, C. E. (1989). *Therapist techniques and client outcomes.* Newbury Park, CA: Sage.

Hill, C. E., Thames, T. B., & Rardin, D. K. (1979). Comparison of Rogers, Perls, and Ellis on the Hill Counselor Verbal Response Category System. *Journal of Counseling Psychology, 26,* 198–208.

Hodges, W. F., & Felling, F. P. (1970). Types of stressful situations and their relation to trait anxiety and sex. *Journal of Consulting and Clinical Psychology, 34,* 333–337.

Hogarth, R. (1985). *Judgment and choice.* New York: John Wiley & Sons.

Holland, J. H., Holyoak, K. J., Nisbett, R. E., & Thagard, P. R. (1986). *Induction: Processes of inference, learning and discovery.* Cambridge: MIT Press.

Horne, G. P., Yang, M. C. K., & Ware, W. B. (1982). Time-series analysis for single-subject designs. *Psychological Bulletin, 92,* 178–189.

Horowitz, M. J. (1979). *States of mind: Analysis of change in psychotherapy.* New York: Plenum.

Horowitz, M. J. (1991). States, schemas, and control: General theories for psychotherapy integration. *Journal of Psychotherapy Integration, 1,* 85–102.

House, W. C. (1980, September). Correlates of outpatients' attributions of their psychological problems. Paper presented at the meeting of the American Psychological Association, Montreal.

Houts, A. C. (1984). Effects of clinician theoretical orientation and patient explanatory bias in initial clinical judgments. *Professional Psychology: Research and Practice, 15,* 284–293.

Hudson, W. W. (1977, June). Elementary techniques for assessing single-subject/single-worker interventions. *Social Service Review, 51,* 311–326.

Hudson, W. W. (1982). *The clinical measurement package: A Field Manual.* Homewood, IL: Dorsey Press.

Hudson, W. W. (1991). *Computer Assisted Social Services.* Tempe, AZ: Walmyr Publishing Co.

Hudson, W. W., & Harrison, D. F. (1986). Conceptual issues in measuring and assessing family problems. *Family Therapy, 13*(1), 85–94.

Imber-Black, E. (1988). *Families and larger systems: A family therapist's guide through the labyrinth.* New York: Guilford.

Imre, R. W. (1984). The nature of knowledge in social work. *Social Work, 28,* 41–45.

Ingram, R. E. (1984). Toward an information-processing analysis of depression. *Cognitive Therapy and Research, 8,* 443–478.

Jack, D. C. (1991). *Silencing the self: Women and depression.* Cambridge, MA: Harvard University Press.

Jayartne, S. (1978, Fall). Analytic procedures for single-subjects designs. *Social Work Research and Abstracts, 14*(3), 30–40.

Jayartne, S., & Levy, R. L. (1979). *Empirical clinical practice.* New York: Columbia University Press.

Johnson, D. J. (1974). The effect of confrontation in counseling. *Dissertation Abstracts International, 34,* 5633A.

Johnson, O. (1976). *Tests and measurements for child development.* San Francisco, CA: Jossey-Bass.

Johnson-Laird, P. N. (1983) *Mental models: Toward a cognitive science of language, inference and consciousness*. Cambridge: Harvard University Press.

Jones, E. E., Cumming, J. D., & Horowitz, M. J. (1988). Another look at the nonspecific hypothesis of therapeutic effectiveness. *Journal of Consulting and Clinical Psychology, 56*, 48–55.

Jones, E. E. & Nesbitt, R. E. (1972). The actor and the observer: Divergent perceptions of causes of behavior. In E. E. Jones, D. E. Kanouse, H. H. Kelly, R. E. Nesbitt, S. Valins, & B. Weiner (Eds.), *Attribution: Perceiving the causes of behavior*. (pp. 79–94) Morristown, NJ: General Learning Press.

Jones, R. R., Weinrott, M., & Vaught, R. S. (1978, June). Effects of serial dependency on the agreement between visual and statistical inferences. *Journal of Applied Behavior Analysis, 11*, 277–283.

Jordan, J. V. (1984). Empathy and self-boundaries. Work in progress. Wellesley College, Stone Center Working Paper Series, Wellesley, MA.

Kagan, N. (1975). *Interpersonal process recall: A method of influencing human interaction*. Unpublished manuscript. College of Education, Michigan State University, East Lansing, MI.

Kagle, J. D. (1991). *Social work records*. Belmont, CA: Wordsworth.

Kahneman, D., Slovic, P., & Tversky. (1982). *Judgment under uncertainty: Heuristics and biases* (2nd ed.). Cambridge UK: Cambridge University Press.

Kazden, A. E. (1976). Statistical analysis for single-case experimental designs. In M. Hersen & D. H. Barlow (Eds.), *Single-case experimental designs: Strategies for studying behavior change* (pp. 265–316). New York: Pergamon.

Kazdin, A. E. (1989). Methodology of psychotherapy outcome research: Recent developments and remaining limitations. In J. H. Harvey & M. M. Parks, *Psychotherapy Research and Behavior Change*. Washington, D.C.: American Psychological Association.

Kegan, R. (1982). *The evolving self*. Cambridge, MA: Harvard University Press.

Kelly, G. A. (1955). *The psychology of personal constructs*. New York: Norton.

Kempler, W. (1980). Some views on effective principles of psychotherapy. In M. R. Coldfried (Ed.), *Cognitive Therapy and Research, 4*, 271–306. [Special issue on psychotherapy process.]

Kent, R. N., & Foster, S. L. (1977). Direct observational procedures: Methodological issues in naturalistic settings. In A. R. Cominery, K. S. Calhoun, & H. E. Adams (Eds.), *Handbook of Behavioral Assessment* (pp. 279–328). New York: John Wiley & Sons.

Kerlinger, F. N. (1973). *Foundations of Behavioral Research*. New York: Holt, Rinehart & Winston.

Kirk, J., & Miller, M. L. (1986). Reliability and validity in qualitative research. Beverly Hills, CA: Sage.

Kirk, S., & Fischer, J. (1976). Do social workers understand research? *Journal of Education for Social Work, 21*(2), 121–124.

Kirk, S., Osmalov, M., & Fischer, J. (1976). Social workers' involvement in research. *Social Work, 12*(1), 63–70.

Kisthard, W. E. (1992). A strengths model of case management: The principles and functions of a helping partnership with persons with persistent mental illness. In D. Saleebey (Ed.), *The strengths perspective in social work practice* (pp. 59–83). New York: Longman.

Kovacs, M., & Beck, A. T. (1978). Maladaptive cognitive structures in depression. *The American Journal of Psychiatry, 135*, 525–533.

Lambert, J. J., Shapiro, D. A., & Bergin, A. E. (1986). The effectiveness of psychotherapy. In S. L. Garfield & A. E. Bergin (Eds.), *Handbook of psychotherapy and behavior change* (3rd ed., pp. 157–211). New York: John Wiley & Sons.

Langer, E. J. (1975). The illusion of control. *Journal of Personality and Social Psychology, 32*, 311–328.

Langer, E. J. (1989). *Mindfulness*. Reading, MA: Addison-Wesley.

Langor, E. T. & Abelson, R. P. (1974). A patient by any other name...: Clinician group difference in labeling bias. *Journal of Consulting and Clinical Psychology, 42*, 4–9.

Larsen, D. L., Attkinson, C. C., Hargreaves, W. A., & Nguyen, T. D. (1979). Assessment of client/patient satisfaction: Development of a general scale. *Evaluation and Program Planning, 2*, 197–207.

Lazarus, A. A. (1971). *Behavior Therapy and Beyond.* New York: McGraw-Hill.

Lazarus, A. A. (1981). *The practice of multimodal therapy.* New York: McGraw-Hill.

Lazarus, R. S. (1991). *Emotion and adaptation.* New York: Oxford University Press.

Lazarus, R. S., & Folkman, S. (1984). *Stress, appraisal, and coping* (pp. 261–285) New York: Springer.

Lerner, H. G. (1985). *The dance of anger: A woman's guide to changing the patterns of intimate relationships.* New York: Harper & Row.

Lerner, H. G. (1989). *The dance of intimacy: A woman's guide to courageous acts of change in key relationships.* New York: Harper & Row.

Levitt, J. L., & Reid, W. J. (1981). Rapid assessment instruments for practice. *Social Work Research and Abstracts, 17*(1), 13–19.

Lieberman, M. A., & Videka-Sherman, L. (1986). The impact of self-help groups on the mental health of widows and widowers. *American Journal of Orthopsychiatry, 56*, 435–449.

Linehan, M. M. (1979). Structured cognitive-behavioral treatment of assertion problems. In P. C. Kendall & S. D. Hollon (Eds.), *Cognitive-behavioral interventions: Theory, research, and procedures.* New York: Academic Press.

Linehan, M. M. (1987a). Dialectical behavior therapy for borderline personality disorder: Theory and method. *Bulletin of the Menninger Clinic, 51*, 251–276.

Linehan, M. M. (1987b). Dialectical behavior therapy: A cognitive behavioral approach to parasuicide. *Journal of Personality Disorder, 1*, 328–333.

Linsk, N., Howe, M. W., & Pinkston, E. M. (1975). Behavioral group work in a home for the aged. *Social Work, 20*, 454–463.

Luborsky, L. (1976). Helping alliances in psychotherapy: The groundwork for a study of their relationship to its outcome. In J. L. Clayhorn (Ed.), *Successful Psychotherapy* (pp. 92–111). New York: Brunner/Mazel.

Luborsky, L., Singer, B., & Luborsky, L. (1975). Comparative studies of psychotherapies. *Archives of General Psychiatry, 32*, 995–1008.

Mahoney, M. J. (1976). *Scientist as subject: The psychological imperative.* Cambridge: Ballinger.

Mahoney, M. J. (Ed.). (1980). *Psychotherapy process.* New York: Plenum.

Mahoney, M. J. (1991). *Human change processes.* New York: Basic Books.

Maluccio, A. N. (1979). *Learning from clients: Interpersonal helping as viewed by clients and social workers.* New York: Free Press.

Marks, I. M. (1987). *Fears, phobias, and rituals.* New York: Oxford University Press.

Markus, H. (1977). Self-schemata and processing information about the self. *Journal of Personality and Social Psychology, 35*, 63–78.

Marlatt, G. A., & Gordon, J. R. (1985). *Relapse prevention: Maintenance strategies in the treatment of addictive behaviors.* New York: Guilford.

Marmer, C. R., Wilner, N., & Horowitz, M. J. (1984). Recurrent client states in psychotherapy: Segmentation and quantification. In L. N. Rice & L. S. Greenberg (Eds.), *Patterns of change* (pp. 194–212). New York: Guilford.

Marsh, J. C., & Shibano, M. (1982). Visual and statistical analysis of clinical time-series data. In G. A. Forehand (Ed.), *New directions for program evaluation: Applications for time series analysis.* (pp. 33–48). San Francisco: Jossey-Bass.

Marsh, J. C., & Wirick, M. (1991). Evaluation of Hull House Teen Pregnancy and Parenting Program. *Evaluation and Program Planning, 14*(1/2), 49–62.

Mayer, J. E., & Timms, N. (1970). *The client speaks: Working class impressions of casework.* New York: Atherton.

McArthur, L. Z., & Post, D. (1977). Figural emphasis and person perception. *Journal of Experimental and Social Psychology, 13,* 520–535.

McGoldrick, M., Anderson, C. M., & Walsh, F. (Eds). (1989). *Women in families.* New York: W. W. Norton.

McGoldrick, M., Pearce, J. K., & Giordano, J. (1982). *Ethnicity and family therapy.* New York: Guilford.

McPhillamy, D. J., & Lewisohn, P. M. (1982). The Pleasant Events Schedule: Studies on reliability, validity, and scale intercorrelations. *Journal of Consulting and Clinical Psychology, 50,* 363–380.

Meichenbaum, D. (1977). *Cognitive-behavior modification.* New York: Plenum.

Meichenbaum, D., & Gilmore, J. B. (1984). In K. S. Bowers & D. Meichenbaum (Eds.), *The unconscious reconsidered* (pp. 273–298). New York: John Wiley & Sons.

Meyer, C. H. (1983). *Clinical social work in the ecosystems perspective.* New York: Columbia University Press.

Miles, M. B., & Huberman, A. M. (1984). *Qualitative data analysis: A sourcebook of new methods.* Beverly Hills, CA: Sage.

Miller, J. B. (1984). The development of women's sense of self. *Work in progress.* Wellesley College, Stone Center Working Paper Series, Wellesley, MA.

Miller, J. B. (1986, May). Women's psychological development: Implications for psychotherapy. Paper presented at the Stone Center Conference on women's development within and toward connections, Wellesley College, Wellesley, MA.

Mintz, J., & Kiesler, D. J. (1982). Individualized measures of psychotherapy outcome. In P. C. Kendall & J. N. Butcher (Eds.), *Handbook of research methods in clinical psychology* (pp. 491–534). New York: John Wiley & Sons.

Minuchin, S., & Fishman, H. D. (1981). *Family therapy techniques.* Cambridge, MA: Harvard University Press.

Mischel, W. (1973). Toward a cognitive social learning reconceptualization of personality. *Psychological Review, 80,* 252–283.

Moos, R. H., & Moos, B. S. (1983). Clinical applications of the Family Environment Scale. In E. E. Filsinger (Ed.), *Marriage and family assessment: A sourcebook for family therapy.* Beverly Hills: Sage.

Mullen, E. J. (1968). Casework communication. *Social Casework, 49*(9), 546–551.

Mullen, E. J. & Dumpson J.R. (1972). *Evaluation of social interventions.* San Francisco: Jossey-Bass.

Murdach, A. D. (1982). A political perspective in problem-solving. *Social Work, 28,* 19–23.

Mutschler, E., & Hasenfeld, Y. (1986). Integrated information systems for social work practice. *Social Work, 31*(5), 345–349.

Nesbitt, R., & Ross, L. (1980). *Human inference: Strategies and shortcomings of social judgment.* Englewood Cliffs, NJ: Prentice Hall.

Newell, A., & Simon, H. (1972). *Human problem solving.* New York: Prentice Hall, 1972.

Nickerson, R. S., Perkins, D. N., & Smith, E. E. (1985). *The teaching of thinking.* Hillsdale, NJ: Erlbaum.

Neisser, U. (1980). Three cognitive psychologies and their implications. In M. J. Mahoney (Ed.), *Psychotherapy process* (pp. 363–367). New York: Plenum.

Norcross, J. C. (Ed.). (1986a). *Casebook of eclectic psychotherapy.* New York: Brunner/Mazel.

Norcross, J. C. (Ed.). (1986b). *Handbook of eclectic psychotherapy.* New York: Brunner/Mazel.

Novaco, R. W. (1975). *Anger control: The development and evaluation of an experimental treatment.* Lexington, MA: Heath-Lexington.

Nulman, E. (1983). Family therapy and advocacy: Directions for the future. *Social Work, 28,* 19–23.

Nurius, P., & Berlin, S. B. (1993). Negative self-concept and depression. In D. K. Granvold (Ed.), *Cognitive and behavioral social work practice.* Belmont, CA: Wordsworth.

Olson, D. H., Portner, J., & Lavee, Y. (1985). FACES-III, Family Social Science, University of Minnesota, 290 McNeal Hall, St. Paul, Minnesota 55108.

Orlinsky, D. E., & Howard, K. I. (1975). *Varieties of psychotherapeutic experience.* New York: Teachers College Press.

Orlinsky, D. E. & Howard, K. I. (1986a). Process and outcome in psychotherapy. In S. L. Garfield & A. E. Bergin (Eds.), *Handbook of psychotherapy and behavior change: An empirical analysis* (3rd edition), (pp. 283-329). New York: John Wiley & Sons.

Orlinsky, D. E., & Howard, K. I. (1986b). The psychological interior of psychotherapy: Explorations with therapy session reports. In L. S. Greenberg & W. M. Pinsoff (Eds.), *The psychotherapy process: A research handbook* (pp. 477–502). New York: Guilford.

Orme, J. G., & Combs-Orme, J. D. (1986). Statistical power and Type II errors in social work research. *Social Work Research and Abstracts, 22* (Fall), 3–10.

Orme, J. G., & Tolman, R. (1986). The statistical power of a decade of social work education research. *Social Service Review, 60*(4), 619–632.

Parloff, M. B. (1986). Frank's "common elements" in psychotherapy: Nonspecific factors and placebos. *American Journal of Orthopsychiatry, 56,* 521–530.

Patterson, G. R., Ray R. S., Shaw, D. A., & Cobb, J. A. (1969). *Manual for coding family interactions* (rev. ed.). (NAPS document 01234). New York: Microfiche Publications.

Patterson, G. R., Reid, J. B., Jones, R. R., & Conger, R. E. (1975). *A social learning approach to family intervention* (Vol. 1). Eugene, OR: Castalia.

Patton, M. Q. (1990). *Qualitative evaluation and research methods.* Newbury Park, CA: Sage.

Paul, G. L., & Lenz, R. J. (1977). *Psychosocial treatment of chronic mental patients: Milieu versus social learning programs.* Cambridge, MA: Harvard University Press.

Peile, C. (1988). Research paradigms in social work: From stalemate to creative synthesis. *Social Service Review, 62*(1), 1–19.

Peiper, M. H. (1981). The obsolete scientific imperative in social work research. *Social Service Review, 55*(3), 371–395.

Peiper, M. H. (1985). The future of social work research. *Social Work Research and Abstracts, 21*(1), 3–11.

Perlman, H. H. (1957). *Social casework: A problem solving process.* Chicago: University of Chicago Press.

Petony, P. (1981). *Models of influence in psychotherapy.* New York: The Free Press.

Pinkston, E. M., Friedman, B. S., & Polster, R. P. (1981). Parents as agents of behavior change. In S.P. Schinke (Ed.), *Behavioral methods in social welfare.* Hawthorne, NY: Aldine.

Pinkston, E. M., & Linsk, N. L. (1984). *Care of the elderly: A family approach.* New York: Pergamon/Allyn & Bacon.

Pinsoff, W. M. (1982). *The intersession report.* Unpublished instrument, Center for Family Studies, Northwestern University, Evanston, IL.

Powell, T. (1990). *Working with self-help.* Silver Spring, MD: NASW Press.

Proctor, E. K. (1990). Evaluating clinical practice: Issues of purpose and design. *Social Work Research and Abstracts, 26*(1), 32–42.

Rapp, C. A. (1992). The strengths perspective of case management with persons suffering from severe mental illness. In D. Saleebey (Ed.), *The strengths perspective in social work practice* (pp. 45–58). New York: Longman.

Rappaport, J., Reischi, T.M., & Zimmerman, M. A. (1992). Mutual help mechanisms in the empowerment of former mental patients. In D. Saleebey (Ed.), *The strengths perspective in social work practice* (pp. 84–97). New York: Longman.

Rappaport, J., Swift, C., & Hess, R. (Eds.). (1984). *Studies in empowerment: Toward understanding and action*. New York: Haworth Press.

Regan, D. T. & Totten, J. (1975). Empathy and attribution: Turning observers into actors. *Journal of Personality and Social Psychology, 32*, 850–856.

Reid, J. B., Taplin, P. S., & Loeber, R. (1981). A social interactional approach to the treatment of abusive families. In R. Stuart (Ed.), *Violent behavior: Social learning approaches to prediction, management and treatment.* New York: Brunner/Mazel.

Reid, W. J. (1985). *Family problem solving.* New York: Columbia University Press.

Reid, W. J. (1990). Change-process research: A new paradigm. In L. Videka-Sherman & W. J. Reid (Eds.), *Advances in Clinical Social Work Research* (pp. 130–148). Silver Spring, MD: NASW Press.

Reid, W. J. & Davis, I. P. (1987). *Qualitative methods in single-case research*. In N. Gottlieb, H. A. Ishisaka, J. Kopp, C. A. Richey & E. R. Tolson. *Perspectives in Direct Practice Evaluation* pp. 56–74. Seattle, WA: Center for Social Welfare Research, School of Social Work, University of Washington.

Reid, W. J., & Epstein, L. (1972). *Task-centered casework*. New York: Columbia University Press.

Reid, W. J. & Shein, A. (1969). *Brief and extended casework*. New York: Columbia University Press.

Renaud, H., & Estess, F. (1961). Life history interviews with one hundred normal American males: "Pathogenicity" of childhood. *American Journal of Orthopsychiatry, 31*, 796–802.

Rice, L. N. (1974). The evocative function of the therapist. In D. Wexler & L. Rice (Eds.), *Innovations in client-centered therapy.* New York: Interscience.

Rice, L. N., & Greenberg, L. S. (Eds.). (1984). *Patterns of change: Intensive analysis of psychotherapy process.* New York: Guilford.

Rice, L. N., & Saperia, E. (1984). A task analysis of the resolution of problematic reactions. In L. Rice & L. S. Greenberg (Eds.), *Patterns of change: Intensive analysis of psychotherapeutic process* (pp. 2–66). New York: Guilford.

Rips, L. J. (1983). Cognitive processes in propositional reasoning. *Psychological Review, 90*(1), 38–71.

Robinson, J. (1989). Clinical treatment of black families: Issues and strategies. *Social Work, 34*, 323–329.

Robinson, J. P., & Shaver, P. R. (1973). *Measures of social psychological attitudes*. Ann Arbor, MI: Institute for Social Research.

Rodwell, M. K. (1987). Naturalistic inquiry: An alternative model for social work assessment. *Social Service Review, 61*(2), 231–246.

Rogers, H. B. M. (1973). Therapists' verbalization and outcome in monitored play therapy. *Dissertation Abstracts International, 34*, 424B.

Rooney, R. H. (1981). A task-centered reunification model for foster care. In A. N. Maluccio & P. A. Sinanoglu (Eds.), *The challenge of partnership: Working with parents of children in foster care* (pp. 135–150). New York: Child Welfare League of America.

Rose, S .M. (1990). Advocacy/empowerment: An approach to clinical practice for social work. *Journal of Sociology and Social Welfare, 17*, 41–52.

Rosen, A., Proctor, E. K., & Livne, S. (1985). Planning and direct practice. *Social Service Review, 59*, 161–177.

Rosenblatt, A. (1968). The practitioner's use and evaluation of research. *Social Work, 13*(1), 53–59.

Ross, L., Greene, D., & House, P. (1977). The false consensus phenomenon: An attributional bias in self-perception: Biased attributional processes in the debriefing paradigm. *Journal of Personality and Social Psychology*, *13*, 279–301.

Rubenstein, H., & Bloch, M. H. (1978). Helping clients who are poor: Worker and client perceptions of problems, activities and outcomes. *Social Service Review*, 69–84.

Ryle, A. (1979). The focus in brief interpretive psychotherapy: Dilemmas, traps and snags as target problems. *British Journal of Psychiatry*, *134*, 46–54.

Ryle, A. (1982). The focus in brief psychotherapy: A cross-fertilization between research and practice. In A. J. Rush (Ed.), *Short-term psychotherapies for depression* (pp. 311–323). New York: Guilford.

Sackett, G. P. (Ed.). (1978). *Observing behavior, volume II: Data collection and analysis methods*. Baltimore: University Park Press.

Safran, J. D., & Greenberg, L. S. (Eds.). (1991). *Emotion, psychotherapy, and change*. New York: Guilford.

Safran, J. D., & Segal, Z. V. (1990). *Interpersonal processes in cognitive therapy*. New York: Basic Books.

Saleebey, D. (Ed.). (1992). *The strengths perspective in social work practice*. New York: Longman, pp. 84–97.

Sandifer, M. G., Hordern, A., & Green, L. M. (1970). The psychiatric interview: The impact of the first three minutes. *American Journal of Psychiatry*, *126*, 968–973.

Schefler, A. (1973). *Communication and structure: Analysis of a psychotherapy transaction*. Bloomington, IN: Indiana University Press.

Schön, D. A. (1983). *The reflective practitioner: How professionals think in action*. New York: Basic Books.

Schön, D. A. (1987). *Educating the reflective practitioner*. New York: Jossey-Bass

Sechrest, L. (1963). Incremental validity: A recommendation. *Educational and Psychological Measurement*, *23*, 153–158.

Sechrest, L. (1984). Reliability and validity. In A. S. Bellack & M. Hersen (Eds.), *Research methods in clinical psychology* (pp. 24–54). New York: Pergamon Press.

Seitz, V., Rosenbaum, L. K., & Apfel, N. H. (1985). Effects of family support intervention: A ten-year follow-up. *Child Development*, *56*, 376–391.

Selye, H. (1956). *The stress of life*. New York: McGraw-Hill.

Sherer, M., Maddox, J. E., Mercandante, B., Prentice-Dunn, S., Jacobs, B., & Rogers, R. W. (1982). The self-efficacy scale: Construction and validation. *Psychology Reports*, *51*, 663–671.

Simon, H. A. (1969). *The science of the artificial*. Cambridge, MA: MIT Press.

Singer, J. L., & Salovey, P. (1991). Organized knowledge structures and personality: Person schemas, self-schemas, prototypes and scripts. In M. J. Horowitz (Ed.). *Person schemas and maladaptive interpersonal patterns* (pp. 69–70). Chicago: University of Chicago Press.

Skinner, B. F. (1974). *About behaviorism*. New York: Knopf.

Sloane, R. B., Staples, F. R., Cristol, A. H. Yorkston, N. J., & Whipple, K. (1975). *Psychotherapy versus behavior therapy*. Cambridge: Harvard University Press.

Slovic, P., Fischoff, B. & Lichtenstein, S. (1977). Behavioral decision theory. *Annual Review of Psychology*, *28*, 1–39.

Smale, G., Tuson, G., Cooper, M., Wardle, M., & Crosbie, D. (1988). *Community social work: A paradigm for change*. London: National Institute for Social Work.

Smith, M. L., Glass, G. V., & Miller, T. I. (1980). *The benefits of psychotherapy*. Baltimore: John Hopkins University Press.

Snyder, C. R., Shenker, R. J., & Schmidt, A. (1976). Effects of role perspective and client psychiatric history on locus of problem. *Journal of Consulting and Clinical Psychology*, *44*, 467–472.

Snyder, M., & Swann, W. B., Jr. (1978). Hypothesis-testing processes in social interaction. *Journal of Personality and Social Psychology, 36*, 1202–1212.

Snyder, M., & Thomsen, C. J. (1988). Interactions between therapists and clients: Hypothesis testing and behavioral confirmation. In D. C. Turk & P. Salovey (Eds.), *Reasoning, inference and judgment in clinical psychology,* (pp. 124–159). New York: Free Press.

Steketee, G., & Foa, E. B. (1985). Obsessive-compulsive disorder. In D. H. Barlow (Ed.), *Clinical handbook of psychological disorders* (pp. 69–144). New York: Guilford.

Stiles, W. B. (1979). Verbal responses modes and psychotherapeutic technique. *Psychiatry, 42*, 49–62.

Stiles, W. B. (1980). Measurement of the impact of a psychotherapy session. *Journal of Consulting and Clinical Psychology, 48*, 176–185.

Stiles, W. B. (1983). Normality, diversity, and psychotherapy. Psychotherapy: *Theory, Research & Practice, 20*, 183–188.

Stiles, W. B., Shapiro, D. A., & Elliott, R. (1986). Are all psychotherapies equivalent? *American Psychologist, 41* (2), 165–180.

Stiles, W. B., & Snow, J. S. (1984). Counseling session impact as seen by novice counselors and their clients. *Journal of Counseling Psychology, 31*, 3–12.

Storms, M. (1973). Video-tape and attribution process: Reversing actors' and observers' points of view. *Journal of Personality and Social Psychology, 27*, 165–174.

Strupp, H. H. (1955). An objective comparison of Rogerian and psychoanalytic techniques. *Journal of Consulting Psychology, 19*, 1–7.

Strupp, H. S., & Binder, J. F. (1984). *Psychotherapy in a new key.* New York: Basic Books.

Stuart, R. B. (1980). *Helping couples change: A social learning approach to marital therapy.* New York: Guilford.

Taylor, S. E., & Fiske, S. T. (1975). Point of view and perceptions of causality. *Journal of Personality and Social Psychology, 32*, 439–445.

Taylor, S. E., & Winkler, J. D. (1980, September). *Development of schemas.* Paper presented at the meeting of the American Psychological Association, Montreal.

Temerlin, M. K. (1968). Suggestion effects in psychiatric diagnosis. *Journal of Nervous and Mental Disease, 147*, 349–357.

Test, M. A., Knoedler, W. H., Allness, D. J., Burke, S. S., Brown, R. L., & Wallisch L. S., (1991). Long-term community care through an assertive continuous treatment team. In C. A. Tamminga & S. C. Schultz (Eds.), *Advances in neuropsychiatry and psychopharmacology, vol. I: Schizophrenia research* (pp. 239–246). New York: Raven Press.

Thomas, E. J. (1978, Winter). Research and service in single-case experimentation: Conflicts and choices. *Social Work Research and Abstracts, 14* 20–31.

Timms, N., & Timms, R. (1982). *Dictionary of social welfare.* London: Routledge & Kegan Paul.

Tolson, E. R. (1977). Alleviating marital communication problems. In W. J. Reid & L. Epstein (Eds.), *Task-centered practice.* New York: Columbia University Press.

Truax, C. B., & Wittmer, J. (1973). The degree of the therapist's focus on defense mechanisms and the effect on therapeutic outcome with institutionalized juvenile delinquents. *Journal of Community Psychology, 1*, 201–203.

Tufte, E. R. (1984). *The Visual Display of Quantitative Information.* Cheshire, CT: Graphics Press.

Tufte, E. R. (1990). *Envisioning Information.* Chesire, CT: Graphics Press.

Tukey, J. W. (1977). *Exploratory data analysis.* Reading, MA: Addison-Wesley.

Turk, D., & Salovey, P. (1988). Reasoning, inference and judgment in clinical psychology. New York: Free Press.

Tversky, A., and Kahneman, D. (1984). Belief in the law of small numbers. In D. Kahneman, P. Slovic, & A. Tversky (Eds.), *Judgement under uncertainty: Heuristics and biases*. New York: Cambridge University Press.

Tversky, A., & Kahneman, D. (1974). Judgment under uncertainty: Heuristics and biases. *Science, 185*, 1124–1131.

Tyron, W. W. A simplified time-series analysis for evaluating treatment intervention. *Journal of Applied Behavior Analysis*, 15, September 1982, 423–429.

Videka-Sherman, L., & Reid, W. (1985). The structured clinical record: A clinical evaluation tool. *Clinical Supervisor, 3*, 45–61.

Videka-Sherman, L., & Reid, W. J. (1990). *Advances in clinical social work research*. Silver Spring, MD: NASW Press.

Wachtel, E. F. & Wachtel, P. L. (1986a). *Family dynamics in individual psychotherapy: A guide to clinical strategies*. New York: Guilford.

Wachtel, E. F., & Wachtel, P. L. (1986b). Active interventions. *In Family dynamics in individual psychotherapy* (pp. 134–176). New York: Guilford.

Wachtel, P. L. (1987). *Action and insight*. New York: Guilford.

Wakefield, J. (1988, June). Psychotherapy, distributive justice, and social work, part 1: Distributive justice as a conceptual framework for social work. *Social Service Review, 62*, 187–210.

Wallace, W. (1971). *The logic of science in sociology*. Chicago: Aldine-Atherton.

Walsh, B. W., & Peterson, L. E. (1985). Philosophical foundations of psychological theories: The issue of synthesis. *Psychotherapy: Theory, Research and Practice, 22*, 145–153.

Waskow, I. E., & Parloff, M. B. (1975). *Psychotherapy change measures*. Rockville, MD: NIMH.

Weick, A. (1987). Reconceptualizing the philosophical perspective of social work. *Social Service Review, 61*(2), 218–230.

Weissbourd, B., & Kagan, S. L. (1989). Family support programs: Catalysts for change. *American Journal of Orthopsychiatry, 59*, 20–31.

Weissman, M. M., Leaf, P. J., Holzer, C. E. III, Meyers, J. K., & Tischler, G. L. (1984). The epidemiology of depression: An update on sex differences in rates. *Journal of Affective Disorders, 7*, 179–188.

Weissman, M. M., Meyers, J. K., Douglas, W., & Belanger, A. (1986). Depressive symptoms as a risk factor for mortality and for major depression. In L. Erlenmeyer-Kimling & N. Millers (Eds.), *Life span research on the prediction of psychopathology* (pp. 251–260). Hillside, NJ: Lawrence Erlbaum.

Wescott, M. R. (1968). *Toward a contemporary psychology of intuition*. New York: Holt, Rinehart & Winston.

Wheelis, A. (1950). The place of action in personality change. *Psychiatry, 13*, 133–148.

Wheelis, A. (1973). *How people change*. New York: Harper Colophon.

Whittaker, J. K., Kinney, J., Tracy, E. M., & Booth, C. (Eds.). (1990). *Reaching high-risk families: Intensive family preservation in human services*. New York: Aldine de Gruyter.

Witkin, S., (1982). Cognitive process in clinical practice. *Social Work, 27*(5), 389–395.

Witkin, S. L. (1991). Empirical clinical practice: A critical analysis. *Social Work, 36*, 158–165.

Witkin, S. L., & Gottschalk, S. (1988). Alternative criteria for theory evaluation. *Social Service Review, 62*, 211–224.

Wood, K. M. (1990). Epistemological issues in the development of social work practice knowledge. In L. Videka-Sherman & W. J. Reid (Eds.), *Advances in Clinical Social Work Research* (pp. 373–390). Silver Spring, MD: National Association of Social Workers.

Yeaton, W. H., & Sechrest, L. (1981) Critical dimensions in the choice and maintenance of successful treatments: Strengths, integrity and effectiveness. *Journal of Consulting and Clinical Psychology, 49*(2), 156–167.

Zajonc, R. B. (1984). On the primacy of affect. *American Psychologist, 39*, 117–123.

Zimmerman, M. A., & Rappaport, J. (1988). Citizen participation, perceived control, and psychological empowerment. *American Journal of Community Psychology, 16*, 725–750.

Zymond, M. J., & Denton, W. (1988). Gender bias in mental therapy: A multidimensional sealing analysis. *The American Journal of Family Therapy, 16*(3), 262–272.

Author Index

Subject Index